Other titles in the series

POSTMODERN LITERATURE

IAN GREGSON

University of Wales, Bangor, UK

A member of the Hodder Headline Group
LONDON
Distributed in the United States of America by
Oxford University Press Inc., New York

First published in Great Britain in 2004 by
Arnold, a member of the Hodder Headline Group,
338 Euston Road, London NW1 3BH

http://www.arnoldpublishers.com

Distributed in the United States of America by
Oxford University Press Inc.,
198 Madison Avenue, New York, NY10016

British Library Cataloguing in Publication Data
A catalogue record for this book is available from the British Library

Library of Congress Cataloging-in-Publication Data
A catalog record for this book is available from the Library of Congress

ISBN 0 340 81371 7

1 2 3 4 5 6 7 8 9 10

Cover image: Mariko Mori *Play With Me*, 1994. Courtesy: Deitch Projects, NY

Typeset in 10 on 13 pt Sabon by Phoenix Photosetting, Chatham, Kent
Printed and bound in Great Britain by CPI Bath

What do you think about this book? Or any other Arnold title?
Please send your comments to feedback.arnold@hodder.co.uk

For Victoria Lill

Contents

Series editor's preface

The plural in the title of this series, *Contexts,* is intentional. Literature, while it emerges from, and responds to, historical, social and cultural moments, also to a large extent establishes its own contexts, through the particular inflection it puts upon its ostensible 'materials', themes and preoccupations. Therefore, rather than offering a traditional 'major works/historical background' parallel discussion, each *Contexts* volume takes its instigation from the ways in which literary texts have defined their areas of reference, and in which they are in active dialogue with key cultural ideas and events of their time. What aspects of a period most concerned writers? What effect upon literary form have various social and cultural trends had? How have different texts responded to single historical events? How do different texts, ultimately, 'speak back' to their period?

Historical background is made readily available in each volume. but is always closely integrated within discussion of literary texts. As such, the narrative woven around each literary historical period in the individual volumes follows no uniform pattern, but reflects their particular authors' sense of the ways in which the contexts of their period establish themselves – generically, thematically, or involving debates about language, gender, religion, or social change, for example. While each volume provides detailed discussion of its period's most studied literary works, it also asks informed questions about the canon and periodisation itself. Each volume also contains a timeline, full bibliography, and several contemporary literary, cultural, or historical documents which provide material for further reflection and discussion.

Steven Matthews

Acknowledgements

The publishers would like to thank the following for permission to use copyright material in this book:

HarperCollins Publishers Ltd for Frantz Fanon, 'Chapter 6 Conclusion', from *Wretched of the Earth*. Reprinted by permission of HarperCollins Publishers Ltd, © Frantz Fanon 1963

University of Minnesota Press for Jean-François Lyotard, 'The Referent, the Name', from *The Differend: Phrases in Dispute*, trans. Georges Van Den Abbeele, vol. 46 of *Theory and History of Literature*. Reprinted by permission of University of Minnesota Press, 1988. Originally published in France as *Le Différend*, copyright 1983 by Les Éditions de Minuit. English translation copyright 1988 by the University of Minnesota

Carcanet Press Limited for Edwin Morgan, 'Message Clear' from *Collected Poems*, Manchester: Carcanet Press, 1990

Columbia University Press for Julia Kristeva, 'Approaching Abjection', from *Powers of Horror: An Essay on Abjection*, New York: Columbia University Press, 1982

Every effort has been made to trace all copyright holders of material. Any rights not acknowledged here will be acknowledged in subsequent printings if sufficient notice is given to the publisher.

Preface

This series, *Contexts*, is premised upon a concept of literary history which depends upon a necessary simplification that divides that history into distinct periods, so that those periods are made to seem self-contained and internally consistent. This simplification is effective because it draws attention to what is genuinely typical of the period in question and to how literature is shaped by the culture and events which are contemporary with it: it is even more effective when the literary historian draws attention to its distortions and points out how these periods are in fact continuous with those before and after it, and how the periods themselves contain contradictions and fissures.

Writers in these periods did not think of themselves under the period headings with which they have been retrospectively labelled, such as 'Renaissance dramatist', 'Romantic poet' – not, that is, until modernism, when the poet Ezra Pound, for example, declared the necessity to 'Make it New'. Modernism inaugurated an unprecedented self-consciousness about writing out of a historical epoch and responding to its cultural conditions. In the postmodern period that self-consciousness has reached highly sophisticated levels and has been incessantly theorised; this process has ramified because it has been endorsed and subsidised by academic institutions and also by the publishing industry. This has meant that the construction of a postmodernist canon has happened much earlier than such canon construction previously occurred. A concept of what it is to be a postmodernist author is widespread in academic circles and this has led to courses being invented on the basis of that concept.

There is a profound paradox underlying this because postmodernism is supposed to be about rejecting canons and subverting orthodoxies of all kinds – yet it has managed to impose this orthodoxy with awesome effectiveness. This is partly because postmodernism is sexy, it is linked with everything which is up-to-the-minute and technological, and its association with popular culture – with film and television and the Anglo-American music industry – has glamorised it so that, while it is dauntingly intellectual, it also appears fun and exciting. It can further impose its paradoxical orthodoxy by reference to a vulgarised version of a concept taken from that dominating poststructuralist theorist Michel Foucault. According to this, a historical period is a sort of system which cannot be escaped; no-one can stand outside their own epoch and therefore it is impossible, now, not to be postmodernist. Foucault's argument is powerful and plausible, but this version of it already contains assumptions about what the postmodern entails and it is these assumptions which need to be questioned.

This book begins by defining, accessibly, what postmodernism is. It does this by exploring its relationship to modernism, to existentialism, and to poststructuralism, and then by discussing, in some detail, thoroughly postmodernist texts like Walter Abish's *How German Is It*, John Ashbery's 'Self-Portrait in a Convex Mirror' and Angela Carter's 'Flesh and the Mirror'. The early chapters are the ones that deal, for the most part, with the texts that fit most comfortably into the postmodernist canon. The chapter on 'Postmodern language' comes first because it is dedicated to discussing the priority which is given in postmodernism to language and textuality. *How German Is It* is especially useful because it refers explicitly to Martin Heidegger and so demonstrates why postmodernists take their symptomatic departure from existentialism. What is crucially involved here is a scepticism about existentialist authenticity, about a true self in a true place where that place is linked to a moral and ideological value placed on Nature. Abish satirises this idea because for him it is inextricably tied to a fascist championing of blood and soil. My discussion of this foreshadows that in my chapter on 'Postmodern Nature' where I indicate why Nature – which appears to postmodernist theorists like Jean Baudrillard and Frederic Jameson to have been superseded by simulacra, by virtual reality and unnatural representation – has in fact been a site of heated textual conflict in the postmodern period.

It is because I think that depicting the transition from existentialism into postmodernism is particularly instructive for understanding postmodernism that I have organised my chapter on the 'Postmodern self' so that it enacts that transition. The argument traces a continuum stretching from Sylvia Plath, through John Berryman, then Frank O'Hara into John Ashbery and Angela Carter. The confessional poets worked in the 1950s and 1960s, when existentialism was fashionable, with a poetic project preoccupied with delving deep (and psychoanalytically) into biographical experiences in order to find the roots of what constitutes the self which is called into being in the diaristic, existential act of the poem. Frank O'Hara, in depicting himself moving minute by minute through the streets of New York, sometimes seems to be involved in confessional writing and at others to be parodying it, and he always avoids its tendency towards portentousness. This makes him a playful existentialist – an oxymoron that suggests how he stands between confessional writing and the thorough postmodernism of John Ashbery, who relentlessly deconstructs notions of a stable self.

What I think is overridingly important is to oppose the insidious process that implies that only thorough postmodernists like John Ashbery, Thomas Pynchon, John Barth *et al.* deserve to be discussed in books and courses dedicated to the postmodern period. A similar mechanism that leads to the necessary simplification I referred to in my first paragraph also leads (much less excusably) to the use of postmodernism as a label which promotes certain writers at the expense of others – this is the 'postmodernist period', so we had better focus on postmodernist writers. Jeanette Winterson has been a conspicuous beneficiary of this process: because her novels conform so readily to the expectations of postmodernist critics and lend themselves so conveniently to discussion by reference to postmodernist concepts like 'magic realism', 'historiographic metafiction', the 'carnivalesque', 'abjection', 'écriture féminine', etc. This has meant that she has achieved a prominence which is dependent upon her conforming to abstract notions of what this type of fiction should be.

The sway that has been exercised in academic circles by postmodernist taste has also tended to obscure the contradictions inside the postmodern. Postmodernist theory is characteristically discussed alongside important postmodern phenomena like postcolonialism and feminism and too little attention is paid to the conflicts between a theorising whose tendency is towards extreme philosophical scepticism and a textual practice which is premised upon the ability to make political commitments. Postcolonial texts like Chinua Achebe's *Things Fall Apart* and Salman Rushdie's *Midnight's Children*, and feminist texts like the novels of Angela Carter, would be impossible unless that ability is assumed and exploited.

A similarly homogenising effect is produced by a tendency to post-modernise the less postmodernist authors and ignore the extent to which they are at odds with the theory. This matters less where the authors flagrantly fail to fit the bill (as in Blake Morrison's attempt to turn Seamus Heaney into a postmodernist). It is more disturbing where this strategy is a half-truth, as in the important case of Toni Morrison, who uses some post-modernist strategies and demonstrates some awareness of poststructuralist theorists like Jacques Lacan and Julia Kristeva but whose political project involves a form of novelistic excavation of African American history and is to that extent significantly anti-postmodernist. In my chapters on 'Postmodern gender' and 'Postmodern race' I treat each author both as an individual case and as part of a wider postmodern context so that the extent of their postmodernism is continually interrogated.

What is conspicuous is that postmodern culture and the influence of postmodernist theory have made the politics of class seem impossibly old-fashioned. There is certainly a link between this and the idea that the post-modern is, in economic terms, the 'postindustrial' – that it is characterised by technology rather than heavy industry. To speak or write about class has become unfashionable, even laughable, otherwise Monty Python's 'Four Yorkshiremen' sketch would not be so famous and so admired. That TV programme was itself a distinctively postmodern phenomenon, its apolitical ('surreal') satire being thoroughly representative – and working, in the esca-lating exaggerations by its Yorkshiremen of their impoverished childhoods, to inflict death by parody on serious attempts to talk about the impact of poverty. Watching the poet Tony Harrison, in a recent television interview with Melvyn Bragg, still talking about the issues of language and class which dominate his early poems I felt uncomfortably that this made him seem terribly out of touch – did he only appear on TV and never watch it? Even more uncomfortably, this made those brilliant poems seem under-mined, however much I knew they should not be.

The odd thing is that it is Britain which is thought to be obsessed with class but it has been the USA which has evolved a form of contemporary literature in which class has become newly important. I am referring to 'dirty realism', a kind of writing associated with Raymond Carver, Richard Ford, Tobias Wolff and Bobbie Ann Mason in which the focus is upon blue-collar characters and settings. Carver is certainly one of the most important writers of recent times and I was determined to discuss his writing in this book, above all for that reason, but also because it constitutes a significant example of a widespread resistance on the part of practising writers to the tenets of postmodernism – a resistance which is ignored by academics. As I show in my chapter on 'Postmodern realism', Carver set out to evolve an idiom of narrative prose which would respect the actual condition of people's lives, and to evolve that idiom in self-conscious opposition to what he saw as the flippantly dismissive anti-humanism of a postmodernist like Donald Barthelme.

This book also deploys a necessary simplification. Its division into chapters, each dedicated to a separate postmodern phenomenon, implies that these phenomena function in isolation from each other. In fact, of course, they are mutually influential and dependent. For this reason I have been at pains to indicate how each eponymous phenomenon overlaps with those in the other chapters. Questions of language, the self and genre are relevant throughout; all three are influenced by gender issues which also have an impact on postcolonialism and the debate about Nature. The deconstruction of racial assumptions is similarly connected to the analogous deconstruction of gender assumptions: both of these have had an important impact on how postmodern authors have deployed generic instabilities in their texts. It is for this reason, too, that I discuss Gayatri Spivak in my chapter on Nature as well as in that on 'Postmodern race': she is an important postcolonial theorist but this concern has led her, recently, to condemn the damage which global capital is inflicting on the environment.

What I most wanted to do in this book was to celebrate the variety of writing that has been produced in the postmodern period. A further effect of this is to juxtapose texts which are not routinely discussed alongside each other – for one thing, poems, novels and plays tend to have different books dedicated to them, but for another there is a kind of deadening fastidiousness found in academic circles which fences off thoroughly postmodernist texts from others which are contemporary with them, but which do not sufficiently match up to the postmodernist script. I think that these juxtapositions defamiliarise these mostly famous texts so that they are seen from a refreshing angle.

Introduction

Postmodernism in context

The dominant attitude in postmodernism is disbelief. The dominant strategy of both postmodernist philosophy and postmodernist aesthetics is deconstruction, which is disbelief put into practice. Deconstruction is an anti-system, or a system that subverts systems; it is a mechanism that exposes mechanisms. Deconstruction unscrews belief systems and uncovers their whirring cogs.

The origins of postmodernist disbelief can be traced back to the Victorian period and the cultural crisis at that time, which involved the waning of Christianity as a result of the power of scientific theories like Darwinian evolution and scientific discoveries, especially in geology. This crisis deepened in the modernist period, and the passage from modernism into postmodernism is far from simple. There are crucial elements of continuity between the two: the influence of science on perceptions of human knowledge and identity; the impact of increasing urbanisation and mechanisation; the accelerating collapse of the social and cultural hierarchies which had traditionally dominated the West.

However, during and after the Second World War there were historical events which further undermined the humanist consensus already subverted by modernism: the holocaust, in particular, has been an obsessive focus for postmodern thinkers and writers. (So Jean-François Lyotard, in the third document at the back of this book, claims that the knowledge of Auschwitz changed language itself.) There were historical and social changes which caused radical shifts in cultural perceptions and therefore caused the break away from modernism: the end of empire; the rise of the women's movement, black power and gay pride; the hugely increasing importance of popular culture; the enormous expansion of secondary and further education. Key economic and social changes are associated with postmodernism which have been identified with 'late capitalism', especially the shift from economic structures based on heavy industry to those based on technology. The impact of the technological media, especially television, on social experience and cultural perception is also a crucial postmodern phenomenon. (This emphasis is the one especially associated with Jean-François Lyotard's *The Postmodern Condition*.)

The roots of the extreme philosophical scepticism which characterises the postmodern are sometimes accounted for in purely philosophical terms, as arising out of a philosophical tradition – in particular as a thorough questioning of metaphysics. However, there are also historical and political reasons why the postmodern is characteristically sceptical. These are best described by J. G. Ballard writing in 1974:

> the balance between fiction and reality has changed significantly in the past decade. Increasingly their roles are reversed. We live in a world ruled by fictions of every kind – mass-merchandizing, advertising, politics conducted as a branch of advertising, the instant translation of science and technology into popular imagery, the increasing blurring and intermingling of identities within the realm of consumer goods, the pre-empting of any free or original imaginative response to experience by the television screen. We live inside an enormous novel.[1]

From structuralism to poststructuralism

Postmodernism means entirely different things to different disciplines. Hans Bertens, in his lucid and helpful book *The Idea of the Postmodern*, points out that it means entirely different things, for example, to architecture and literature:

> For Robert Venturi, Denise Scott Brown, Charles Jencks and other theorists, modernist architecture is the purist self-referential architecture of the Bauhaus – Mies van der Rohe, Gropius, and others – and of the corporate architecture of the postwar International Style. Postmodern architecture turns away from this self-absorbed and technocratic purism and turns to the vernacular and to history, thus reintroducing the humanizing narrative element that had been banned by the Bauhaus group and its corporate offshoots.[2]

However, for many of the American literary critics who brought the term postmodernism into circulation in the 1960s and early 1970s, postmodernism is the move *away* from narrative, from representation.

The focus of this book is on literary postmodernism, so the complexities of the term can at least be reduced this far: humanising narratives are anti-postmodernist for these purposes, and the move is very much *away* from representation.

The key background of literary postmodernism is in poststructuralism. The best way of accounting for its origins, therefore, is by referring to the linguistic theories of Ferdinand de Saussure, and my book's first document (pp. 153–7) is taken from his *Course in General Linguistics*. This considerably predates the postmodern period, having been published in 1915 after Saussure's death. But it forms a crucial reference point for all the most important poststructuralist thinkers – Jacques Derrida, Jacques Lacan, Roland Barthes and Michel Foucault, amongst others – and constitutes the crucial premise of deconstruction.

That premise is located in Saussure's discussion of the relationship between language and the 'real world': the impact of his theories is to emphasise the distance between them. The anti-realism which characterises postmodernism can be helpfully explained by reference to this basic idea (though it also has a much longer history in Western philosophy). Saussure's theories call radically into question the common-sense idea that language is simply the means we use to tell each other real things about reality. For Saussure, language is an artificial construct.

Saussure refers to real things like trees and horses as 'referents' and stresses that these are nowhere present in words, or linguistic 'signs'. He divides the sign into the 'signifier' and the 'signified'. The signifier is the sound of the word ('sound-image') and the signified is what the sound is trying to say (the 'concept'). The most important point for the anti-realist input into postmodernism is that the relationship between signifier and signified is arbitrary. There is no natural or real connection between the sound of the word 'tree' and the concept 'tree'. Saussure says that this principle 'dominates all the linguistics of language', but its dominance extends much further than this. The gap this opens between language and the world is the space into which all postmodernist theorising, and explicitly postmodernist literature, enters.

Individual signs are meaningless; they acquire meaning only because they form part of a much larger structure. Because this structure is imposed upon the world it means that the world can only be understood in a structured, as opposed to a 'real', way.

So postmodernist disbelief is extended first and foremost to language. For literature, the most important impact of this is to question, and even to pour scorn upon, realism. The common-sense value placed upon a text being 'realistic' is opposed and often mocked. For literature Saussure's points are further intensified because literature has evolved its own special languages.

Saussure refers to language being a 'master-pattern' for other semiological systems. Literature, as well as deploying language itself, is also such a system which contains within it specifically literary signs and codes – for example, imagery in poetry, or soliloquies in drama. These further codify what literature does to the real and impose further alien structures upon the world.

John Barth deconstructs such codes in his story 'Lost in the Funhouse', which is a famous example of early postmodernist fiction (published in 1968). He introduces his character Ambrose and then places him in the back seat of his family's car, adopts his point of view and then introduces Magda G— and says:

> Initials, blanks, or both were often substituted for proper names in nineteenth-century fiction to enhance the illusion of reality . . . Interestingly, as with other aspects of realism, it is an *illusion* that is being enhanced, by purely artificial means. Is it likely, does it violate the principle of verisimilitude, that a thirteen-year-old boy could make such a sophisticated observation?[3]

Fifty years, and enormous social and literary changes, separate Saussure's text from Barth's. I am simplifying strategically at this point when I say that their dominant idea is the same because I want to dwell on its dominance. That dominant idea is that there is no direct access to the real, which can only be problematically mediated by language and textuality. Magda G— is not a person but a fragmentary name; the use of 'initials' or 'blanks' is meant, according to a nineteenth-century convention, to make us believe in her, but the effect of drawing attention to them is to make us aware of how they enact an absence – the sense that the real Magda is missing from the text and replaced by a sign whose inadequacy is visible on the page. This insistence that Magda G— is not real but textual exemplifies the starting-point of the most characteristic postmodernist thinking. It is this which leads to deconstruction because it motivates the characteristic desire to reveal that what claims to be real or natural is actually artificial, is actually fabricated. It is this which leads to a constitutive suspicion of all claims to authenticity, all claims to direct expression of the truth.

There is a further exemplary point in both the Saussure and the Barth texts – both stress that what appears to be real is in fact structural. That is, what appears to point to something 'out there' in the world actually refers back on itself to an internally coherent structure of meanings. This means that the appearance of realness is an effect produced by an understanding of that structure of meanings. This effect is so familiar that it is not noticed as such; the familiarity transforms it into a pane that is so transparent that we seem to be in living communion with the outside world.

Deconstruction points to the pane and the flaws in the glass; it reveals that what we are experiencing is a structure. Poststructuralism is dominated by the idea that we live inside multiple structures which are so familiar that they appear natural. Poststructuralists, especially Jacques Derrida, acknowledge the importance of Saussure's structuralism but question many of the assumptions that underlie it. Most importantly for postmodernism, they question the possibility of standing outside the structure in a position from which the structure can be properly understood. Saussure's linguistics implies that it is possible to fly above the landscape of language so that all its structural features can be discerned; poststructuralism insists that such a privileged vantage point is unavailable, that we are stranded in the landscape of language and too surrounded by its features for their ultimate shape to be knowable. Deconstruction emerges, above all, from the poststructuralist sense that this landscape of language is inescapable, that all we can see is the language, and not the landscape.

This difference exemplifies an important contrast between modernism and postmodernism. Saussurian linguistics is characteristically modernist in an anti-realism which is nonetheless able to discern hierarchies and patterns of meaning. Arbitrariness is important at the level of the individual sign, but even so becomes the necessary premise of an overriding structure in which those signs find their proper place. Poststructuralism is characteristically postmodernist in the way it flattens these hierarchies and subjects these patterns to subversive questioning; structure, for postmodernists, arouses endless suspicion.

So Jacques Lacan, by deploying both Freudian psychoanalysis and structuralist linguistics, allows each to infiltrate the other so that both are interrogated as systems of thought. This collision of structures has been especially important for a characteristically postmodernist anxiety about the self – Lacan's theorising is directed above all at exploring how identity is constructed by language. This produces perhaps the biggest postmodernist affront of all to common sense because, in applying anti-realism to identity questions, it insists that the self is a linguistic construct, so that its reality is as inaccessible as the reality of Saussure's tree. The 'I' is a sign amongst other signs.

Freud's impact on literary modernism was enormous and Lacan's impact on postmodernism is comparable. Characterisation in modernist novels was profoundly affected by the idea of the unconscious, the idea that the self contains within it irrational drives which are hidden and alien to that self. Lacan's re-readings of that idea, via structuralist linguistics, have profoundly affected how postmodernist writers treat the crucial issue of identity, especially in relation to notions of desire.

This is an obsessive theme and characteristically postmodernist in its anti-humanist tendency – a point which becomes clearer if it is contrasted with the value placed upon love by classic realist novelists. The centrality of its role in novels by Jane Austen and George Eliot, for example, is tied to a celebration of the human capacity for imaginative sympathy and self-transcendence, and the narrative linking of love and marriage reinforces a sense of social stability based upon individual happiness. Postmodernist desire contrasts starkly with this humanist concept; it is an anarchic force that tears selves apart. This is evident, for example, in the work I discuss in this book by J. G. Ballard and Angela Carter, who share an interest in pornography – combined, in Carter's case, with an obsession with de Sade.

It is through Lacan's potent hybrid of Freudian psychoanalysis and structuralist linguistics that postmodernist desire has been most extensively explored. This results in an even more thorough questioning of ontological coherence than the modernist anxiety provoked by the unconscious. Lacanian thought takes up the focus upon the subversion of any unitary or coherent self by repressed and displaced desire but it then intensifies that subversion by its insistence that the unconscious is structured like a language:

> what the psychoanalytic experience discovers in the unconscious is the whole structure of language. Thus from the outset I have alerted informed minds to the extent to which the notion that the unconscious is merely the seat of the instincts will have to be rethought . . .
>
> This simple definition assumes that language is not to be confused with the various psychical and somatic functions that serve it in the speaking subject – primarily because language and its structure exist prior to the moment at which each subject at a certain point in his mental development makes his entry into it.[4]

Lacan's emphasis on the priority of language and his focus on the powerful but secretive workings of desire combine to depict a psyche which is thoroughly enmeshed in structures which pre-determine what it is possible to think and feel. This is one of a number of postmodernist strands of thought which oppose liberal humanist assumptions (which have been so powerful in Western thought that they appear to be simply common sense) about individual freedom of expression and thought. For Lacan the psyche is so occupied by structures of language and desire that the self is not itself.

For this reason his use of the phrase 'speaking subject' is significant: it simultaneously refers to subjectivity and subjection. This telling combination of meanings is also highly significant in the use of the word 'subject' in the work of Michel Foucault, whose earliest writings (1961–80) were focused upon how the subject is constructed socially and institutionally. As with the other poststructuralists, the reference to 'subjects' is firstly a reference to linguistic structures, because it refers to 'I' as the subject of a sentence. What is implied in this is again (as in Lacan) an insistence on how language exists before it is entered by individuals: the 'I' of the sentence is there before I enter it. For Foucault the most important issues raised by this are political: to speak as the 'I' of a sentence is to adopt a position of power. His work is focused above all on how linguistic structures and power structures are ideologically entangled with each other.

This means that Foucault is particularly concerned with how systems of thought, like medicine, psychopathology, economics or jurisprudence, establish themselves as forms of objective knowledge but impose themselves as ideological structures. He calls these systems of thought 'discourses' and insists on their historical specificity and their political role as institutions in constructing the human subject: they work by establishing norms and categories as though they were universal and natural so that their political impact is concealed. This Foucauldian concept has been especially important to postcolonial thinkers like Edward Said, whom I discuss in my chapter on 'Postmodern race'. Foucault's focus on the interactions of knowledge and power, and of textuality and power, has also exercised a crucial influence on New Historicists like Stephen Greenblatt.

Theories of the postmodern

Poststructuralism is an important postmodern phenomenon, but none of these major poststructuralists explicitly theorised postmodernism. Their self-reflexivity does not extend into analysing the cultural origins and motives of their own deconstructive practices. However, for all the major theorists of postmodernism – Jean-François Lyotard, Fredric Jameson and Jean Baudrillard – poststructuralism is a major point of departure. This is because postmodern theory stresses, above all, issues of representation – it focuses upon how the 'real' is constructed through language, how it is everywhere transformed into textuality, and how what appears literal is in fact metaphorical.

The most famous statement by a postmodernist theorist is Lyotard's definition of the postmodern as an 'incredulity towards metanarratives'.[5] There are acute problems with this as a generalisation. What is powerful in Lyotard's writing, however, is how – despite this problem – he links his theorising so closely to historical events:

the very basis of each of the great narratives of emancipation has, so to speak, been invalidated over the last fifty years. All that is real is rational, all that is rational is real: 'Auschwitz' refutes speculative doctrine. At least that crime, which was real, was not rational. All that is proletarian is communist, all that is communist is proletarian: 'Berlin 1953, Budapest 1956, Czechoslovakia 1968, Poland 1980' (to mention only the most obvious examples) refute the doctrine of historical materialism; the workers rise up against the Party. All that is democratic exists through and for the people, and vice versa: 'May 1968' refutes the doctrine of parliamentary liberalism. If left to themselves, the laws of supply and demand will result in universal prosperity, and vice versa; 'the crises of 1911 and 1929' refute the doctrine of economic liberalism.[6]

Auschwitz is a crucial event for Lyotard because its stark, appallingly cruel irrationality destroys the belief in rational human progress achieved through increasing knowledge. The collapse of this metanarrative, associated with nineteenth-century idealist philosophy, especially Hegel, has enormous cultural consequences. As my third document shows (pp. 161–3), Lyotard insists that Auschwitz shatters the possibility of a liberal consensus premised upon shared humanist assumptions. It is here that he deploys his concept of 'the differend' which I discuss at length in my chapter on 'Postmodern genres'. Behind it are Saussurian premises – Auschwitz is a sign and its referent is lost. But Lyotard goes far beyond Saussure in his insistence on the loss of this historical reality. Structuralist linguistics implies a shared understanding of the sign, but Auschwitz has destroyed that and replaced it with stark mutual incomprehension. When that name is spoken, the response is not that this is a problem that can be resolved; it is that the problem cannot even be named in the first place because there is no common language in which it can be formulated: 'it is the sign that something remains to be phrased which is not, something which is not determined' (Document 3, p. 162).

Fredric Jameson emerges from a different tradition to Lyotard. His Marxism leads him to associate postmodernism with what he calls 'late capitalism', so that he premises his discussion upon sociological theories such as those of Daniel Bell about 'postindustrial society': 'consumer society, media society, information society, electronic society or high tech'.[7] Jameson, like other Marxists, is sceptical about these theories which associate modernism with heavy industry and postmodernism with technology because they imply that the emphasis on class struggle is no longer relevant. He prefers the term 'multinational' to 'postindustrial'

(p. 35). However, he is more willing than other Marxists to explore at length the implications of the idea of a cultural break from modernism which is based upon these symptomatic changes in economic structure.

Jameson's theories are highly applicable to literature, especially because he himself applies them provocatively to specific literary texts. His analyses of the contexts and meanings of postmodernist irony and parody (or what he calls 'pastiche') are especially valuable and their linking to what he calls a 'new depthlessness' does help to explain the impact of much post-modernist literature. This is an important point of departure for my own discussion throughout this book. In particular, he names four depth models which have been repudiated:

> (1) the dialectical one of essence and appearance (along with a whole range of concepts of ideology or false consciousness which tend to accompany it); (2) the Freudian model of latent and manifest, or of repression . . .; (3) the existential model of authenticity and inauthen-ticity whose heroic or tragic thematics are closely related to that other great opposition between alienation and disalienation, itself equally a casualty of the poststructural or postmodern period; and (4) most recently, the great semiotic opposition between signifier and signified, which was itself rapidly unraveled and deconstructed during its brief heyday in the 1960's and 1970's. What replaces these various depth models is for the most part a conception of practices, discourses, and textual play . . . here too depth is replaced by surface, or by multiple surfaces.
>
> (p. 12)

This depthlessness is linked to other losses: the withering away of Nature, the decline of a historical consciousness, and the 'waning of affect' (p. 10). Jameson's emphasis on multiple surfaces can be compared to Jean Baudrillard's emphasis on the postmodern dominance of simulation, on a culture so influenced by the technological media that any sense of the real is lost and replaced by the multiplying of signs and representations. Depthless simulacra are so all-pervading that they create a sense that experience cannot be real unless it is represented, preferably by television. In Don Delillo's *White Noise* a man carries a TV set into a room occupied by others, like him, who have taken refuge from a chemical cloud (or 'airborne toxic event'). He displays its blankness to the others and then utters a lament over the failure of TV to represent their suffering:

> Are they so bored by spills and contaminations and wastes? Do they think this is just television? 'There's too much television already – why

show more?' Don't they know it's real? Shouldn't the streets be
crawling with cameramen and soundmen and reporters? Shouldn't we
be yelling out the window at them, 'Leave us alone, we've been
through enough, get out of here with your vile instruments of
intrusion.'[8]

Jameson, as a Marxist, is acutely uncomfortable with what he calls the
'essential triviality' (*Postmodernism*, p. 46) of postmodernism and often
seems hard pressed not to betray his impatience with its tendencies towards
the amoral and the apolitical. He is much more preoccupied than
Baudrillard (and Delillo) with how 'the logic of the simulacrum' (p. 46) has
been deployed by global capitalism as a weapon which is all the more potent
because of its mercurial elusiveness. His official position is ambivalent.
Given that postmodernism is a historical phenomenon, he considers that
attempts at moral condemnation of it are a 'category mistake' (p. 46) and
that the only way to regard it is by analogy with Marx's ambivalence to
capitalism, that it is both the best and the worst thing that has ever
happened to the human race (p. 47).

Jameson does to some extent genuinely sustain this position and it is
evident that he does (almost guiltily at times) enjoy much postmodern art.
Frequently, however, his irritation is all too clear and what are often highly
illuminating insights can be marred by a simultaneous tendency towards
generalisation and dismissiveness. These attitudes are only possible because
Jameson ignores some crucial postmodern phenomena – especially feminism
and postcolonialism. An attention to these highly political movements
would surely require him to modify his insistence on triviality; his engage-
ment with them would be especially interesting because their relationship to
postmodernism is as ambivalent as his own. As I show in my chapters on
'Postmodern gender' and 'Postmodern race', feminists and postcolonialists
are beneficiaries of the postmodern collapsing of traditional hierarchies but
are chary of postmodernist underminings of political activism.

Jameson's version of postmodernism, as it relates to literature, is oriented
towards camp and the Lyotardian 'sublime'. He mentions Susan Sontag's
importance as a theorist of camp. She played an important role, for this
reason, in the early evolution of a postmodernist sensibility, at a point
before it was even labelled as such. In her 'Notes on Camp'[9] she says:

Camp sees everything in quotation marks. It's not a lamp, but a
'lamp'; not a woman but a 'woman'. To perceive Camp in objects and
persons is to understand Being-as-Playing-a-Role. It is the farthest
extension, in sensibility, of the metaphor of life as theater.

(p. 109)

Surrealism had similarly drawn attention to the painterliness of painting, and the textuality of texts, and, like camp, had made witty play with the sophisticated frisson of recognition that this arouses. Where the two differ is that surrealism contains the vestige of a modernist surface versus depth model – being premised on the concept of the unconscious – whereas camp is thoroughly postmodern in its confrontational depthlessness. Its Wildean preference for style rather than sincerity (Sontag, 'Notes on Camp', p. 116), its emphasis on codes rather than self-expression, question whether there actually exists any 'real' self beneath the coded behaviour.

Jameson suggests combining camp with the sublime and refers to that idea – which looms so large in Romantic literature – of a kind of sublime awe which combines pain and enjoyment so that it creates a severe problem of representation. He strangely fails, at this point, to mention Lyotard who has most famously redeployed this idea in the context of postmodern representation connected to 'a shattering of belief' and a 'discovery of the "lack of reality" of reality, together with the invention of other realities' (*The Postmodern Condition*, p. 77). And Lyotard continues:

> Moreover, the postmodern is that which puts forward the unpresentable in presentation itself; that which denies itself the solace of good forms, the consensus of a taste which would make it possible to share collectively the nostalgia for the unattainable; that which searches for new presentations, not in order to enjoy them but in order to impart a stronger sense of the unpresentable. A postmodern artist or writer is in the position of a philosopher: the text he writes, the work he produces are not in principle governed by preestablished rules, and they cannot be judged according to a determining judgement, by applying familiar categories to the text or to the work.
>
> (p. 81)

These notions of camp and the unpresentable sublime which Jameson collides (p. 34) are very helpful when explaining the most thoroughly postmodernist writing – the poetry of John Ashbery, for example, which I discuss in my chapter on the 'Postmodern self'. The problem with Jameson's totalising tendencies, however, is that they depict a postmodern condition – and a postmodernist aesthetics evolved in response to that condition – which are much more uniform than the actual condition and the actual aesthetics. In the interests of creating a coherent argument Jameson depicts a late capitalist culture – oddly for a Marxist – which is much more coherent, much more lacking in contradictions than it actually is. The depthless phenomena which he identifies interlock to present such a consistent picture that it is highly persuasive and all the more so because those phenomena are undeniably important aspects of postmodern culture.

Jameson is also a very eloquent writer; so, referring to one of his recurrent themes, the 'radical eclipse of Nature' (p. 34), he says:

> Heidegger's 'field path' is, after all, irredeemably and irrevocably destroyed by late capital, by the green revolution, by neocolonialism and the megalopolis, which runs its superhighways over the older fields and vacant lots and turns Heidegger's 'house of being' into condominiums, if not the most miserably unheated, rat-infested tenement buildings.
>
> (pp. 34–5)

The deconstruction of Heidegger is an important point of departure for postmodernism, important most conspicuously for Derrida in opposing existential notions of authenticity. Walter Abish, as I show in my chapter on 'Postmodern language', associates Heidegger with a specifically German valorising of Nature which is inextricable from a sinister ideology. However, Jameson's equation of Nature and Heidegger here is simply a rhetorical strategy designed to consign Nature to what (given his emphasis throughout on postmodern factitiousness, on the dominance of technology and the consequent dominance of representation and simulacra) is its inevitable grave.

Jameson needs Nature to be tidied away. But this is a telling point at which postmodernist theory reveals its tendency to simplify the postmodern condition. However important simulation is, and however exemplary that importance is of the kind of culture created by 'late capitalism', Nature has still been a crucial issue in postmodern culture. This is partly because it has been so much under threat from the forces with which postmodernists are preoccupied, but the effect of the ecological lobby has been to draw attention to the meaning of Nature, so that its meaning has been a constant source of debate. What the postmodernist tidying away of Nature ignores is that a key aspect of postmodern culture lies in the interaction between technology and Nature. Contemporary news reflects this in its coverage of stories related to test-tube babies, the genetic modification of crops, cloning, the human genome, and so on. Literature reveals its superiority to theory in this context in its refusal of tidiness, and its refusal to conform to what theorists say it should be. My chapter on 'Postmodern Nature' is dedicated to showing how fiction and poetry have dwelt on an issue which postmodernist theory has consigned to the dustbin.

Jameson is disdainful of science fiction (see pp. 283–4) yet this is a postmodernist genre in which the interaction between Nature and technology has been a central issue. This is evident in J. G. Ballard's *Crash* which I analyse in my chapter on 'Postmodern genres'. However, it is evident above all in the figure of the cyborg where the boundary between the biological and the technological is opened to repeated question. The photograph by Mariko Mori on the cover of this book illustrates this point with particular sharpness: the young Japanese woman who is its central subject has dressed herself up as a cyborg and is posed next to a Sega computer console which is decorated with cartoon figures. The woman and the computer are the same height and echo each other's metallic colouring: one is a human masquerading as a machine, the other is a machine displaying half-human representations. Together they resemble an alien couple who are hybrids of the biological and the cybernetic.

The title of the photograph is 'Play With Me': this is significantly poised between postmodernism (where it would signify amoral play) and feminism (where it would express an anxiety about commodification – the equation of the woman with the computer game). This indicates a crucial debate in the postmodern period in which gender theory has been similarly poised.

It has been gender theorists who have most concerned themselves with the role of Nature because gender in the postmodern period has raised questions about the role of biology in determining identity. Donna J. Haraway has expressed a confrontational preference for cyborgs over goddesses and done so in response to an organicist feminism of the sort championed by Susan Griffin and Adrienne Rich. This debate has to be seen in the context of a wider concern with gender 'essentialism' which includes post-Lacanian feminists like Luce Irigaray who have been accused by Anglo-American feminists of tying feminine identity too closely to the female body. While this accusation has some truth, the post-Lacanian exploration of the relationship between the self and the body has produced insights which have been powerfully suggestive, and have helped to transform attitudes to gender.

These issues have been formulated in a different way by Julia Kristeva, whose emphasis has always been upon the body and its relationship to subjectivity and identity formation. These theories are important in their own right but they also form part of a range of postmodern thinking about ontological and gender questions which are profoundly at odds with the Jamesonian/Baudrillardian account of postmodernism. Nature, in the form of the body – especially the maternal body – plays a key role in these discussions and there is certainly no lack of affect because these subjects arouse a full range of often uncontrollable emotions. Kristeva's theory of 'abjection' has been especially important for literary studies where it has been used to theorise about bodily and gender identity. My fifth document (pp. 165–9) is an extract from Kristeva's definitive statement of the theory, which she took, originally, from the anthropological writings of Mary Douglas concerning rituals surrounding bodily waste. Kristeva uses it to explore the way that identity is formed in relation to the mother as the desired and despised source of succour, and in relation to the threat of the other in the form of death and sickness. Disgust, fear and horror are aroused by the abject:

> There looms, within abjection, one of those violent, dark revolts of being, directed against a threat that seems to emanate from an exorbitant outside or inside, ejected beyond the scope of the possible, the tolerable, the thinkable. It lies there, quite close, but it cannot be assimilated. It beseeches, worries, and fascinates desire, which, nevertheless, does not let itself be seduced.[10]

This concept is especially relevant to Toni Morrison's *Beloved* where the central narrative event is the killing of a baby ('Beloved') by her slave mother, Sethe, so that slavery has a similar impact to that which Kristeva attributes to Auschwitz, because, in both, death interferes with childhood which 'is supposed to save me from death' (p. 4). This is linked to identity issues which are especially acute in Morrison's novel because it focuses on the loss of identity which slaves suffer because they do not own themselves; this means that they are deprived of subjectivity and their selves are invaded by an oppressive and alien otherness. Slavery is an abjection because it is a form of living death and Beloved is intensely abject because she has been forcibly expelled by her mother so that she is defined entirely in terms of loss. Her return as a ghost is therefore a source of particular horror and is depicted repeatedly in terms of abject imagery; before long she starts falling apart. This starts with the loss of a tooth – but childhood and death are mingled in this because this ordinary childhood event is linked to a terminal process: 'Among the things she could not remember was when she first knew that she could wake up any day and find herself in pieces. She had two dreams: exploding and being swallowed.'[11]

The work of Toni Morrison, who is certainly one of the most important writers in the postmodern period, sharply rebukes the depthless, affectless, ahistorical vision of postmodernity. Her career has been dedicated to evoking the presence of African Americans inside American history and above all to making that presence and that history *felt*. Her work is also exemplary of much literature in the period in containing elements which conform to the postmodernist norm – as defined by both theorists of postmodernism and by postmodernist literary critics – and others which conspicuously do not. *Beloved*, for example, is a self-consciously fragmentary narrative which displays its own textuality and makes political points about fictiveness, especially about the meaning of the narrative point of view (as, for example, in the sharp jolt when it switches to the point of view of whites, p. 148). On the other hand its most important premise – and here it has to be considered alongside Morrison's other novels – is that history is retrievable and continues to be important (and even 'real') for African Americans as a constitutive part of their late twentieth-century identity.

This indicates where the problem lies for a thoroughly postmodernist literature. The loss of the referent leads to a writing which is pure textual play: fiction like Barth's 'Lost in the Funhouse' extended to great self-reflexive length, and poetry like John Ashbery's epics of camp irony (like *Flow Chart*). When the real entirely disappears there is nothing for irony or parody to brace itself against and the result is monotonous, however paradoxically polyphonous. This is why so many writers angrily object when they are labelled as postmodernist: it is part of the business of a writer to want to say something about actual experience, and often this is what drives a writer to write in the first place. Readers also tend to object to the multiplying of fictions: in fact the best-selling books, currently, are not fictions at all but 'true-life' accounts of one sort or another. The taste for 'reality TV' may have similar origins: both accounts of the real are obviously only representations of the real, but their prominence suggests a hunger for the referent which may even have its origins in the cultural dominance of Baudrillardian simulacra.

What this suggests is that the cultural dominance of simulations and constructs leads to a deconstructive sensibility in which the relationship between the constructed and the real is constantly interrogated. This means that much of the most powerful literature in the period focuses on that relationship, which requires it to draw upon traditional realist techniques at the same time as it calls them into question with postmodernist techniques. This, as I show in my chapter on 'Postmodern realism', is what happens in Morrison's novels, so that a fractured gendered and racial identity is depicted in its interactions with a textual history through which real history can be problematically glimpsed.

A differently oriented mingling of postmodernism and realism also has an exemplary presence in the still undervalued poetry of Edwin Morgan whose concrete poem 'Message Clear' is my fourth document (p. 164). This is one of a group that Morgan has termed 'emergent poems', ' where everything comes out of, but at the same time mounts towards, the last line'.[12] Each of these poems seems to move through numerous attempts to arrive at the complete articulacy represented by this last line, but this eludes them because they have spaces where most of their letters should be. What this does is to focus on the signifier which it visibly deconstructs, so that the physical nature of the sign is revealed and its relationship to the signified is interrogated as words assemble, before the last line, across the spaces. So 'Message Clear', with its spaces removed, reads:

> Am I?/ if/ I am he,/ Hero,/ Hurt/ There and/ Here and here/ And there,/ I am rife/ in/ Sion and/ I die:/ A mere sect/ A mere section/ of/ The life/ of/ men./ Sure, / The die/ Is set and/ I am the surd – / At rest/ O life! / I am here:/ I act,/ I run,/ I meet,/ I tie,/ I stand;/ I am Thoth,/ I am Ra,/ I am the Sun/ I am the Son – / I am the erect one: if/ I am rent,/ I am safe/ I am sent,/ I heed,/ I test./ I read/ A thread,/ A stone,/ A tread,/ A throne./ I resurrect/ a life:/ I am in life;/ I am resurrection;/ I am the resurrection and/ I am;/ I am the resurrection and the life.[13]

To remove the spaces from the poem like this, though, destroys it, for the spaces are as important as the letters – they are cognate with the silences that have preoccupied modernist and postmodernist literature. The letters strive for stability because, when they emerge, they always do so in the place they occupy in the last line. The spaces, however, undermine this stability – they keep shifting in the line, so that each line has a different shape, and its sounds and its silences (and therefore its meanings) vary each time.

What is exemplary about 'Message Clear' is that it is an act of deconstruction which at the same time reconstructs, and finds alternative and plural meanings within its traditional message. Each line is a brief variant shape and the poem's multiple fissurings cause the words to sit with their feet hanging over a void, but they are not anxious about this emptiness – they use it as a background for their own expressiveness so that where previously there was a single monolithic meaning, the poem discovers numerous other possibilities. So the splinters from the Christian message build tentative other messages ('I am the surd/ . . . I am Thoth,/ I am Ra,/ I am the Sun').

Therefore, what begins by looking like postmodernist scepticism about language ends by celebrating the range of expressive capabilities it contains. So everywhere in his poetry Morgan responds optimistically and playfully to the postmodern as a fascinating challenge – his poetry is self-consciously various because it responds to a sense of its period as quickly changing with a quick-change art. In this process he juxtaposes postmodernist strategies with realist ones so that they interrogate each other. In his poem 'Not Playing the Game' he says:

> – Although a poem is
> undoubtedly a 'game'
> it is not a game.[14]

Which is to emphasise that poetic playfulness is also serious and however much the 'real' is deconstructed, it is vital that the poem can evoke it. This is why Morgan is also a poet of place who has written starkly realist poems about Glasgow.

The work of Toni Morrison and Edwin Morgan exemplifies a range of writing in the postmodern period which contains both postmodernist and anti-postmodernist elements. While there are obviously others whose work can be comfortably discussed in the terms defined by Lyotard, Jameson and Baudrillard, writers like John Barth and Don Delillo, whom I have referred to here, and others like John Ashbery and Walter Abish, whom I discuss elsewhere in this book, there are yet others who are entirely anti-postmodernist. The poetry of Seamus Heaney, who is generally regarded as one of the most important contemporary poets, has its roots in a Romantic poetic preoccupied with nature and lyric emotion. His work constantly refers to Irish history and associates it with an organic metaphor of depth which is obsessively recurrent. The fiction of Raymond Carver, as I show in my chapter on 'Postmodern realism', is profoundly opposed to the post-modernism of his American predecessors such as Donald Barthelme, and he made explicit statements saying so. Carver is one of a number of American writers, including Richard Ford, Tobias Wolff and Bobbie Ann Mason, who have used the short-story form to powerful realist effect; the short story form has been especially important in this period and I refer throughout this book to three important anthologies which contain some of the most fascinating postwar fiction: *Fictions*, edited by Joseph F. Trimmer, *The Penguin Book of Modern British Short Stories*, edited by Malcolm Bradbury and *The Oxford Book of American Short Stories*, edited by Joyce Carol Oates.

Bobbie Ann Mason's story 'Shiloh' illustrates the simultaneous truth and untruth of postmodernist theory. The lives of 'Shiloh's' protagonists are so dominated by trivia that they seem like personifications of depthlessness. Norma Jean Moffitt works at the Rexall drugstore and is very knowledge-able about cosmetics; she does weight-training and plays the electric organ. Her husband Leroy is a truckdriver who is unemployed because he has an injured leg; he smokes marijuana and makes things from craft kits. Any knowledge they have comes from TV programmes like *Donahue*. Their rela-tionship seems entirely shallow but the story takes on another dimension when Norma Jean starts to grow away from Leroy when she starts to do evening classes. Feminist points could have been made about this but Mason deflects these by viewing the story from Leroy's point of view, so that his plight arouses sympathy, especially in the climactic scene where the couple visit Shiloh and Norma Jean says she wants to leave him. The story deviates most tellingly from postmodernism as the battleground acquires epiphanic significance when Leroy

> tries to focus on the fact that thirty-five hundred soldiers died on the grounds around him. He can only think of that war as a board game with plastic soldiers . . . General Grant, drunk and furious, shoved the Southerners back to Corinth, where Mabel and Jet Beasley were married years later, when Mabel was still thin and good-looking. The next day, Mabel and Jet visited the battleground, and then Norma Jean was born, and then she married Leroy and they had a baby, which they lost, and now Leroy and Norma Jean are here at the same battleground. Leroy knows he is leaving out a lot. He is leaving out the insides of history.[15]

On the one hand this confirms the Jamesonian point about the loss of the historical referent. Leroy is aware only of the pop history outlines of the Civil War battle – he has a shallow contemporary mind on whom these historical depths are mostly lost. This is so easy to say that it is almost a truism. What is more arresting in this passage is the mental effort Leroy makes to understand this history and to enter into it fully as an experience. This is amplified because it has come to be entangled with his own history and especially that of his marriage, so that the 'insides of history' come to be equated with the 'real inner workings of a marriage'. This indicates the extent to which it is important (and also inevitable) that the 'real', and even 'real history', are going to be reached after, and that human thought requires it because otherwise experience cannot be even remotely understood. It is worth noting that Mason's first book was *Nabokov's Garden: A Guide to Ada* (1974) and that Nabokov was one of the godfathers of postmodernist fiction. Mason's own response, by contrast, but similarly to Raymond Carver, is to evolve a form of realism that is aware of postmodernism but insists on the human need to reach out for 'the insides' of the referent, however ungraspable it finally is.

What I have aimed to do, above all, in this book, is to represent the full range of writing in the postmodern period. Otherwise, key elements of the literary world in that period get lost. One flagrant sign of that is how at odds with postmodernism is the most famous literary story in postmodern times – the Plath/Hughes affair. The two poets both emerged out of a tradition of nature poetry and continued to draw upon the characteristic imagery of that tradition throughout their careers, adapting it, nonetheless, to deal with characteristically postmodern concerns with the self. Their clash in the 1960s, and the subsequent clashes of Hughes' attackers and defenders – drawn up around opposed gender attitudes – is characterised by an overload of affect. This arises from contrasting attitudes to what is conspicuously a love story, however painful: a story which (like Hughes, in Plath's account, forcibly stripping off her earrings) strips the postmodern quotation marks from around the word 'love' and leaves it standing naked again.

Notes

1 J. G. Ballard, 'Introduction to the French Edition of *Crash*', reprinted in *Crash* (London: Flamingo, 1993), p. 8.
2 Hans Bertens, *The Idea of the Postmodern* (London: Routledge, 1995), pp. 3–4.
3 John Barth, 'Lost in the Funhouse', in Joseph F. Trimmer and C. Wade Jennings (eds), *Fictions* (Fort Worth: Harcourt Brace, 1998), p. 269.
4 Jacques Lacan, 'The Agency of the Letter in the Unconscious or Reason since Freud', in *Ecrits: A Selection* (London: Tavistock, 1977), pp. 147–8.
5 Jean-François Lyotard, *The Postmodern Condition: A Report on Knowledge*, trans. Geoff Bennington and Brian Massumi (Manchester: Manchester University Press, 1984), p. xxiv.
6 Andrew Benjamin (ed.), *The Lyotard Reader* (Oxford: Blackwell, 1989), p. 318.
7 Fredric Jameson, *Postmodernism or, The Cultural Logic of Late Capitalism* (London: Verso, 1991), p. 3. All references to Jameson are to this volume.
8 Don Delillo, *White Noise* (London: Pan, 1986), p. 162.
9 Susan Sontag, 'Notes on Camp', in *A Susan Sontag Reader* (Harmondsworth: Penguin, 1983), pp. 105–19.
10 Julia Kristeva, *Powers of Horror: An Essay on Abjection* (New York: Columbia University Press, 1982), p. 1.
11 Toni Morrison, *Beloved* (London: Pan Books, 1988), p. 133.
12 Edwin Morgan's note on his poem 'Seven Headlines', in Emmett Williams, *An Anthology of Concrete Poetry* (New York: Something Else Press, 1967). The book is unpaginated, but organised alphabetically according to the names of contributors.
13 A 'translation' of the poem by Heather Bremer which first appeared in the *TLS* on 3 February 1966, incorporating two corrections by Morgan that appeared on 10 February. See Geoffrey Summerfield (ed.), *Worlds: Seven Modern Poets* (Harmondsworth: Penguin, 1974), pp. 275–7. This book also includes a selection of poems by Morgan and a note by him on the origins of and motives for his writing.
14 Edwin Morgan, *Collected Poems* (Manchester: Carcanet, 1990), p. 277.
15 Bobbie Ann Mason, 'Shiloh', in Joseph F. Trimmer and C. Wade Jennings (eds), *Fictions* (Fort Worth: Harcourt Brace, 1998), p. 882.

1

Postmodern language

As I indicated in the Introduction, language is a key issue in postmodernism, so language and textuality are even more central to postmodernist litera- ture. There are continuities with modernism here in the movement away from the realist view of language as an unproblematic medium of self- expression and communication. Continuities with modernist 'formal desperation' are also evident, and postmodernist authors often press these concerns playfully and self-reflexively further.

J. G. Ballard's point, which I quoted in the Introduction, about living in 'a world ruled by fictions of every kind'[1] is crucial because it indicates why a contemporary sensibility is inevitably deconstructive. Don Delillo's *White Noise* is a brilliant example of how postmodernist authors have described the impact on language of the technological media, especially television, and of consumer capitalism: its title refers to the overwhelming cacophony of technological voices which bombard the postmodern viewer and consumer.

The historical experience of the postmodern constantly imposes the knowledge that we are surrounded by representations rather than truth, that what we are told has been pre-packaged by ideological distortion – this makes acts of deconstruction a constant and inevitable mental habit. It means that 'mass-merchandizing, advertising, politics conducted as a branch of advertising' are so omnipresent that it is impossible to function mentally without deconstructing their claims. In particular, this is a period in which propaganda, misinformation and 'spin' have played a conspicuous and crucial role, a period in which, as Noam Chomsky has said, political elites have been notably 'dedicated to indoctrination and thought control, a major and largely neglected theme of modern history'.[2]

Before 1990 the Cold War confrontation of two ideologies and the conflicting claims of capitalism and communism made the workings of ideology starkly obvious. But the idea that things are not what they seem is everywhere in contemporary culture and is vividly represented in the figure of the spy, or undercover agent, which obsesses cinema, popular literature and TV. The recurrence of this shady figure reveals the presence of hidden agendas and alternative versions of the truth.

For Jean-François Lyotard the historical events that have shaped post-modernity, especially the holocaust, have put language under extreme pressure and thoroughly undermined the rationalist consensus upon which it depends. In my third document (pp. 161–3) he says that the silence that surrounds the phrase 'Auschwitz was an extermination camp' is not a 'state of mind . . . it is a sign that something remains to be phrased which is not, something which is not determined'.[3] I discuss this passage elsewhere in this book, but well before Lyotard something very like Lyotardian 'dissensus' had shaped what Martin Esslin labelled 'absurd drama'. In plays such as Samuel Beckett's *Waiting for Godot* and Harold Pinter's *The Caretaker*, the grounds of consensus upon which communication depends are radically deconstructed. Beckett's plays, which were first performed in the 1950s, are early expressions of postmodernist anxieties about the loss of metanarratives and the damage that loss inflicts on language:

> *Long silence*
> VLADIMIR: Say something!
> ESTRAGON: I'm trying.
> *Long silence*
> VLADIMIR: (*in anguish*). Say anything at all!
> ESTRAGON: What do we do now?
> VLADIMIR: Wait for Godot.
> ESTRAGON: Ah!
> *Silence.*
> VLADIMIR: This is awful![4]

Beckett's plays stand in a liminal position between modernism and post-modernism. They inherit from modernism their deployment of a fragmentariness whose self-consciousness indicates that only fragments are now possible; a fully coherent work would imply that it is possible, still, to make extensive sense of the world into which human beings are thrown. The language issue is inevitably involved in this because the collapse into fragmentariness indicates that language is faced with an impossible struggle to cope with that systemic failure to comprehend, and find significance, which underlies the modern experience.

Beckett intensifies this with a mid-century existentialism which focuses upon the post-Christian predicament: without God human beings are thrown into lives that are without any defining context. His plays are most telling for the ways they dramatise this loss of context and for how they invent settings which are non-settings – a stage bare except for a single tree (*Waiting for Godot*), or a single room where the characters are in a wheelchair or immobile in dustbins (*Endgame*), or the main character is buried in sand (*Happy Days*). This is a form of anti-theatre because it defies expectations that plays will provide action that occurs in identifiable locations; this is also where it subverts consensual assumptions. Beckett's settings, and the passivity of his characters, are a refusal of the forms of recognition that reassure audiences that the world of the theatre is also the world that they routinely inhabit.

The passivity of the characters indicates the point at which Beckett deviates from existentialism. As I show below in relation to Walter Abish, and in the next chapter in relation to confessional poetry, this deviation point is crucial in indicating the beginnings of postmodernism. Existentialism requires human action in the face of the void; it insists that human beings can determine their own fate through their ability to make crucial life choices and then to act upon them. Beckett's plays are not existential in this sense. Instead they are postmodernist in depicting characters who are thoroughly stalled and at a loss – so thoroughly at a loss that they are depicted as having had all character drained out of them. Like Beckett's settings and plots, they are defined by an absence which deconstructs the presence of such components in theatrical tradition.

These ideas are a key starting-point for Harold Pinter's plays, which first appeared in the early 1960s. However, this English playwright also draws upon social realism, and even at times upon references to the thriller, so that his work produces effects of generic instability which contrast with the austere purity of Beckett's theatre. His realism can be illustrated by contrasting the tramp Davies from *The Caretaker* with Vladimir and Estragon from *Waiting for Godot*. Beckett's tramps are taken from silent film comedies and their status refers metaphorically to a concept of existential homelessness. Pinter's tramp is depicted much more closely as a character who has spent his life outside social norms; his need to get to Sidcup to retrieve his papers indicates the anxious insecurity that such a life arouses, as does his indignant racism, and it is crucial to the play's plot that living continuously under the same roof is terribly alien to him.

This kind of realism, which is also present in Pinter's famous mimicry of colloquial speech, might be thought to arouse a consensual recognition on the part of audiences. However, that form of consensus is thoroughly unsettled by the ways that language in these plays is deployed politically (in the broadest sense) as an instrument of mystification and oppression. Pinter's characters evade communication systematically as a strategy in power struggles which require them to circumvent direct disclosures of a kind that might promote mutual understanding and sympathy. It is this which makes these plays most identifiably postmodernist.

It is at this point too that the influence of Beckett on Pinter is joined by that of Franz Kafka, because these linguistic mystifications arouse an atmosphere of anxious and disorienting suspiciousness that resembles that of novels like *The Trial* and *The Castle*. There is a satirical tradition with its origins in those novels which is important in postmodernist fiction – it contributes an important strain to the work of Joseph Heller and Don Delillo in the form of a systemic paranoia which is by turns deadly serious and blackly comic. In Pinter it takes the form of his 'comedy of menace' which resembles the Kafkaesque elements in Heller and Delillo in rendering the threat insidiously as a form of fantasy, but at the same time indicating that it is all too real – and thereby complicating it by making it harder to locate and define. One important effect of this is to evoke a much larger unlocatable threat which relates it to power systems operating in society as a whole. Heller does this in *Catch-22* by unsettling what is superficially a war novel with postwar references that satirise the American industrial–military complex; Delillo does it in *White Noise* by evoking how a single household is invaded by an insistent plurality of media and advertising voices. In Pinter's plays language is manipulated by the characters with a knowing obliqueness that infuses it with a much larger political dimension, so that it hints synecdochically at systemic power struggles which have created the contexts out of which they speak.

1.1 Language after the holocaust: Walter Abish

The document from Lyotard (pp. 161–3) is especially relevant to Walter Abish who focuses upon issues of representation in relation to the holocaust in his novel *How German Is It*. Abish's most powerful deconstructive strategies are those which are brought to bear on German culture and those which satirise what he sees as German amnesia about war crimes. These are especially helpful for my purposes because they dwell upon ideas of naturalness and the familiar. So they indicate how deconstruction is above all designed to reveal the constructedness of cultural norms which have established themselves so powerfully that they have come to be experienced as not cultural at all, but inevitable and natural.

Abish is unusual for a literary writer in applying his philosophical analysis with such coherence and consistency. That analysis is premised upon a critique of a German philosopher whom he calls Brumhold but who is obviously in fact Martin Heidegger. What is again very revealing here for deconstruction is that Abish's relationship to Brumhold is symmetrical with Derrida's relationship with Heidegger: both Abish and Derrida draw upon their German philosophers to carry them a necessary philosophical distance, but then both carefully differentiate themselves from what they see as crucial failings in Heideggerian thought. Christopher Norris is characteristically lucid in his account of Derrida's debt to Heidegger's deconstructive practices and of the point at which Derrida parts company from Heidegger, which is

> at the point where Heidegger locates the source and ground of authentic thought, that is, in the moment of Being or plenitude which precedes articulate discourse. For Derrida this can only represent another classic case of the familiar metaphysical hankering after truth and origins. Heidegger's entire hermeneutic is founded on a notion of truth as self-presence which ultimately seeks to efface, or claims to precede, the play of signification. Where Nietzsche looked back beyond Socrates to a diverse and shifting prehistory of thought, Heidegger looks to a source of authentic truth in the unitary ground of Being. His 'destruction' of metaphysics is intended not, like Derrida's, to release a multiplicity of meaning, but to call meaning back to its proper, self-identical source. Heidegger thus stands as Derrida's nearest tactical ally and yet – by this crucial divergence – as his major modern antagonist.[5]

Thus, in both his short story 'The English Garden' and his novel *How German Is It* Abish refers to the figure of Brumhold in order to deconstruct the ordinary phenomena and routine activities of the citizens of the new city which is named after him, Brumholdstein – but then turns on the German philosopher and deconstructs the unexamined assumptions behind his philosophy. He says that Brumhold is part of the tradition of Western metaphysics in questioning the 'intrinsic meaning of a *thing*' and then applies a similar interrogation to the things of which Brumholdstein is composed: 'fire department, post office, library, school, medical facilities, cinema, theatre, flower shop, restaurant, coffee shop, bookstore, etc.'[6] What this interrogation of things also interrogates is the problematic relationship between things and the words which are used to represent them – that is, the relationship between language and the world and how language structures that world in the ways implied by the list of Brumholdstein things.

In dwelling on this interrogation, Abish is also drawing attention to how the representative metonymies of narrative fiction evoke a sense of place and thereby a sense of the real. In other words he is drawing upon Brumhold in order to reflect self-consciously on the language of fiction, so that his own self-consciousness as a fiction writer is incorporated into his fiction and is made exemplary of a more general deconstructive attitude. Malcolm Bradbury is referring to this aspect of Abish when he refers to his

> curiosity about the relation between language (or to put it more grandly, semiotics) and narrative. So what he has been doing has been very consistent with a developing revolution in contemporary intellectual and critical thought which has put the problem of language at the centre of current understanding.[7]

These issues of representation are further explored, in both the short story and the novel, by the key image of the colouring book, which is referred to at the start of 'The English Garden' and then repeatedly afterwards. Abish lists the scenes that the colouring book contains in order to show how it represents (like Abish's own fiction) the 'things' out of which Brumholdstein is composed. To this extent it is accurately representative and its childlike aspect may also suggest that it reflects an earnest and open-minded attempt to depict the German city. However, what it more obviously suggests is distortiveness in the caricatural crudeness of its drawings, so that the tone is clearly satirical when the first-person narrator declares that the people in the colouring book only need 'a bit of colour to come to life and embrace each other' (Abish, p. 4).

Nonetheless, it is the lack of colour which Abish focuses upon as depriving the colouring book of verisimilitude – the word 'colour' is repeated throughout 'The English Garden'. This sense of a component crucially missing is evoked in order to represent the gap between the text and the 'real', between the signifier and the referent. This alludes to what is crucially missing in Brumholdstein, which is an acknowledgement of its history and its relationship to Durst, the neighbouring city which contained a concentration camp where Jews were systematically killed. Abish refers to this with characteristic deadpan flatness when he notes the difference between the current colouring books and those dating from 1940, for in the current ones, 'the heavy emphasis on the military, on strange salutes, on enthusiastic crowds watching tanks roll by, has been de-emphasized' (p. 9). The sense of something eerily missing is evoked at much greater length in *How German Is It*, but in both the story and the novel it is linked to a systematically emotionless tone, an impression of universal loss of affect.

In the novel it is also linked to a continual reference to the hermeneutic code of detective stories and this generic reference implies the interrogation of clues which will lead to the missing piece that will solve the problem. So Ulrich thumbs through the pages of the colouring book which here summarise some of the novel's key scenes (while adding enigmatic others) and wonders,

'Could one read anything into these drawings? Was it a message?'[8] However, these generic references only draw attention to the differences between Abish's text and the classic detective story: instead of unmasking a guilty individual, *How German Is It* unmasks a murderous culture.

It is in the process of this satirical unmasking that Abish distances himself from Brumhold just as Derrida distances himself from Heidegger. The references to the colouring book and to the detective story indicate the impact of the play of signification, of the multiplicity of meaning, and form part of a critique of the mystifications involved in Heideggerian hankerings after truth and origins. Abish is explicit about this when he paraphrases a posthumous interview with Brumhold in which he has the philosopher declare that:

> The forest continues to beckon to us. For in the forest are located our innermost dreams and desires. In order to re-establish our roots and our purpose and return to a simplicity of life that can no longer be found in the German community, we turn to the forest. We wander off by ourselves, packs on our backs, haphazardly selecting one path, then another not knowing where the forest is leading us, but willing to let our instincts and chance dictate our journey and confident that in what we are doing, we are coming closer to our past, to our history, to our German spirit.
>
> (p. 167)

This is a very helpful passage for understanding postmodernism because it focuses upon a key debate about Nature to which I dedicate a later chapter. To put this starkly: anti-postmodernists like Margaret Atwood, Adrienne Rich, Ted Hughes and Seamus Heaney are consistent defenders of Nature, believers in the power of instinct, propounders of an organicist ideology. By contrast, postmodernists like Abish are deeply sceptical about appeals to naturalness on precisely the grounds that Norris defines in Derridean thought – that they are premised upon a hankering after origins and self-identical authenticity.

Such appeals are especially disturbing in the German context which Abish is defining because they suggest a link to a fascistic championing of blood and soil. This is the point he is making when he has Brumhold stress not just rootedness in the forest but specifically German rootedness there. Deconstruction is especially appropriate in this context because it uncovers the hidden agenda behind the call to return to the forest – what appears to be natural is actually cultural; what appears to be innocent is actually ideological.

Abish's deconstructive strategies in *How German Is It* are focused upon habitual patterns of thought whose familiarity makes them appear inescapable, and therefore not patterns of thought at all but inevitable ways of perceiving the world. The novel contains a continual discussion of familiarity which is especially explicit in the passage (pp. 119–23) where the schoolteacher Anna Heller writes the word 'familiar' on the blackboard and then discusses with her pupils the elements in the environment of their school and city to which the word would most readily be applied. In conducting this discussion Anna is relying upon elements of consensus amongst the pupils, and between herself and the pupils, and this is itself exemplary of the role that familiarity plays in communication and indicates how language structures a regulated understanding of the world. There is once again a self-reflexive element here because the realist novel also relies upon these structured recognitions in order to produce a consensus between author and reader out of which a sense of the real is evoked.

This point is confirmed later when Franz visits the Brumholdstein library. He is making a model of the Durst concentration camp out of matchsticks, an image which makes similar points about distortive representation as the colouring book, though more grotesquely. André Brink has pointed out how library scenes are repeatedly present in postmodernist texts by 'Borges, Calvino, Eco and others . . . a world of Books and of Literature, the make-believe and self-constructions of language'.[9] The library is 'a familiar picture, and in that respect a reassuring one' (Abish, p. 155) and its catalogue represents an Enlightenment attempt to comprehend and categorise the whole of human experience. This seems especially inhuman when applied to the holocaust: 'see Brumholdstein, see Concentration camps/Germany, see World War II Effort, and see Railroads/German' (p. 156).

These linguistic constructions are even further removed from the historical reality of the concentration camp than Franz's matchstick versions. Abish's parody of the catalogue register reveals what happens to experience when it is subsumed in the play of signification. This is a vast distance from notions of truth as self-presence of the sort propounded by Brumhold/Heidegger; the historical reality of the holocaust is effectively nullified by its repeated representation in blandly familiar forms of thought and distortive linguistic structures – so much so that Germans can wonder whether or not it really happened: 'It's too much. It's more than one can bear' (p. 191). What *How German Is It* does most powerfully is to evoke these distortive structures so systematically that it reveals how they conspire with a pervasive ideology which can flourish because it insinuates itself routinely everywhere. In doing this the novel deconstructs an insidiously nationalistic and implicitly violent concept of Germanness which promotes itself as natural and which makes it impossible not to acknowledge or recognize in everything German the intrinsic *Standpunkt*, the German point of view, the unique German way of seeing and appraising an object: a house, a barren hill, a tree in bloom, or something as evanescent as a passing cloud – and also the way in which this appraisal, this mere looking at as well as recognizing the true property or quality of what is seen, can be said to reflect a society, a culture, a particular people.

(p. 123)

1.2 Language and politics: 'language' poetry

There are also political motives behind the deconstructive practices of much of the American language poetry which has been developing since the 1970s. Fredric Jameson notices this in a poem he discusses by Bob Perelman – 'China', he says, 'is in some curious and secret way a political poem',[10] thereby indicating the obliqueness which is a consistent characteristic of the politics of these poems. This arises because this poetry is not focused upon social structures or institutions but upon how language is thoroughly infiltrated by their oppressive presence. The obliqueness is the product of how language poems focus upon representing this linguistic effect instead of focusing upon the underlying politics.

The best introduction to this poetic movement is in the important anthology *Postmodern American Poetry*[11] which places it in the context of its most important precursors and includes some of the key theoretical statements by language poets as well as a good selection of poems. The theoretical statements are important because they help to connect this poetic to an American tradition of poetic theorising which dates from the middle of the nineteenth century and which has itself always contained political motives of its own.

American poets have always regarded poetic form as a political issue. Walt Whitman's long free verse line was deployed explicitly in favour of democratic American openness and against what he saw as the tyrannies implied in European verse forms. William Carlos Williams was later involved in a similar declaration of poetic independence in inventing a free verse line explicitly designed to evoke an American voice. The proliferation of poetic manifestos which characterise American poetry in the twentieth century, the energetic explosion of competing *isms* – Imagism, objectivism, projectivism, the Beats, the New York school, etc. – reflect not just restless experimentalism but fervent attempts to bring a poetic into being by acts of will and in explicit competition with the prescriptions of competitors. These power struggles are premised upon a political attitude to poetic expression which is peculiarly American: this becomes even clearer when it is contrasted with the absence of such competitive theorising in Britain where poetic expression has rarely been thought of as political.

The crucial aspect of this poetic politics is its assumption that poets are inevitably engaged in acts of opposition and protest and that it is through these acts that they will achieve self-definition. The theoretical version of this American attitude is most articulately expressed by Harold Bloom in his depiction of poets in an Oedipal struggle with a powerful precursor whose influence must be overcome before poets can acquire their own poetic power. Language poetry is best understood in this context, which explains why American poets would be so sensitive to the idea of a secret politics in the activities of the language itself, given that in their tradition poetic language has been such a site of struggle as both a source of conformist oppression and a potential means of expressive liberation. What is also crucially important here is that this struggle is part of a much wider political dialectic in American culture between an official ideology of individualism and a *de facto* authoritarianism.

Language poetry repeatedly enacts this key dialectic and often refers it, self-reflexively, to the aesthetic struggles I have been describing by alluding to the struggle for poetic freedom. In Charles Bernstein's 'Of Time and the Line' (pp. 570–1), for example, different kinds of 'line' are listed but all of them are associated with a pressure to conform and all of them refer back, since they are incorporated in a poem, to the poetic line which, in aesthetic terms, shapes them into a structural conformity. This is made explicit when the poem refers to the iambic line whose prestige is said to have declined because 'I am' is a much less confident statement than it used to be. The pun on the first two syllables of 'iambic' is playful but it also suggests the link between poetic structures and ontological issues and insists that traditional versification is inseparable from traditional ideologies of the self. Bernstein introduces a manifesto component into this discussion when he significantly widens it into a prescription: 'When/ making a line', he says

> better be double sure
> what you're lining in & what you're lining
> out & which side of the line you're on; the
> world is made up so (Adam didn't so much
> name as delineate). Every poem's got
> a prosodic lining, some of which will
> unzip for summer wear.

There is an allusion here to the structuralist view that language structures the world which is 'made up' by the delineations imposed on it by the act of naming. Bernstein is worried by this because it threatens an oppressiveness; delineation means that meanings are instituted arbitrarily and too exclusively; the phrase 'made up' implies the possibility of imaginative construction which is important to poets, but it also suggests that a subjective vision of the world can too easily be imposed and rigidly maintained. It is characteristic of the American tradition I have been describing that it is this prospect which most arouses a political anxiety and which requires in response an urgent need to be aware of the political choices that must be consciously made to prevent the made-up truths imposing a stifling conformism. Poets must be aware that, whether they like it or not, they are making a political choice in the very process of structuring the poem: the lines are drawn up before the poem is written and its structure will place them on one side of the line or another. Once the prosodic lining is recognised it is possible for its restrictiveness to be deflected, for its unzipping to allow a half-liberation into a hinted-at nudity which evokes a return even to a Whitmanian pre-linguistic primitiveness, but significantly repackaged in a camp form closer to the New York poets – not mystically nude but more lightly clothed in linguistic 'summer wear'.

The theoretical writings by the language poets all draw upon post-structuralist theories. Bruce Andrews finds traditionally radical writing inadequate because it contains too many assumptions about language as a simple means of communication and fails to look at the medium itself:

> in an era where the reproduction of the status quo is more & more dependent upon ideology & language (language in ideology & ideology in language), that means that it can't really make claims to comprehend and/or challenge the nature of the social whole; it can't be political in that crucial way.
>
> (p. 669)

Lyn Hejinian extends these arguments in a feminist direction, so that the structures of social authority which she identifies are specifically patriarchal. She draws upon post-Lacanian French feminists like Luce Irigaray in order to make an 'identification of language with power and knowledge – a power and knowledge that is political, psychological, and aesthetic – and that is identified specifically with desire' (p. 656). And she finds an affinity between the view of language propounded by these theorists and that expressed in the avant-garde texts by the writers she most admires – 'including an interest in syntactic disjunctures and realignments, in montage and pastiche as structural devices, in the fragmentation and explosion of subject' (p. 657).

What is conspicuous, however, is that when these poets apply these French theories to the writing of poems they take on a distinctly American colour derived from the tradition I have been outlining. Their applications notably soft-pedal that materialist aspect which is crucial in the French thought because of its dialogue with Marxism. When these poets envisage what their poems should do in response to the ideological power of linguistic structures, they tend to revert to an American model of poetic protest. Andrews wants writing to be a '*counter*-reading'; he wants to reshape poetic language 'to make it possible to become *less* of an exile in our own words'; he wants to confront 'the restrictions of constraining rules' (p. 671) in a move that looks very like a postmodern version of Whitman's liberationist revolt. Charles Bernstein refuses to accept the loss of the referent and is determined to invent 'ways of releasing the energy inherent in the referential dimension of language' (p. 676).

All of these language poets want to move (if hesitantly) beyond the authoritarian oppressiveness of language and into a renewed form of expression that will provide a new freedom. Their poststructuralism gets oddly edged with a utopian and idealist striving. The inevitable failures of such striving are responsible for crucial elements of this poetic: the sense it constantly contains of irreconcilable elements in tense and open-ended conflict with each other. Lyn Hejinian speaks about the constant longing 'to close the gap between ourselves and things' and how while 'failing in the attempt to match the world, we discover structure, distinction, the integrity and separateness of things' (p. 658).

Frustration, then, is not just a major characteristic of language poetry but crucially constitutive of it. Hejinian's reference to failure draws attention to the repeated sense these poems convey of trying to say something that refuses to be said, and in which that refusal becomes the point of the poem because it deconstructs what the language always does with attempts to speak freely about the world. Frustration arises from the clash between the American striving to penetrate to the origin of all poems, the real stuff of experience, and the insistence of poststructuralist theory that such authenticity is unattainable. And every attempt these poets make to shape the poem individualistically is thwarted by the authoritarian pressures which the language always and everywhere exerts.

Bob Perelman's 'Chronic Meanings' illustrates this vividly:

> They won't pull that over.
> Standing up to the Empire.
> Stop it, screaming in a.
> The smell of pine needles.

Economics is not my strong.
Until one of us reads.
I took a breath, then.
The singular heroic vision, unilaterally.

Voices imitate the very words.
Bed was one place where.
A personal life, a toaster.
Memorized experience can't be completely.
(p. 503)

There is a stark dialectic in this poem between the stuff of lyric experience –
the natural, the personal – and the apparatuses of social and political life;
the clash between the two half-gags the former. This is reflected in the
poem's form which looks, at first glance, like a traditional lyric poem, even
a song, divided into quatrains and with short lines – but turns out to be very
unpoetically organised because each line is simply limited to five words. By
contrast with metrical arrangements or even syllabic structure, this
organisation of the line implies a structure imposed from outside of poetry
altogether, just as the state apparatuses impose themselves on the lyric
experiences which the poem evokes. This structuring of the poem's expression limits it so severely that many of its statements remain unfinished, so
that it enacts an inescapable disappointment.

So language poetry contains a powerful vision of the sort articulated by
Michel Foucault – a vision of the human subject imprisoned by social and
political institutions in dominant discourses which determine and limit what
it is possible for that subject to think. Perelman's reference to 'bed' as the
'one place' may even allude to Foucault's 'archaeological' delvings into the
history of sexuality in which he demonstrates how even sexual feelings and
experiences – which might be regarded as the most private and personal,
and the least political – have been shaped by dominant discursive formations. Especially relevant here is Foucauldian theorising about the limits of
thought imposed by different periods and different cultures, and an
especially vivid statement of it in the preface to Foucault's book *The Order
of Things*, where he discusses a passage quoted from a 'certain Chinese
encyclopaedia' by Borges which declares that

animals are divided into: a) belonging to the Emperor, b) embalmed, c)
tame, d) sucking pigs, e) sirens, f) fabulous, g) stray dogs, h) included
in the present classification, i) frenzied, j) innumerable, k) drawn with
a very fine camelhair brush, l) etcetera, m) having just broken the
water pitcher, n) that from a long way off look like flies.[12]

As Foucault points out:

> In the wonderment of this taxonomy, the thing we apprehend in one great leap, the thing that, by means of the fable, is demonstrated as the exotic charm of another system of thought, is the limitation of our own, the stark impossibility of thinking *that*.
>
> (p. xv)

That others can order the world so differently calls into question our own way of ordering it, especially because these orderings become so oppressively powerful and limiting. Language poets continually push against the boundaries of the categories of thought which are imposed by the order of things and continually, therefore, baulk at the impossibility of thinking what their time and place refuses to allow them to think. Their most important achievement is in providing fragmentary glimpses of the nature of that impossibility.

1.3 In dialogue with postmodernist language

A recurrent experience when reading the critical and theoretical writings of poets and novelists is to find a shared resistance to postmodernist theorising, especially in its more extreme forms. So A. S. Byatt feels it necessary to insist: 'I do believe language has denotative as well as connotative powers', and to recommend the reconsideration of 'the idea of truth, hard truth, and its possibility'.[13] So, where the Derridean concepts of deconstruction, decentring, supplementarity and free play work well for discussing writers like Abish and Ashbery, they work much less well for writers in the period who are still preoccupied with denotation and evoking a sense of the real. Not all of these writers are by any means straightforwardly realist, but the extent of their postmodernism needs to be carefully weighed. Here it seems to me that the Russian critic Mikhail Bakhtin is much more helpful than Derrida, and especially Bakhtin's concepts of the dialogic and of heteroglossia. Implied here are radically different views of subjectivity to those of John Ashbery, behind whose work lies the crucial influence of the surreal which undermines any stable sense of social context.

Writers like A. S. Byatt are reluctant postmodernists. Like Bakhtin, they regard subjectivity as socially constituted (and inseparable, therefore, from intersubjectivity). As Bakhtin says: 'Each person's inner world and thought has its stabilised social audience that comprises the environment in which reasons, motives, values and so on are fashioned.'[14] Bakhtin retains much of the materialist emphasis of his Marxist context in the Soviet Union and sees subjectivities defining each other by the way they interact in socially and historically defined contexts; he emphasises the multiplying of discourses but insists that they must be finally understood by reference to the historical and social setting of specific language users.

This Bakhtinian negotiation between stabilities and instabilities is the most accurate way of accounting for many important texts in the postmodern period – and not primarily because their authors often insist on those stabilities but because the texts themselves make that insistence. Brian McHale refers to how

> Baxtin has shown us how dialogue among discourses is a staple of all polyphonic novels. Postmodernist fiction, by heightening the polyphonic structure and sharpening the dialogue in various ways, foregrounds the ontological dimension of the confrontation among discourses, thus achieving a polyphony of worlds.[15]

This is a very accurate description of the impact that A. S. Byatt's *Possession*[16] makes in the end. But it makes this polyphonic impact by systematically destabilising a key set of stabilities which it works very hard to establish. Much of the writing in the novel, at a local level, is realist – it contains very painstaking descriptions of its characters and its settings (especially bathrooms). The characters are depicted, on one level, in conventional ways, and are made to be vividly particular.

Realist characterisation is a key stability in the novel. What is crucial though is how this stability, like all the others in the novel, is placed in dialogue with instability. It is not thoroughly subverted, because there is an important sense in which it remains in force, but in a radically modified form: this is a vital feature of the dialogic. In fact, what Byatt does first of all is to reinforce the idea of the realist self by exaggerating it by reference to the novel's controlling metaphor of 'possession'. This refers to the idea of one self being invaded by another – sexually, emotionally, linguistically and intellectually.

Such ontological invasions are the motive force of the novel's most telling instabilities. However, in order for this to make its full impact, the concept of an autonomous self has to be fully established, and Byatt achieves this implicitly through her realist strategies of characterisation and, more explicitly, through depicting the self as a kind of fortress. The novel tells the story of two sexual relationships which are depicted through significant symmetries; both women in these relationships, Maud Bayley and Christabel La Motte, have names which refer to fortifications (see p. 502) and which therefore suggest a conventional pattern of wooing in which the man must penetrate the woman's defences in order to 'possess' her. This idea is further articulated in a letter to Maud by her ex-lover Fergus Wolff, a poststructuralist literary critic who suggests that the allusions to castles in La Motte's poem about Melusina can be explained by reference to Lacan's assertion that ego formation is symbolised in dreams 'by a fortress or stadium' (p. 138).

This idea of the self as an ontological stronghold is the stable premise which makes possible the novel's key instabilities – it makes the instabilities meaningful by providing them with a telling context. In such a stronghold only one language would be spoken and only one point of view would hold sway. It is upon this stability that the controlling metaphor of possession goes to work by infiltrating it with multiple languages and points of view so that it is dialogised by the vision of the novelist. The novel as a form works by juxtaposing languages and points of view and so shattering the fortress of the self with linguistic hordes. For Bakhtin the ideal paradigm of this vision is provided by Dostoevsky who, he says, saw

> many and varied things where others saw one and the same thing. Where others saw a single thought, he was able to find and feel out two thoughts, a bifurcation; where others saw a single quality, he discovered in it the presence of a second and contradictory quality . . . In every voice he could hear two contending voices, in every expression a crack, and the readiness to go over immediately to another contradictory expression; in every gesture he detected confidence and lack of confidence simultaneously; he perceived the profound ambiguity, even multiple ambiguity of every phenomenon. But none of these contradictions ever became dialectical, they were never set in motion along a temporal path or in an evolving sequence: they were, rather, spread out in one plane, as standing alongside or opposite one another, as consonant but not merging . . . as an eternal harmony of unmerged voices or as their unceasing and irreconcilable quarrel. Dostoevsky's visualising power was locked in place at the moment diversity revealed itself – and remained there, organizing and shaping this diversity in the cross section of a given moment.[17]

The narrative of *Possession* is directed above all towards opening up single voices so that they are made to incorporate significant others. The most obvious way it does this is through the influence of love which is traditionally the force which can most effect self-transcendence. All four lovers influence each other in this way. The two academics in the 1980s, Maud Bailey and Roland Mitchell, learn to modify their gender and class biases in the process of a collaboration which acquires the increasingly intense associations of a romantic quest. Both of them feel profound identification with their respective objects of study – Maud with Christabel La Motte, Roland with Randolph Henry Ash – and these identifications both imply that they have already been invaded by alien perspectives. However, in the process of their collaboration they both read the other's hero and so learn to incorporate another voice which had previously not appealed to them. This requires a more difficult form of identification because it involves overcoming gender prejudice, and the novel clearly takes this as exemplary and important.

The novel's focus on love as an exemplary source of self-transcendence suggests a link with John Bayley's book *The Characters of Love*[18] which proposes that authors need to feel a form of love for their characters if they are to depict them with convincing substance and depth. This link to Bayley's vivid statement of a liberal humanist view confirms a sense that Byatt herself has some unreconstructed sympathy with liberal humanism, but it must also be stressed that her own treatment of these themes is mediated through an evident knowledge of the shaping force of linguistic representation. This is conspicuous in *Possession* because of the self-consciously wide range of registers which the novel parodies, especially registers of a conspicuously textual kind such as poetry and literary criticism. Byatt is extremely skilful in the plausibility of her discriminations between the varieties of idioms in these discourses. It is also important that one of the most important effects of the love between the two Victorian poets is that their poetic languages start to interpenetrate each other. Byatt indicates bifurcations here and consonances which, however, remain unmerged, so that each poet is coloured by the other yet remains themself.

So, by incorporating a version of Victorian poetry into her novel, Byatt places poetry and the novel in dialogue with each other. It is further dialogised because the 'Victorian' poetry is actually written by Byatt, so that it is 'double-voiced' as all parody is. What this involves is an enacting, in *Possession*, of the process of 'novelisation'; for the novel's influence on other genres, Bakhtin says, is to make them

> more free and flexible, their language renews itself by incorporating extraliterary heteroglossia and the 'novelistic' layers of literary language, they become dialogised, permeated with laughter, irony, humour, elements of self-parody and finally – this is the most important thing – the novel inserts into these other genres an indeterminacy, a certain semantic openendedness, a living contact with unfinished, still-evolving contemporary reality.[19]

One of Byatt's most impressive achievements in this novel is how she registers the cultural changes taking place in the Victorian period which have already made the writing of purely lyric poetry seem outdated. She makes the dialogising of Ash and La Motte enact this, and also shows them referring to the momentous intellectual upheavals of their time, especially in science, which make lyric utterance seem insufficient.

So Ash, who resembles Robert Browning without exactly being him, tells La Motte, in a letter, that he has written 'dramatised monologues' on historical figures. This reference to the poetic form with which Browning is most associated is highly significant because it indicates a shift away from Romantic self-expression towards a novelised poetic form which requires the poet to inhabit another mind and speak the poem in a language associated with that mind. Ash says that he is at ease reviving historical figures and the objective facts of their circumstances ('hair, teeth, fingernails, porringer, bench, wineskin, church, temple, synagogue') and then evoking their patterns and processes of thought: 'the incessant weaving labour of the marvellous brain inside the skull' (*Possession*, p. 158). This also provides a key paradigm for similar acts of sympathetic identification which drive the novel's plot and its repeated overlappings of languages – its 'confrontation amongst discourses', to use McHale's phrase – which produces a 'polyphony of worlds'.

Dramatic monologue is an important analogue of these linguistic crossovers because, despite its name, it is a dialogic idiom which works in the ironic gaps which open up between the explicit statements of the monologuist and the implied attitudes of the implied author. Usually, in Browning, there is also a significant collision of cultural histories between the contemporary Victorian moment and the period of the monologuist. This is also a crucial effect of Byatt's novel which repeatedly places the Victorian and the postmodern in a contrastive juxtaposition. This is achieved through the intellectual activities of the academic characters who are shown in the process of thinking, speaking and writing about their Victorian objects of study who are therefore able to speak through them, speaking in their Victorian idioms but mediated through the language of postmodern literary criticism.

Roland and Maud have a conversation (p. 254) in which they discuss the effort of imagination required to enter the Victorian mind and the impossibility of escaping your own time: Maud says that for their own time it is the inescapability of Freudian psychology which dominates, and this moves them to think through the historical process which leads from Victorian 'self-value' into what Maud calls our 'horrible over-simplification'. Moments like this indicate Byatt's stubbornly anti-postmodernist attempt to get at the truth, to strive with a tenacious imaginativeness towards an historical referent. This again looks like a striving for stability of a kind which a thorough postmodernist would regard as worryingly nostalgic. But, like the other stabilities which Byatt establishes, this striving for 'real' history is placed in dialogue with powerful forces which destabilise it. Most important of these are the novel's romance elements: *Possession* is subtitled 'A Romance', and its plot is accordingly organised around the theme of quest and contains references to 'the Gothic extravagance of churchyards and castles and midnight terrors, the trials and tribulations of lovers, [and] magnificent melodramatic excess in the final reunion between father and daughter' (Brink, p. 292).

Possession sustains a dialogue throughout between the genres of romance and classic realism: this is also connected to its dialogue between the genders because the genres are stereotypically gendered as masculine (realism) and feminine (romance). This is why Roland feels so disoriented when he finds himself trapped in a text which he feels to be thoroughly alien to him: 'He was in a Romance, a vulgar and a high Romance simultaneously, a Romance was one of the systems that controlled him' (p. 425). This realisation comes towards the end of the novel and is the product of all the textual overlappings which precede it. One especially significant moment immediately precedes it:

> Roland thought, partly with precise postmodernist pleasure, and partly with a real element of superstitious dread, that he and Maud were being driven by a plot or fate that seemed, at least possibly, to be not their plot or fate but that of those others. And it is probable that there is an element of superstitious dread in any self-referring, self-reflexive, inturned postmodernist mirror-game or plot-coil that recognises that it has got out of hand, that connections proliferate apparently at random, that is to say, with equal verisimilitude, apparently in response to some ferocious ordering principle, not controlled by conscious intention, which would of course, being a good postmodernist intention, *require* the aleatory or the multivalent or the 'free', but structuring, but controlling, but driving, to some – to what? – end. Coherence and closure are deep human desires that are presently unfashionable. But they are always both frighteningly and enchantingly desirable.
>
> (pp. 421–2)

The labyrinthine syntax of this passage evokes a vacillation that marks the whole of *Possession*. This represents the novel's significant hesitation in the face of postmodernism – its refusal to allow postmodernism thoroughly to possess it combined with its horrified fascination with postmodernism's threatening seductiveness. This is mirrored in Roland's simultaneous pleasure and dread at the prospect that his fate, and Maud's, might be wholly possessed by that of Ash and La Motte – the prospect, that is, that their own selves might be so thoroughly breached and invaded that they will be ontologically erased. Coherence and closure are still desired and there is still the wish to make yourself into an ontological stronghold which can resist the colonising power of alien invasion, or of a chaotic otherness which will disrupt any stable sense of individuality.

However, the novel crucially differentiates between two models of ontological possession. These are represented by the metaphors of ventriloquy and the seance which are especially important in Chapter 20. Ash's biographer, Mortimer Cropper, has written a book on the poet called *The Great Ventriloquist*. Ventriloquy threatens the most self-erasure in those who are invaded by the voices of other people – it implies that the dramatic monologuist becomes the mere puppet of the poet. The metaphor of the seance is introduced via references to Ash's attendance at such an event conducted by a Mrs. Lees in the house of Miss Olivia Judge (p. 389) and to the resultant poem 'Mummy Possest' which is printed in full as Chapter 21. This metaphor is far less oppressive: it implies that a dead voice speaks through a living body, but only briefly, and in a way that can lead to 'dispossession, or perhaps the word was exorcism' (p. 480).

It is this image which is significantly dominant at the end of the novel. Moreover, its metaphorical importance is more precisely located by being combined with another image which has been recurrent throughout and which now more powerfully reasserts itself – the image of liminality (p. 506). This is the concept with which Maud Bailey is associated in her approach to La Motte: it refers to the idea of a fortress which is present in both women's names, but by referring to the image of a threshold it evokes the possibility of looking simultaneously inwards and outwards. It suggests the image of a validated vacillation. This in the end is the novel's answer to postmodernism, which is calculatedly ambiguous in precisely Bakhtinian terms: the novel's languages are consonant but not merging, and the novel is consonant with postmodernism but stubbornly unmerged with it.

Notes

1 J. G. Ballard, 'Introduction to the French Edition of *Crash*', reprinted in *Crash* (London: Flamingo, 1993), p. 8.
2 Noam Chomsky, *Deterring Democracy* (London: Vintage, 1992), p. 382.
3 Jean-François Lyotard, *The Differend: Phrases in Dispute*, trans. Georges Van Den Abbeele (Minneapolis: University of Minnesota Press, 1988), pp. 56–7.
4 Samuel Beckett, *Waiting for Godot* (London: Faber, 1965; first published 1956), p. 63.

5 Christopher Norris, *Deconstruction* (London: Methuen, 1982), pp. 69–70.
6 Walter Abish, 'The English Garden', in *In the Future Perfect* (London: Faber, 1984), p. 8.
7 Malcolm Bradbury, 'Introduction', to *In the Future Perfect*.
8 Walter Abish, *How German Is It* (London: Faber, 1982), p. 178.
9 André Brink, *The Novel: Language and Narrative from Cervantes to Calvino* (Basingstoke: Macmillan, 1998), p. 293.
10 Fredric Jameson, *Postmodernism or, The Cultural Logic of Late Capitalism* (London: Verso, 1991), p. 29.
11 Paul Hoover (ed.), *Postmodern American Poetry* (New York: Norton, 1994). All subsequent references to language poetry are to this volume.
12 Quoted in the preface of *The Order of Things* by Michel Foucault (London: Tavistock, 1974), p. xv.
13 A. S. Byatt, *Passions of the Mind: Selected Writings* (London: Chatto and Windus, 1991), p. 24.
14 V. N. Vološinov, *Marxism and the Philosophy of Language*, trans. Ladislav Matejka and I. R. Titunik (New York and London: Seminar Press, 1973), p. 133. Bakhtin is now generally thought to have been the actual author of this book.
15 Brian McHale, *Postmodernist Fiction* (London: Methuen, 1987), p. 166.
16 A. S. Byatt, *Possession* (London: Vintage, 1991).
17 M. M. Bakhtin, *Problems of Dostoevsky's Poetics*, trans. and ed. Caryl Emerson (Manchester: Manchester University Press, 1984), p. 30.
18 John Bayley, *The Characters of Love: A Study in the Literature of Personality* (London: Constable, 1960).
19 M. M. Bakhtin, *The Dialogic Imagination: Four Essays by M. M. Bakhtin*, trans. Caryl Emerson and Michael Holquist (Austin: University of Texas Press, 1981), p. 7.

2

The postmodern self

The most important postmodernist take on identity questions arises from the deconstruction of concepts of inner or underlying essence. What is being deconstructed, therefore, is the idea of a stable core of self (like a soul) which is present throughout an individual's life and which constitutes their true being. It is the assumption of such a self that underlies Romantic concepts of 'self-expression', but 'common-sense' attitudes also tend to assume that everyone is blessed with this essential core.

The calling into question of realist and liberal humanist notions of the self was a feature of many modernist texts. The impact of Freudian thought and its insistence on the 'unconscious' and therefore on a fractured self was explored, for example, by D. H. Lawrence in *The Rainbow* and after. These preoccupations have been pressed further by postmodernist writers, so that a stable sense of identity has been persistently undermined. This has been accompanied by a deconstruction of the ideological assumptions behind traditional views of identity and their link to the dominance of Western European, liberal and masculine values; these deconstructions are linked to the profound social and political changes described in the Introduction.

Postmodernism depicts the self as a social and ideological construct which is endlessly in process, and identity as being constituted performatively, by what the self does. Theorists of gender and race have been especially focused upon the importance of opposing essentialist attitudes. Gender theorists have attacked conventional beliefs in rigid gender categories defined by reference to biology; they have attacked the assumption that masculinity and femininity can be determined solely in terms of hormones and body shape, and insisted on multiplying the range of gender formations by referring to 'masculinities' and 'femininities'. Theorists of race, similarly, have attacked definitions of racial identity based upon assumptions about 'roots', about an essential identity which is organically linked to a native origin. They have rejected, for example, attempts to define African American identity purely by reference to an African provenance and stressed the importance of a specifically American experience with its origins in slavery, and stressed the importance of viewing that identity as constantly evolving in dialogue with dominant American culture and with other American ethnicities.

In opposing concepts of ontological essence, postmodernism was influenced by existentialism which exercised a powerful philosophical sway in the 1950s and 1960s – but it takes ontological scepticism much further. Existentialism was important for its attempts to explore the impact on identity of a post-Christian loss of transcendent meaning; but it looked to find forms of personal authenticity and even heroism which might be invented in the face of that loss. Postmodernist thought has been especially dismissive about such notions, and can be helpfully understood as representing a much more extreme scepticism that follows the exhaustion of existentialism. The movement from existentialism into postmodernism can be clearly traced in the distinctions I make in this chapter between the poetic practice of confessional poets like Sylvia Plath and that of a thoroughly postmodernist poet like John Ashbery; Frank O'Hara is interesting because he is situated somewhere between the two as a sort of playful existentialist.

2.1 The fractured self: Sylvia Plath

Sylvia Plath deserves her fame because she invented a powerful set of characteristic images which evoke, with highly memorable vividness, a tellingly symptomatic sense of a contemporary self – a sense of a self as eerily diminished or fissured. The form her fame has taken has distorted this achievement because it has attributed her depiction of this self to the poet's own mental illness. Plath's posthumous celebrity is a postmodern phenomenon which has reinvented her work in the light of a crude sensationalism which draws upon populist myths of the poet as madly inspired and self-consumingly driven. This has meant that the precision of her poetic acts of self-deconstruction has been popularly blunted by a Plathian myth of banal self-destruction.

Plath's depiction of the self evolved out of a version of Nature poetry which arose originally out of a post-Darwinian anxiety that Nature was not, as the Romantics thought, a benevolent and nurturing force which reflected God's own benevolence, but a mechanical and often cruel set of processes in which individuals and even individual species were treated with massive indifference. Alfred Lord Tennyson wrote early poems in this tradition, referring to a Nature red in tooth and claw, and there is some of this as well in the work of Emily Dickinson who combined it with an obsessiveness about death – a combination that suggests interesting comparisons with her later compatriot. More directly relevant, however, is the work of Dylan Thomas with its focus on natural processes of fertility and death, and – in particular – Theodore Roethke whose poems express bewildered and anxious awe at a proliferating fertility that at the same time creates life and erases it.

Plath's 'Mushrooms'[1] expresses a similar bewilderment. In a characteristic manoeuvre, Plath gives the mushrooms a voice so that the poem is already premised upon a defamiliarising perspective. The mushrooms' point of view implies something missed by humans, something happening behind our backs, which itself arouses a sense of disturbance, an anxiety that we are not as in control of our environment as we like to think. This is heightened by the alienness of these fungi and the sense that this mode of life is so different from the human that its difference alone poses a threat. Plath reinforces this by insinuating a creepy violence into her mushroom imagery; this is not the energetic, open violence of Ted Hughes' pike or even his thrushes, but a secret violence happening invisibly and quietly. The mushrooms use their 'hammers' but they are 'Earless and eyeless'; they are humble and unassuming; they do not intend to be violent but the force of their proliferating numbers makes them in fact powerful colonists who will 'Inherit the earth'.

The spectacle of this proliferation has profound implications for human identity because it overwhelms any idea of individual uniqueness; it undermines the liberal humanist sense of personal specificity by exposing it to the daunting knowledge of relentless biological processes. What mushrooms do is inevitably mushroomy: they have no individual volition. The implication of all this activity happening behind our backs is that it contains a message that humans are unaware of – humans are also more a part of such processes than we recognise. This is also implied in how the mushrooms are compared to human body parts, to toes and noses, partly this evokes the otherness of the mushrooms because these are scattered body parts, but it also introduces a reminder about human bodies and their connection to cycles of generation and decomposition.

There are some similar ideas in Plath's short sequence about bee-keeping, and it is significant that a swarm of bees, like a crowd of mushrooms, makes Plath think of human body parts. When she looks through the grid of the beehive she declares it has the 'swarmy feeling' of shrunken African hands (p. 213). The idea of swarminess which is aroused by both the mushrooms and the bees produces the anxious image of *disjecta membra*, so that the association clearly indicates that swarminess threatens the coherence of the self; it makes the self feel that it is disintegrating under the pressure of massed biological numbers. Consequently, when Plath imagines bees sacrificing themselves for the sake of the collective, she says:

> They thought death was worth it, but I
> Have a self to recover, a queen.
> Is she dead, is she sleeping?
>
> (p. 215)

In the face of the swarmy feeling, individuality is a rare and elusive privilege; it is a strangeness that turns its unique owner into a chimera with a 'lion-red body' and 'wings of glass'.

Plath's identification with the queen represents a wish-fulfilment of transcending the biological process, so that in the final stanza of this poem she imagines the queen surviving her own death and flying angrily above the hive, magnificently exempt from the common fate. This is an exceptional moment in Plath where the wish-fulfilment helps to stress her obsessive depiction elsewhere of being locked into a process that effaces her; it is especially exceptional because the queen bee is female and Plath's poems insist repeatedly that female biology is especially inescapable. It is a gendered consciousness that she adds to the Roethkian theme because her treatment of the themes of pregnancy and motherhood depicts the speakers of her poems as personally swept along in the biological current, riding 'the train there's no getting off' ('Metaphors', p. 116).

The nine lines of 'Metaphors', each with nine syllables, present their speaker as programmed by the nine months of her pregnancy, and so thoroughly unrecognisable to herself that she is transformed into an elephant, a house, a melon, a loaf, a pregnant cow. Biology has turned her into an object of use, reduced her to a 'means'. This idea is amplified in 'Morning Song' (pp. 156–7) where the speaker compares her relationship with her baby to that of a cloud with the puddle it creates which then reflects it being torn apart by the wind. She sees in the baby merely a reflection of her future death, and the word she uses for this, 'Effacement', is characteristic and linked to an obsessive imagery in Plath that depicts self-fragmentation and erasure.

These processes cannot be comprehended by the individuals they co-opt to serve their purposes. Childbirth is bewildering but so too is miscarriage: 'Parliament Hill Fields' is addressed to a miscarried foetus, so that its use of the word 'you' is as defamiliarising as the use of the word 'we' in 'Mushrooms' – in both poems the use of these pronouns contains an implied questioning about what constitutes a self. This is intensified in 'Parliament Hill Fields' when the speaker's daughter is referred to as the sister of the dead foetus, stressing the loss of similar potential for life. The idea of the draining away of the amniotic fluid is represented in the landscape where 'the spindling rivulets/ Unspool and spend themselves' and leads to a baffled sense of a similar draining away of part of the self. A syntactical ambiguity therefore allows both the speaker and the foetal addressee to be reduced to the 'Ghost of a leaf, ghost of a bird'.

In that image, too, death and life are anxiously conflated so that what is conspicuously natural – a leaf, a bird – is transformed into something unnatural. This represents how natural processes are felt by the overwhelmed self to be unsettlingly unnatural because they place the self uncannily at odds with itself. Identity, when it is subjected to biology's purposes, becomes unrecognisable to itself and this is the most important reason why Plath's surreal references are so telling – because they insist that the self contains profoundly alien materials. For surreal imagery carries with it the associations that the practitioners of surreal painting and poetry themselves bestowed upon it in their manifestos – associations with Freudian psychoanalysis and its theorising about the unconscious, about irrational drives and about a rich cache of unsettling symbols fraught with ambiguities and paradoxes.

Plath's surrealism differs markedly from that of French poets like Paul Eluard and Robert Desnos whose poems invent surrealist contexts: in Plath the context is more often realist but insinuatingly undermined by surreal twists and inflections. 'Mushrooms', for example, is premised upon an unremarkable woodland scene, but this is transformed by how the mushrooms are estranged by being half-humanised, endowed with a consciousness, however alien, and transmuted into bits and pieces of human bodies. This poem and the bee-keeping sequence both refer to the Freudian concept of latent and manifest. In 'Mushrooms' the earth out of which the mushrooms emerge suggests a latent depth; in the bee-keeping poems, the hive is evoked as a sinister enclosure – a dangerous latency out of which disturbing revelations may (and do) erupt. These references to the Freudian model confirm the sense that the images in these poems represent an uncanniness inside the self, that the mushrooms and the bees are manifestations of the self's most shadowy corners.

For Plath, however, these images of latency are also intricately bound up with the image of pregnancy in an image cluster that associates both the earth and the hive with the womb. The cloud/mother in 'Morning Song' is another example of this cluster, in which the cloud/mother and the puddle/baby are also versions of latent and manifest. One important and queasy effect of this set of associations is to intensify the anxieties that pregnancy arouses in Plath's poems: if the womb is figured as a site of Freudian latency, then its contents are made horrifyingly open to question.

The potentially Gothic consequences of this are realised in 'Elm' (pp. 192–3) where the womb is represented as a bird's nest so that pregnancy can be imagined as being 'inhabited by a cry'; as having a 'dark thing' sleeping inside the self. Allowing the tree to speak the poem in this case produces a woman/tree hybrid, like the creatures in Ovid's *Metamorphoses*, except that in the Plathian context I have been describing it is yet another image that evokes the predicament of feeling yourself metamorphosed by feminine biology into a sort of chimera, of feeling yourself so colonised by the alien process that you become only half yourself. All of these poems evoke a sense of how frightening this is, but in 'Elm' it is especially powerful, and especially preoccupied with how it leaves the self reduced.

This leads Plath to introduce the image of the moon here, as she often does elsewhere, to measure by implication how far femininity has declined from a notion of itself as rendered transcendently powerful by its biological role. The moon is a traditional symbol of that mysterious and formidable potency, but in Plath's poems it is depicted as cold, scarred, isolated and, as here, 'diminished' – in this case 'as after radical surgery'. In 'Parliament Hill Fields' the moon reference is made to follow the reference to 'spindling rivulets' and the day emptying its images so that it is associated with ontological leakage. These characteristic images of liquefaction form a stark contrast with the characteristic images of hard containment in Ted Hughes. So too her elm is anxiously multiple and fragmented, whereas Hughes' most famous monologuist, his hawk, is a masterful monolith, a masculine wish-fulfilment of self-contained and frightening power.

But however much these images have a gendered origin, their ontological significance acquires a much more general relevance. Certainly the woman/tree's consternation at how she breaks up 'in pieces that fly about like clubs' is one of the most powerful images in the postmodern period of a fractured sense of identity that is crucially symptomatic of how it feels to be living now. What is also significant in this image is the way that the pieces of the self that break up are transformed into weapons: these clubs refer to a dynamic of violence that is insufficiently recognised in Plath's poems. Ted Hughes is famous for his preoccupation with the violence of Nature, but this element is less noticed in Plath because it is quieter and more complex, being connected to an angry response to a perceived or actual threat. Plath's identification with the furious queen bee provides a clue to this, especially because she becomes an object of both fear and awe.

It is this combination of fear and violent anger which drives her two most famous poems, 'Daddy' and 'Lady Lazarus'. Their fame is distortive to some extent because they are uncharacteristic in being so starkly confessional, but her choice of this idiom is entirely appropriate because confessional writing is focused on social relationships and these are the poems by Plath which are most socially and politically oriented. This is also the source of their anger. They are premised upon a rage against the dominating presence, in contemporary culture, of social pressures and political events – this also makes them key texts for the postmodern, because they explicitly refer to historical events which have been crucially formative in the period. The controversial references to the holocaust in both poems are best understood in these terms – they are not a self-dramatising appropriation of an atrocity for purely personal purposes, but an evocation of the relentless and unavoidable impact of mid-twentieth-century history on the lives of individuals.

This is a theme that Plath shares with Robert Lowell and John Berryman who both juxtapose confessional writing with political and historical references in order to stress the interpenetration of the personal and the public. This early postmodern idiom can be tellingly compared with modernist 'impersonality' which can best be understood as an aesthetic response to urbanisation and mechanisation in the modernist period: the invention of a self-consciously 'constructed' text which implies that lyric writing is outmoded in a time dominated by urban and industrial life. The existential and psychoanalytic assumptions of confessional writing reintroduce an emphasis on the personal life but in a context in which 'personality' itself is deconstructed, and placed in an interrogative dialogue with much larger, collective forces which infiltrate and continuously shape it.

The sense of being invaded by these forces is itself a source of anger in Plath's confessional poems; the implications of this writing are that social and political relationships have superseded natural ones. This is itself a key postmodern issue and one which I explore extensively in my chapter on 'Postmodern Nature'. Fredric Jameson defines postmodernism as 'what you have when the modernization process is complete and Nature is gone for good'.[2] And Plath's horrified shift of emphasis towards events like the holocaust and the atom bombing of Hiroshima is significant in indicating a preoccupation with the denaturing of contemporary culture.

There are clear signs that Plath associates this process with the destructive dominance of patriarchal values – 'Daddy' and 'The Applicant' (pp. 221–2), Plath's most explicitly feminist poem, were written very close to one another (the latter on 11 October, the former on 12 October 1962). 'Daddy', like the earlier 'The Colossus' (pp. 129–30), massively enlarges and generalises the actual father until he becomes a representative figure, and this is why he can be convincingly indicted of war crimes and literally demonised. The comparison of the father/daughter relationship to that, in the holocaust, of Nazis to Jews, transforms both relationships so that they can be made to participate symbolically in much larger patterns of relationships centred on dominance and submission. This implies the symptomatic universalising of power relationships – a diagnosis of a cultural sickness arising from the inescapability, anywhere, of transactions centred on power. The consequences of this are focused for Plath on the denaturing of women: 'The Applicant' begins with a series of references to prosthetic body parts and ends by transforming the eponymous woman into marital currency ('paper', 'silver', 'gold'). The second and third stanzas of 'Lady Lazarus' depict the parts of the poet's body transformed into objects of Nazi use.

The origin of all this, and the implied premise of confessional writing, is that the contemporary cultural dominance of political relationships produces a form of ontological exposure. The self is now very far from the spiritual haven that the Romantics took it to be and is instead the vulnerable site of historical and social conflicts. Both Plath and Berryman have key images that express this sense of psychic nakedness and even surgical anatomising. Plath refers to a 'peanut-crunching crowd' which invades her hospital convalescence in order to witness her 'big strip tease' (p. 245). In the first of his *Dream Songs*, John Berryman imagines his persona, Henry, being 'pried/ open for all the world to see'.[3]

2.2 The confessional self

Berryman, like Plath, wrote poems premised upon this idea of the opening up of the self. Like her, too, he insists on the problematic ground on which the self is based. The central figure of Henry is the only feature of *The Dream Songs* that gives them any coherence and yet Henry's own coherence is undermined by continuous interventions from his unconscious. Berryman's premises for this are largely Freudian and, as Helen Vendler has pointed out, 'there is no integrated Ego in *The Dream Songs*: there is only Conscience at one end of the stage and the Id at the other, talking to each other across a void, never able to find common ground'.[4] This makes poetry writing analogous to the psychotherapeutic talking cure, so that each Dream Song is

> eighteen lines long, and is divided into three six-line irregularly rhyming stanzas – an isometric form one might associate, looking backward, with Berryman's debt to the meditative Petrarchan and Shakespearian sonnet sequences or, looking forward, to the therapeutic fifty minutes, with the inflexible and anecdotal psychiatric hour.
>
> (Vendler, p. 36)

themselves towards this wondering about fullness. Similarly, all O'Hara's activities in 'The Day Lady Died', after the first reading, seem to reach towards the last-mentioned one, his purchase of a *New York Post* with a photograph of Billie Holiday on it, which leads to the poem's crucial last shift:

> and I am sweating a lot by now and thinking of
> leaning on the john door in the 5 SPOT
> while she whispered a song along the keyboard
> to Mal Waldron and everyone and I stopped breathing
>
> (p. 325)

O'Hara's deployment of free verse fluidity and openness is aimed at improvising an identity and is related to 'projectivist' notions of shaping the poem as an organism that is a living representation of the poet's breath and body. The phrase 'stopped breathing' is self-reflexive as the final phrase of a poem composed of the poet's own breathing (as well as referring to Billie Holiday's death and a reaction of awe to her performance). The insistence in O'Hara's 'I do this, I do that' poems on the poet's moving body and speaking voice refers them to existential notions of personal authenticity.

O'Hara's poems therefore are negotiations between projectivist organicism and camp artifice. John Ashbery, by contrast, has none of the former and expands the latter systematically, so that everything inside his text and out of it is placed between quotation marks.[8] This is extended much more thoroughly than in O'Hara to include the sense of the poet inside his poem. O'Hara can be accurately understood by reference to Heideggerian explorations of 'being in the world'.[9] Ashbery's work, by contrast, is post-existentialist in the sense that it is, like Derrida's, endlessly sceptical about the metaphysics of presence and wants to explore how much the sense of 'presence' is constructed by language. This makes him much more thoroughly postmodernist. Perhaps the clearest example of this is how Ashbery's poem 'The Tennis Court Oath'[10] refers to David's 1781 painting of the same name in which figures were erased and replaced as they fell out of favour with the government. Ashbery has therefore written a text with a problematic relationship to its title which refers to a deeply problematic representation of history which was itself finally abandoned. All of this therefore calls thoroughly into question any sense of the 'real' and of authentic ontological continuity.

This constellation of radical concerns has made Ashbery the most challenging poet of the last twenty years, so that what is above all a gay sensibility has been profoundly influential and become more widely exemplary of a more general postmodern sensibility. His 'Self-Portrait in a Convex Mirror' (pp. 196–212) centres on the self-portrait by the Mannerist Francesco Parmigianino, and thus is premised upon a historical examination of the beginnings of modern masculine self-fashioning in the Renaissance. But it extrapolates from this premise in order to explore much more broadly the issue of self-constructedness.

It describes how the painter cut in half a ball of wood and then copied his reflection from a convex mirror onto it: the result is that his image is 'sequestered' and 'Glazed, embalmed' (p. 196). So Ashbery is drawing upon references to portraiture in order to explore how identity is thoroughly involved in issues of representation and thus is neither spontaneous nor natural. Painting is invoked as a language with its own sign system in order to demonstrate how a 'self-portrait' simultaneously draws upon assumptions about the self and constructs a version of a self by exploiting the resources of portraiture as a system of codes. Parmigianino's mannerism is especially helpful in this argument because mannerism is one of those aesthetic movements that critics of postmodernism refer to when they want to prove that postmodernism's self-reflexivity and self-conscious unrealism are by no means new. Ashbery himself refers to how the self-portrait deploys the 'consonance of the High Renaissance' but distorted by the mirror (p. 202), and he quotes the art critic Sydney Freedburg pointing out how the painting's realism paradoxically produces 'a *bizarria*' (p. 201).

The poem focuses then on these issues: language and representation, the 'real' and constructions of the self. The relaxed brilliance with which it deals with these most central of postmodern preoccupations makes it one of the most important postmodernist texts. The comparison with Frank O'Hara is very helpful in defining this particular aspect of postmodernism. O'Hara's vivid evocation of himself walking and talking is an evocation of a full and authentic presence in a particular place and time. His poems define themselves as the equivalent of a phone call to a friend; they are as alive and breathing as 'Lucky Pierre', the middle body in an act of troilism (O'Hara, p. 499).

All these organicist ideas are treated with extreme scepticism by Ashbery's poetic which holds them at a poststructuralist arm's length. In the case of this poem the most relevant sceptical thinker is Jacques Lacan because he has done the most influential theorising about mirrors and self-representation. He is especially relevant because the emphasis in his theories has been upon the aesthetic nature of the mirror stage, the earliest moment of self-recognition. Lacan stresses, that is, that when the baby first realises that the image in the mirror is its own self, that what it is seeing is a representative fiction – it is not its 'real' self but a mere reflection:

The *mirror stage* is a drama whose internal thrust is precipitated from insufficiency to anticipation – and which manufactures for the subject, caught up in the lure of spatial identification, the succession of phantasies that extends from a fragmented body-image to a form of its totality that I shall call orthopaedic – and, lastly, to the assumption of the armour of an alienating identity, which will mark with its rigid structure the subject's entire mental development.[11]

Much of Ashbery's poem is occupied with exploring the 'lure of spatial identification', for which the self-portrait provides a perfect metaphor because it depicts a self-consciously distorted mirror image, a 'reflection, of which the portrait/ Is the reflection once removed' (p. 196). The painting represents two acts of attempted self-recognition – firstly in a mirror and secondly in a portrait; both inevitably fail to recognise a real self and, taken together, multiply the distance that the act of recognition must attempt to cross. This is all then further compounded by the necessary addition of the observer of the self-portrait who interposes another self to complicate what is being recognised in the mirror:

> What is novel is the extreme care in rendering
> The velleities of the rounded reflecting surface
> (It is the first mirror portrait),
> So that you could be fooled for a moment
> Before you realize the reflection
> Isn't yours. You feel then like one of those
> Hoffmann characters who have been deprived
> Of a reflection, except that the whole of me
> Is seen to be supplanted by the strict
> Otherness of the painter in his
> Other room.
>
> (pp. 202–3)

The surreal disorientation aroused by the idea of looking into the mirror and seeing someone else's face reflected there introduces the concept of alienation. Identity is supplanted by the experience of its own otherness and fragmentation: the separation of the self from itself that occurs because the self feels itself to be entirely different from the self as it is represented in language. This leads to the self adopting the 'armour of an alienating identity', and perhaps the most memorably vivid imagery in this poem is that which evokes this armour. So the self is depicted as imprisoned in its representation, a 'captive', frozen into immobility and an artificial pose (pp. 196–7):

> Actually
> The skin of the bubble-chamber's as tough as
> Reptile eggs; everything gets 'programmed' there
> In due course
>
> (p. 201)

The poem demonstrates how this particular kind of self-regard gets thoroughly enmeshed with an ideological system which makes its vision seem 'natural'. Ashbery draws on discursive modes derived from Wallace Stevens and W. H. Auden to explore the implications of this, and then on his own characteristic imagery (which is edged with surrealism) to contrast this hard enclosedness with an alternative emphasis on openness and fluidity. Deployed together, these modes produce a camp mastery that deconstructs mastery and advocates an improvisatory responsiveness, and this is certainly one of the great achievements in postwar poetry.

2.4 The self and desire

The most influential theoretical formulations for postmodernist perspectives on identity have been those of Lacan and his feminist critics, with some important interventions by Derrida. To generalise: these have crucially involved combining Freud and deconstruction. The post-Lacanian theorising of Julia Kristeva has exercised an especially powerful influence on literary critics, and the extract from her book on abjection which constitutes my fifth document (pp. 165–9) is vivid in its account of the origins of desire in a constitutive lack, related to exile from the body of the mother, in which the self is depicted as coming into being through an 'inaugural *loss*'.

So the self has become a site of theoretical conflicts, but underlying these there is a broad consensus amongst theoretically inclined critics about onto-logical fragmentation: deconstructions of liberal humanist celebrations of the unitary self have become routine exercises. So A. S. Byatt in her novel *Possession* depicts her central character Roland Mitchell, a young academic, reflecting on this 1980s' orthodoxy: he had learned

> to see himself, theoretically, as a crossing-place for a number of sys-
> tems, all loosely connected. He had been trained to see his 'self' as an
> illusion, to be replaced by a discontinuous machinery and electrical
> message-network of various desires, ideological beliefs and responses,
> language-forms and hormones and pheromones.[12]

The jaded tone that Byatt adopts here reflects a sense that this post-modernist view of the self could potentially become a deadening truism.

What must be stressed, however, is the gulf between how these theories appear in their abstract and reiterated literary critical formulations compared with their vivid particularity in a number of postmodern literary texts. Salman Rushdie, for example, presents Saleem Sinai, the protagonist of *Midnight's Children*, as physically disintegrating because he has been 'buffeted by too much history'.[13] This powerful image is deployed as part of the postcolonial intertextuality of the novel: its implicit satire of the unstated ideology of the West's classic realism whose depiction of 'well-rounded' autonomous individuals is premised upon a systematic marginalising of social and political forces. By contrast with those nuanced and organically developing characters, Saleem Sinai is so helplessly bound up with the fate of his country, India, that he must share its deeply fissured identity and have his head telepathically infiltrated by the terrible clamour of its multiple voices and languages (see, for example, p. 168).

The postmodern incoherent self has also been very vividly represented in contexts where gender has been the central focus. Here, the principal source of incoherence has been sexual desire. Philip Roth has been especially acute, throughout his career, on the ontological distortions inflicted on both men and women by masculine sexuality. In *Portnoy's Complaint*[14] the protagonist is driven by a sexual compulsion, a restless 'horniness' (p. 102):

> I have desires – only they're endless. Endless! And that, that may not be such a blessing, taking for the moment a psychoanalytic point of view . . . But then all the unconscious can do anyway, so Freud tells us, is *want. And* want! *And* WANT!
>
> (p. 103)

This novel acquired considerable notorious celebrity in a 1960s' context when the culture was being progressively sexualised. Roth himself, however, was very far from sharing the optimistic humanism of the popular culture of that period; his work has always been characterised by mordant, confrontationally aggressive and often misanthropic satire. *Portnoy's Complaint* is an early work and is propelled by youthful and colloquial energy but its narrator is already so deeply unsettled and guilty about male drives that he is convinced that just to be in possession of a penis (like both himself and his father) makes you the '*culprit*' (pp. 85–6). Sexual compulsiveness also means that the self is reduced to a mere machine of repetitive wanting or a helpless appendage to an overweening body part: a synecdochic 'schlong' where the part does not so much stand for the whole as usurp it. Degraded eroticism threatens to turn Portnoy into 'one of the fragmented multitude' (p. 186).

In Roth's much more recent work, *Sabbath's Theatre*,[15] the shocking endlessness of masculine desire is personified in the central, obsessively transgressive figure of Sabbath who continues to be sexually driven despite being sixty-four years old. Throughout his adult life Sabbath has performed carnivalesque puppet shows and the key motif of puppetry works as a metaphor for the idea that human beings are at the mercy of larger forces which mechanise and control them. The mind is a 'perpetual motion machine' (p. 297) and people and puppets become indistinguishable from each other because people are thoroughly reified by desire. Having sex with his frighteningly voracious girlfriend Drenka, Sabbath feels his own identity to be nullified by her desire – 'he needn't have been there' – and to such an extent that he might as well 'have been one of those antique marionettes with a long wooden dick'. Exhausted, Sabbath tells Drenka that, for her, 'Coming is an industry', that she is 'a factory' (p. 132).

These issues are similarly central to the work of Angela Carter for whom the 1960s were also formative. In a retrospective, prefixed note to her essay 'Notes for a Theory of Sixties Style'[16] she says 'I learned how to look at things in the sixties, and I have carried on looking' (p. 84). Carter was much more attuned to that decade than Roth and welcomes the social changes it introduced, especially contraception and equal pay, which she sees as having emancipated women 'from the stiff forms of iconic sexuality' (p. 90). Most relevantly to the issues of postmodern identity, she welcomes 1960s' fashions as a form of playful disguise which allows

> a relaxation from one's own personality and the discovery of maybe unsuspected new selves. One feels free to behave more freely. This holiday from the persistent self is the perpetual lure of fancy dress. Rosalind in disguise in the Forest of Arden could pretend to be a boy pretending to be a seductress, satisfying innumerable atavistic desires in the audience of the play. And we are beginning to realise once again what everybody always used to know, that all human contact is profoundly ambiguous.
>
> (p. 87)

It is precisely this preoccupation with highly self-conscious role-playing which grips the heroine of Carter's story 'Flesh and the Mirror'.[17] She is obsessed with style in the sense that she is desperate to construct herself as 'a three-dimensional art object' (*Nothing Sacred*, p. 86); to be observed by others but, above all, by herself. Desire is the motive force for this self-dramatising because her reinvention of herself as an object of desire shapes her subjectivity: she performs herself and voyeuristically watches her own performance. The preoccupation with personal style is mirrored in the prose style which is symmetrically involved in similar acts of narcissistic self-reflection as the heroine dresses herself in black in the role of being in love and weeping and 'walking through the city in the third person singular' ('Flesh and the Mirror', p. 363). The metafictional strategies which are such a marked feature of postmodernist fiction are drawn upon here to evoke destabilised identity: desire is desired by the heroine as a way of finding 'unsuspected new selves', and the switch from one self to another is reflected in the switching of narrative voices as the heroine slips out of the first person and into the third: 'however hard I looked for the one I loved, she could not find him anywhere' (p. 364).

This sexual role-playing leads Carter's heroine, as it does Roth's Sabbath, into a 'puppet theatre' (p. 363). What this implies is a power struggle – a conflict fought over who is pulling the strings, who is the subject and who is the object of desire. Here Carter is broaching themes which have preoccupied feminist theory, especially in its indictment of the reifications inflicted by the male gaze, but her own treatment of the theme is characteristically ambiguous. Where feminists would indicate how the male gaze turns women into its puppets, and Philip Roth satirises that feminist line by depicting his horny old hero transformed into a marionette by his girl-friend's sexual demands, Carter evokes a theatre where the roles of puppet-master and puppet are endlessly switching. Her heroine's lover – even more than that heroine herself – is constructed as a fiction to be manipulated both by the female author and her female protagonist. He resembles the lovers of Gabriel García Márquez' famous story 'Eyes of a Blue Dog' – lovers who only ever meet in their dreams and who spend their waking lives fruitlessly trying to track each other down: 'he was plainly an object created in the mode of fantasy. His image was already present somewhere in my head and I was seeking to discover it in actuality, looking at every face I met in case it was the right face' (pp. 366–7).

For Carter these gender power struggles are inevitably linked to issues of sadism and masochism, as her controversial book *The Sadeian Woman* extensively proves. 'Flesh and the Mirror' is memorable for the risks it takes in this disturbing area, and its Japanese setting confirms that this theme is a key preoccupation behind the story – for it is also a repeated pre-occupation of her writings on Japan, where she lived in 1969. So, in a piece on Japanese tattooing, she refers to Japan as a culture whose rigorous repressiveness encourages a sadomasochistic dynamic (*Nothing Sacred*, p. 38). In creating her lover as a puppet, Carter's heroine is too preoccupied with the needs of her own fantasy life to care whether or not she hurts him: her power over him is so complete that she can dismember him like 'a clockwork toy' (p. 367).

What this means, above all, is that her lover's 'self and, by his self, I mean the thing he was to himself, was quite unknown' to her (p. 367). Desire is all-consuming: it consumes both the heroine's self and that of her lover. Both characters become its puppets just as, self-reflexively, they are the puppets of the author, however much the heroine tries to become the author of both herself and her lover. Authorial power is represented textually by the power of the mirror; in the power struggle between flesh and the mirror it is the mirror which is always victorious because it reflects the power of desire and its multiple representations:

> During the durationless time we spent making love, we were not ourselves, whoever that might have been, but in some sense the ghost of ourselves. But the selves we were not, the selves of our own habitual perceptions of ourselves, had a far more insubstantial substance than the reflections we were. The magic mirror presented me with a hitherto unconsidered notion of myself as I. Without any intention of mine, I had been defined by the action reflected in the mirror. I beset me. I was the subject of the sentence written on the mirror.

(p. 364)

Notes

1 Sylvia Plath, *Collected Poems* (London: Faber, 1981), pp. 121–2. All Plath references are to this volume.
2 Fredric Jameson, *Postmodernism or, The Cultural Logic of Late Capitalism* (London: Verso, 1991), p. ix.
3 John Berryman, *Selected Poems 1938–1968* (London: Faber, 1972), p. 69.
4 Helen Vendler, 'John Berryman', in *The Given and the Made* (London: Faber, 1995), p. 36.
5 See Stephen Frosh, *Sexual Difference: Masculinity and Psychoanalysis* (London: Routledge, 1994), p. 13.
6 Frank O'Hara, *Collected Poems* (New York: Knopf, 1979), pp. 257–8. Henceforth O'Hara.
7 Bryan S. Turner, 'Introduction' to Christine Buci-Glucksmann, *Baroque Reason: The Aesthetics of Modernity* (London: Sage, 1994), p. 27.
8 See Susan Sontag, 'Notes on Camp', in *A Susan Sontag Reader* (Harmondsworth: Penguin, 1983), p. 109.
9 See Roger Gilbert, *Walks in the World* (Princeton, NJ: Princeton University Press, 1991), p. 182.
10 John Ashbery, *Selected Poems* (London: Paladin, 1987), pp. 31–2. Subsequent references are to this volume.
11 Jacques Lacan, 'The Mirror Stage as Formative of the Function of the I as Revealed in Psychoanalytic Experience', in *Ecrits: A Selection*, trans. Alan Sheridan (London: Tavistock, 1977), p. 4.
12 A. S. Byatt, *Possession* (London: Vintage, 1991), p. 424.
13 Salman Rushdie, *Midnight's Children* (London: Vintage, 1995), p. 37.
14 Philip Roth, *Portnoy's Complaint* (London: Vintage, 1995; first published 1968).
15 Philip Roth, *Sabbath's Theatre* (London: Vintage, 1996).

16 Angela Carter, 'Notes for a Theory of Sixties Style', collected in *Nothing Sacred: Selected Writings* (London: Virago, 1982), pp. 85–90.
17 Angela Carter, 'Flesh and the Mirror', in Malcolm Bradbury (ed.), *The Penguin Book of Modern British Short Stories* (London: Penguin, 1988), pp. 362–9.

|3|

Postmodern genres

The postmodern preoccupation with language and textuality has led to an insistently parodic culture. This is also evident in popular culture, such as a film like *Galaxy Quest*. As a result, postmodernist authors have been led to adopt generic modes which can be exploited for their familiarity but at the same time deconstructed and extended in unfamiliar and often much more sophisticated directions, sometimes introducing philosophical preoccupations which are alien to the genre. Paul Auster's detectives are like postmodern *flâneurs*: nihilistic observers of New York, detached wanderers and gazers at a city whose meaning baffles them. The incongruity that results from the collision of the populist and the philosophical is often comic, as in Tom Stoppard, but can also be exploited for political ends. The latter accounts for some of the uses which feminist writers have made of the Gothic mode. Similarly, science fiction has been exploited to explore the ontological boundaries of the human – boundaries which are in evidence in TV and cinema versions of the genre, for example, in the human/cybernetic boundary personified in the Borg in *Star Trek*.

Jacques Derrida is preoccupied, in his discussions of genre, with its paradoxical qualities. He says that:

> As soon as the word 'genre' is sounded, as soon as it is heard, as soon as one attempts to conceive it, a limit is drawn. And when a limit is established, norms and interdictions are not far behind: 'Do', 'Do not' says 'genre', the figure, the voice, or the law of genre.[1]

But he protests against this textual authoritarianism and is preoccupied with how genre contains within itself – because of its own tendencies towards impurity and excess – inevitable subversions of these norms. So the law of genre for him implies simultaneously both normativeness and the end of norms.

For Jean-François Lyotard the notion of that 'end' acquires much bigger implications and is associated with an apocalyptic postmodernity. For him, genre is linked to his concept of the 'differend', which is 'a case of conflict' which 'cannot be resolved for lack of a rule of judgement applicable to both arguments'.[2] The background to this is that the collapse of metanarratives (which I discussed in the Introduction) leaves only a range of competing narratives, each of which has as much legitimacy as any other. This means that there can be no metalanguage in which a thoroughly reliable judgement can be made.

Lyotard's focus is on legal and political questions but his discussion of genre in the context of differends is relevant to postmodern literature because it provides insights into the political reasons why that literature is so concerned to enact the fissures that open up between one genre and another. The impossibility of resolving the dispute arises because the dispute takes place as it were *between* genres so that a judgement cannot be made that would be just for both sides. To make such a judgement would be as impossible as ruling on a dispute between a character in a legal report and a character in romance. A universal genre, which would provide the language required for resolving the dispute, is as unavailable as a grand narrative that explains all of human experience. So what is left is an urgent sense of generic relativity; the political task in the face of this is to detect differends and to invent the idiom that is required to phrase them, even though such an idiom is 'impossible' (p. 142).

This prevailing emphasis on impossibility is tied to a repeated and ambiguous sense of the apocalyptic in Lyotard – of being (half in hope, half in despair) at the end of history:

> Could it be that 'we' are no longer telling ourselves anything? Are 'we' not telling, whether bitterly or gladly, the great narrative of the end of great narratives? For thought to remain modern, doesn't it suffice that it think in terms of the end of some history? Or, is postmodernity the pastime of an old man who scrounges in the garbage-heap of finality looking for leftovers, who brandishes unconsciousnesses, lapses, limits, confines, goulags, parataxes, non-senses, or paradoxes, and who turns this into the glory of his novelty, into his promise of change?
>
> (pp. 135–6)

3.1 Science fiction

Lyotard's concept of the differend, his emphasis on the irreconcilable clash of linguistic worlds, works well when applied to Edwin Morgan's science fiction poems. The opportunity which the genre provides to enact the thoroughly bewildered encounter of irreconcilably different cultures is exploited by Morgan so that he invents radically disjunctive texts which display this irreconcilability linguistically. This connects these poems to Morgan's experience of writing sound and concrete poems, a point which is well illustrated in this book by the printing as one of its documents (p. 164) of his 'emergent' poem 'Message Clear' – a poem I discuss in the Introduction. This avant-garde experience is drawn upon in the science fiction poems so that the visual and aural materials of language are thoroughly exploited in them.

This allows him, in 'The First Men on Mercury',[3] to invent a literally impossible idiom for the aliens who inhabit the eponymous planet, and to juxtapose it with the English of the space-travelling earthlings, so that a differend opens up between them in the space of their Lyotardian 'phrases in dispute':

> – We come in peace from the third planet.
> Would you take us to your leader?
>
> – Bawr stretter! Bawr. Bawr. Stretterhawl?
>
> (p. 267)

The platitudinous and patronising language of the earthlings reveals human complacency which is thoroughly unsettled by the profound alienness of the natives of Mercury. The two languages start to infect each other but so bewilderingly that it is frightening for both the earthlings and the mercurians, and desperately urgent that they leave each other to live separately in their irreconcilable othernesses.

Mostly, however, Morgan uses science fiction in a paradoxically humanist way to suggest the huge range of potential human adaptiveness. So 'In Sobieski's Shield' (pp. 196–8) imagines a kind of technology similar to that of the transporters in *Star Trek*. This treats human material in the most radical possible way – dismantling it atom by atom, dispatching the atoms to a distant planet and reassembling them. In the end, however, this process emphasises the resilience of the human in surviving even this, and demonstrates how human beings can draw strength by transforming change itself into renewal.

'In Sobieski's Shield' refers twice to a 'second life' and shows how this can be achieved against terrible odds, and how even shock and pain can become ways of seeing ourselves from a new perspective, so defamiliarising and thereby reaffirming ourselves. So the speaker carries with him a race memory of the First World War and finds a tattoo from a dead soldier on his arm. There is human continuity in this but there is also change. The memory is altered by the radically different context in which it interferes; the tattoo, which is seen in Flanders as a symbol of tenuous hope – 'a heart still held above the despair of the mud' – becomes a much more substantial symbol of hope in 'In Sobieski's Shield': 'my god the heart on my arm my second birth mark'.

Fredric Jameson compares science fiction to the historical novel, finding the two genres to be symmetrical opposites:

> For if the historical novel 'corresponded' to the emergence of historicity, of a sense of history in its strong modern post-eighteenth-century sense, science fiction equally corresponds to the waning or blockage of that historicity, and, particularly in our own time (in the postmodern era), to its crisis and paralysis, its enfeeblement and repression.[4]

This argument is linked to Jameson's depiction of the loss of depth in post-modernism and its accompanying multiplying of surfaces. What it fails to notice is the importance in the postmodern period of the historical novel as practised by Gore Vidal, William Golding, Anthony Burgess, Rose Tremain, Margaret Atwood, Peter Ackroyd, Peter Carey and many others. Much of this writing takes a conventionally realist form and concerns itself hardly at all with the 'disappearance of the historical referent' (p. 25) which Jameson considers to be a central preoccupation of American novelist E. L. Doctorow. Here, as elsewhere amongst postmodernist theorists, the internal demands of theorising have led to a conspicuous ignoring of the contradictions in the culture and the variety of aesthetic practice. If historicity had been as enfeebled in the period as Jameson suggests, then this historical writing would not have been as vigorous and inventive as it has been; nor would it have found such a lucrative market.

Moreover, this negative view of the role of science fiction fails to take account of how important its resources have been to the postmodernist novel. Brian McHale is accurate in his substantial and detailed account of what the genre has meant to recent fiction, and his analysis of the symmetry between science fiction and postmodernism is illuminating:

> Science fiction, like postmodernist fiction, is governed by the onto-logical dominant. Indeed, it is perhaps *the* ontological genre *par excellence*. We can think of science fiction as postmodernism's noncanonized or 'low art' double, its sister-genre in the same sense that the popular detective thriller is modernist fiction's sister-genre.[5]

Novelists who have made important use of science fiction include William Burroughs, Kurt Vonnegut, the Angela Carter of *Heroes and Villains* and

The Passion of New Eve, the Alasdair Gray of *Lanark,* the Marge Piercy of *Body of Glass* (which draws upon Donna J. Haraway's cyborg theorising) and the recent work of Will Self, especially *Great Apes.*

However, the most consistently powerful deployment of the genre has been in the work of J. G. Ballard, who started out in the 1960s writing inventive apocalyptic narratives, and developed, by the end of that decade, through *The Atrocity Exhibition,* an experimental collection of short pieces, into *Crash,*[6] his most challenging and important work. Its challenge arises from its being sited on a differend. Its central subject matter is car crashes: elsewhere in the culture these are conventionally treated, if at all, in the language of realist reportage, and the conventional response to them is fear, horror and sympathy. By antagonistically treating this subject matter in the language of pornography and science fiction, and describing, in his characters, responses to it that combine fascination and sexual arousal, Ballard confronts his readers with a terrifying gap between generic worlds.

Lyotard's redeployment, in relation to the differend, of the Kantian sublime is urgently relevant here. When Lyotard says that the sublime 'entails the finality of a nonfinality and the pleasure of a displeasure' (p. 165), his language seems entirely apt to *Crash,* as it does when he refers to the need to 'supply a presentation for the unpresentable, and therefore, in regard to Ideas, to exceed everything that can be presented' (p. 166). Such Kantian references have become fashionable, as Jameson points out (p. 34), but their use is exceptionally valid in a discussion of a novel whose own author considers its material 'extreme', as 'a kit of desperate measures only for use in an extreme crisis'.[7] This novel's transgressiveness is a calculated strategy deployed in order to invent an impossible idiom that can express the differend that drives its subject matter: sexual perversity is invoked in order that the novel can think the unthinkable.

Science fiction is drawn upon generically, therefore, to provide the literary conventions that enable the invention of an alternative world in which norms are reversed. *Crash* refers repeatedly to styles and rituals which combine sex and car crashes, as though this combination were so routine that there were institutionally imposed modes of behaviour that reflected that routineness. So, when an injured young woman is helped out of her crashed car, and the action requires the opening of her thighs, the narrator (who has also been injured in the crash) is immediately aware of the sexuality of her posture, but what he remembers is 'the stylization of the terrible events that had involved us, the extremes of pain and violence ritualized in this gesture of her legs' (p. 22). The firemen reach their hands towards him 'in a series of coded gestures' and the ambulance attendants have 'stylised gestures' which get associated with a bite inflicted on him by 'a tired prostitute irritated by [his] hesitant erection' (p. 23). Later, when he imagines penetrating the anus of Vaughan (who becomes the principal instigator of car-crash eroticism) in the back seat of Vaughan's car, he imagines the event as 'stylised and abstracted' (p. 82), and he celebrates a 'marriage of sex and technology' when he observes Vaughan, again in a car, masturbating against a prostitute's hand as though 'in a dance of severely stylised postures' (p. 110).

This set of highly esoteric associations, by being evoked as a set of styles and rituals, is transformed by *Crash* into the marker of a radically altered everydayness. In this novel to associate car crashes and sex is normal. This is how it finds an impossible idiom for a differend. In the 'ordinary' world which we inhabit, any styles and rituals which are associated with car crashes would be dedicated to sterilising them and segregating them thoroughly from eroticism. Their routine combination in *Crash* indicates an extreme reconfiguring of what it means to be human.

So the novel's most important dispute with the ordinary world is with that world's ordinary attitudes to identity: the crucial concerns of *Crash*, as of science fiction generally, are (as McHale points out) ontological. Where 'ordinary' attitudes to the self assume it to be unitary and organic, *Crash* depicts it as fragmented (sometimes all too literally) and mechanised. The novel's key premise is that its characters, as a consequence of the traumata inflicted on them in car crashes, have been ontologically infected by cars as though by a technological virus. So Gabrielle has been photographed by Vaughan in the crash that has crippled her and in which she has been 'reborn':

> The crushed body of the sports car had turned her into a creature of free and perverse sexuality, releasing within its twisted bulkheads and leaking engine coolant all the deviant possibilities of her sex. Her crippled thighs and wasted calf muscles were models for fascinating perversities.
>
> (p. 79)

Ballard provides a realist explanation for this at the level of personal psychology when he refers to 'that period of unthinking promiscuity through which most people pass after a bereavement' (p. 94), but this moment is uncharacteristic, and his emphasis is elsewhere very much focused on diagnosing much larger cultural forces. In particular, this transformation of the human psyche is linked to the idea of 'autogeddon', the 'end of the world by automobile' (p. 43). It can be compared as such to Ballard's self-confessed 'obsession with nuclear weapons', which he discusses in an interview with Will Self – 'a glamorous apocalypse', the 'idea that the human spirit might be somehow transfigured by an apocalyptic nuclear war'.[8]

The crucial image in *Crash* is of a car/human hybrid. Its characters, after their crashes, bear scars whose imprint can be read so that their bodies remain inscribed with the car parts with which they have collided. More than this, however, they are metaphorically invaded by cars, so that their identity has been colonised by car technology. So, in his sexual encounters with Gabrielle, the narrator explores 'the tender causeways driven through her flesh by the handbrake' and her 'sexual apertures formed by fragmenting windshield and dashboard dials' (p. 137); watching his wife Catherine have sex with Vaughan, the narrator 'wants to adjust the contours of her breasts and hips to the roofline of the car, celebrating in this sexual act the marriage of their bodies with this benign technology' (p. 125).

That narrator is called Ballard, and this suggestion of personal investment in the story orients the image of the car/human hybrid towards issues of the personal and the impersonal. *Crash* diagnoses the way that technology invades personal space and renders it impersonal. This is also an important key to the novel's generic references to pornography which focuses upon the sexual – generally regarded as the most personal of human responses – but depersonalises and reifies it. The novel's pornographic imagery is therefore surprisingly symmetrical with its car-crash imagery: both transform the human body by treating it as a thing. This is part of an image cluster in which new symmetries are discovered between cars – and the landscape which cars create – and the eroticised body. These symmetries arise when technology is humanised and the human is technologised. In this context Ballard reinvigorates dead metaphors, as when he says 'the sluggish traffic moved like blood in a dying artery' (p. 115), and redeploys them punningly, as when he has the narrator visualise Vaughan following Catherine 'through car-washes and traffic detours, moving ever closer to an intense erotic junction' (p. 163).

Science fiction and pornography conspire with each other generically in *Crash* to evoke a post-human apocalypse. The novel occasionally reprises Ballard's earlier apocalyptic fictions but works much more powerfully than them because it situates its anxieties in a recognisably contemporary culture which it renders simultaneously both frighteningly strange and luridly familiar. Finding the roads, near the end of the novel, strangely empty, the narrator is reminded of a lunar landscape – 'a still-life arranged by a demolition squad' – and then thinks of a deserted city 'with an abandoned technology left to its own devices' (p. 162). Throughout the novel, however, there is a subtler and more insinuating apocalypse underway in the reconfiguring of the human from within. It is not aliens who are the body snatchers in *Crash*; it is technology that appropriates human material for its own purposes. The consequences of this are most insistently represented in the image of dolls which haunts the narrative – dolls, mannequins and crash-test dummies are referred to obsessively. The science fiction implication of this is that human beings may look as they always did but only their shell is human: they are hollow, or they have been replaced by something horrifyingly other.

So a nurse's assistant is described as 'a middle-aged woman with the small face of a corrupt doll' (p. 31). The narrator, after his accident, is said to have a 'mannequin-like face', and the lowering of his right eyebrow seems to give him an eye-patch that conceals his 'new character' (p. 32). Catherine seems to the narrator to be 'as inert and emotionless as a sexual exercise doll fitted with a neoprene vagina' (p. 44), and 'like some demonstration model of a beautiful woman's face' (p. 89). When Vaughan, Helen Remington and Ballard go to watch a crash-test experiment, involving 'a family of four mannequins' with crash zones inscribed on their bodies, the several hundred human observers take on 'the appearance of mannequins' (p. 96), and the 'dream-like reversal of roles' make them eventually seem 'less real than the mannequins in the car' (p. 101).

The associations of this image reinforce those of the references to styles and rituals in implying unthinking behaviour, automatic responses. They also reinforce the associations of the car/human hybrid image in suggesting the mechanising of the human, the quiet replacement of human beings by cyborgs. So the narrator, after his accident, is steered around in his wheel-chair like 'one of those elaborate humanoid dummies fitted with every conceivable orifice and pain response' (p. 35). And when Catherine and Vaughan perform a sex act in a car as it goes through a car wash they resemble 'two semi-metallic human beings of the distant future making love in a chromium bower' (p. 124).

3.2 The detective story

Brian McHale's points about the relationship between postmodernism and science fiction are helpful. However, the other part of his argument in this context – like Jameson's generalisations about historicity – is belied by the literary facts. The equation of science fiction and the ontological dominant of postmodernism works well, but the accompanying argument, which equates detective fiction with the epistemological dominant of modernism (see p. 9), collapses in the face of the enormous importance which detective fiction, and the thriller to which it is generically related, have achieved in the postmodern period. Paul Auster's *New York Trilogy* is not mentioned by McHale, but it is a key postmodernist text which focuses upon, and parodies, detective stories.

McHale does not discuss poetry but a consideration of Paul Muldoon's 'Immram'[9] would also have made him aware of the inadequacy of his argument, because this is an important postmodernist poem which draws upon the detective story. Stylistically, 'Immram' is a hybrid of epic and Chandleresque novel. Muldoon has spoken in an interview about how the title of his poem refers to voyage tales and how the most famous of these is 'Immram Mael Duin',

> In which the hero sets out to avenge his father's death, goes through many fabulous adventures, and at the end discovers an old hermit sitting on a rock – who turns out to be a Howard Hughes figure in my version – who tells him that he should turn the other cheek.[10]

The preoccupation with the father figure, which also dominates a number of Muldoon's other poems, indicates that identity issues dominate 'Immram': its narrative is driven by a search for fatherly origins (frustrated though that search is, in the end). This further unsettles McHale's generalising categories because Muldoon's poem draws upon detective story references in order to explore ontological questions. Muldoon is interested in what detective stories share in common with voyage tales: what he calls 'the heroic mode' (*Viewpoints*, p. 139) and, connected with this, their sense of purpose – the quest in epic, the search for a solution in the detective story. Both genres focus on actions and events and claim to describe them objectively.

This might be called the poem's 'palimpsestic' aspect. In placing the voyage tale as an undercurrent below the contemporary narrative, Muldoon is drawing upon a strategy favoured by modernist authors – most famously James Joyce in *Ulysses*, which uses the Homeric epic to underpin its story about early twentieth-century Dublin. Muldoon's poem is postmodernist, however, precisely because it deploys its palimpsest in a self-consciously and playfully textual manner that draws upon references to genre in order to stress textual relativity. The apparent objectivity of both genres is called into question by dwelling on how they are composed out of language and stock literary effects. The generic instability of 'Immram' unsettles expectations and cuts off both the speaker and the reader from the reassurances that are singly offered by epic and detective story, and so suggests a restless refusal on the part of experience itself to be too easily packaged. One key effect here is the way the, as it were, wateriness of the voyage tale is partly denied by the landlocked nature of the detective story but, nonetheless, keeps surreally infiltrating itself:

I did a breast-stroke through the carpet,
Went under once, only to surface
Alongside the raft of a banquet-table –
A whole roast pig, its mouth fixed on an apple.

(*Viewpoints*, p. 62)

The way the setting of 'Immram' hesitates between sea and land is roughly equivalent to the way it hesitates between the solidity of the 'real world' and the deliquescence of dream or hallucination, sometimes explicitly drug-induced. Individual images within each scene loom up with vivid particularity but the scenes are linked by a problematic series of 'dissolves' and each scene is itself vulnerable to undergoing a 'sea-change'. Ultimately, the hesitation between detective story and voyage tale constitutes a differend: the two genres are irreconcilable and this produces constant ruptures in a text which is a hybrid whose generic (or genetic) components never thoroughly fuse. This enacts in the end a postmodernist idea of identity in process – especially gender identity because the poem's self-conscious textuality deconstructs heroic images and therefore masculine self-constructions, masculine adoptions of personal styles and postures.

Tom Stoppard has parodied detective stories mostly in order to produce effects of comic incongruity. *The Real Inspector Hound* has a lot of metatheatrical fun with Agatha Christie's *The Mouse Trap*: here, and also in *Jumpers*,[11] his characteristically postmodernist concern is to mock the simplifying effect of the detective story plot and its reassuring structure in which an initial mystery leads to a thorough solution. The central themes of *Jumpers* are acted out through the generic clash between the detective story and moral philosophy. The assumption that a detective can clear up all the questions and, by the end of the story, know the absolute truth in all its ramifications, is thoroughly unsettled by the insistent asking of the most difficult moral questions. The most telling moment for this clash comes when the central character, the moral philosopher George Moore, explains moral relativism to the play's detective, Inspector Bones. Invested with all the stable values of his own genre, the detective is astonished to learn that mainstream philosophy does not believe 'in good and bad as such' (p. 48).

In a conventional detective story plot the focus would be upon the murder of Professor McFee and the discovery of his murderer by Bones. In Stoppard's postmodernist mingling of genres, however, this plot is relegated to a background role. Much closer to the play's surface is a farcical stage action: this generic mix suggests the influence on Stoppard of Joe Orton, and there are hints at times of satirical metatheatricality in Stoppard's pastiche which confirm this suggestion. Farce as a genre is traditionally as conservative as the detective story – both genres draw strategically upon apparent confusion which is dispelled when the truth is finally discovered and order is restored. Orton, like Oscar Wilde, deployed farce but shattered its conservatism by multiplying confusions (especially gender confusions) and terminally unsettling order; he thereby attacked the stable conformities of straight society from an explicitly gay perspective.

Farcical action is spectacularly multiple in *Jumpers*: a cabaret performance, a striptease on a swing, gymnastic displays, a giant screen showing a political victory parade and a moon landing, George's stage business with his philosophical props (his tortoise and his hare, and his bow and arrow) and the ambiguous visits of Archie (the university vice-chancellor) to the bedroom of George's wife, Dotty. All of this overwhelms the murder plot which becomes simply another action in the farce. This makes its own point about moral relativism – a murder seems to become no more worthy of attention than any of the other activities, and in fact much less eye-catching than most of them. The murder mystery also remains significantly unresolved and it is unclear at the end whether McFee was murdered by a colleague or by the secretary with whom he was having an affair.

The play's coruscating hyperactivity is tellingly symptomatic of postmodernism. It vividly illustrates Jameson's point about loss of depth and the multiplying of surfaces: someone has been murdered in the midst of all this frantic display but his murder is flattened into another visual image for theatrical consumption:

> DOTTY *is standing in the Bedroom. She hasn't moved at all. She is dressed in a blood-stained party frock, holding up a corpse dressed in yellow trousers and singlet. She is composed, looking about her, clearly trying to decide what to do with the body.*
>
> (p. 22)

What is also intriguing is that Stoppard wanted his play to oppose this postmodernist loss of depth. As Benedict Nightingale has written, 'Stoppard's own mistrust of materialist philosophy is on record, as is his belief that there must always be "a moral standard, a consistent idea of what constitutes good and bad in the way human beings treat each other".'[12] This is remarkable because it means that this author who seems – because of his apparent playfulness and his love of theatrical excess – amongst the most conspicuously postmodernist is actually a thorough anti-postmodernist.

Given Stoppard's stated view of the play, it is clear that we are meant to take George's side of the argument, and meant to take seriously his polemics against moral relativism and in favour of God. Stoppard has also said that the play is 'theist' and that he 'wanted to suggest that atheists may be the

magic realism: oral expression and thought is '(i) Additive rather than subordinative' (p. 37); '(ii) Aggregative rather than analytic' (p. 38) and '(iii) Redundant or "copious"' (p. 39).

The textual miming of pre-textual structures which is deployed by Márquez, Rushdie and Carter (amongst others) constitutes a form of parody which is highly characteristic of magic realism:

> Colonel Aureliano Buendia organized thirty-two armed uprisings and he lost them all. He had seventeen male children by seventeen different women and they were exterminated one after the other on a single night before the oldest one had reached the age of thirty-five. He survived fourteen attempts on his life, seventy-three ambushes, and a firing squad. He lived through a dose of strychnine in his coffee that was enough to kill a horse . . . Although he always fought at the head of his men, the only wound that he received was the one he gave himself after signing the Treaty of Neerlandia, which put an end to almost twenty years of civil war. He shot himself in the chest with a pistol and the bullet came out through his back without damaging any vital organ.[18]

This is certainly additive, aggregative and copious and it also parodies that tendency in oral cultures towards what Ong calls 'fulsome praise' which 'strikes persons from a high-literacy culture as insincere, flatulent, and comically pretentious' but which is inevitable in 'the highly polarized, agonistic, oral world of good and evil, virtue and vice, villains and heroes' (p. 45).

Magic realist parody produces a generic instability which interrogates the structures of thought which Western textual culture imposes – this has made it an especially important idiom for exploring postcolonial issues. These oral structures function partly by what they are not. Their lack of subordinativeness and analysis, and their refusal to conform to the discreet economies of realist discourse, indicate how that discourse imposes its hierarchical and rationalist assumptions. In Márquez' influential case, this forms part of a thoroughgoing critique of Western values and how they have been imposed by colonialists: a critique in which the 'magic' of the colonised is contrasted with the 'realism' of the colonisers. Magic carpets are more believable to the villagers of Macondo – where *One Hundred Years of Solitude* is set – than the Western technology which descended upon them and 'changed the pattern of the rains, accelerated the cycle of harvests, and moved the river from where it had always been and put it with its white stones and icy currents on the other side of the town, behind the cemetery' (p. 188).

A number of feminist writers have drawn upon the resources of magic realism in order to deploy its fantastical effects against the rationalist ideology of patriarchy. Angela Carter in *The Bloody Chamber* refers to that ideology explicitly and in terms that connect her feminist critique to post-colonial critiques, when she has the heroine of 'The Tiger's Bride' say that 'I was a young girl, a virgin, and therefore men denied me rationality just as they denied it to all those who were not exactly like themselves, in all their unreason.'[19] Carter could easily be referring to Márquez here because she is making common cause with him against a rationalist hegemony that is both Western and masculinist and oppresses its colonial and gender victims by insisting that they are inferior to the universalising model which that hegemony imposes, and insisting that their inferiority is related, in particular, to their primitive or feminine lack of Western and masculine rationality.

Carter's cycle of short stories draws upon the satirical effects of the generic hybridity of magic realism in order to subvert these claims to rationality. Its principal generic references are to fairy tale, especially to 'Beauty and the Beast' and 'Little Red Riding Hood', so that rational masculinity finds itself at a disorienting generic disadvantage. Carter's satirical strategy here is symmetrical with that of postcolonial writers who use references to oral structures to disrupt the subordinative and analytic structures of Western technological textuality. Fairy tale as a genre assumes that there are dark, primitive forces at work as represented, for example, by the forest in 'Little Red Riding Hood'. There is also a tendency for fairy tales to be told from a feminine point of view, and Carter's choice of tales emphasises this.

Generic hybridity in itself poses a problem to masculine rationalism which wants to present itself as a powerful monolith. The linguistic instability of these stories already compromises that dominant ideology, but it is further compromised because the males in the stories are presented as human/animal hybrids – they are men but they are also simultaneously lions, tigers and wolves. The crucial satirical point here is that masculine claims to rationality are subverted by the consequent focus upon masculine appetites, especially sexual appetites. This means that hybridity paradoxically simplifies the males because it satirically reduces them to a set of simple drives:

> I never saw a man so big look so two-dimensional, in spite of the quaint elegance of The Beast, in the old-fashioned tailcoat that might, from its looks, have been bought in those distant years before he imposed seclusion on himself; he does not feel he need keep up with the times. There is a crude clumsiness about his outlines, that are on

the ungainly, giant side; and he has an odd air of self-imposed restraint, as if fighting a battle with himself to remain upright when he would far rather drop down on all fours. He throws our human aspirations to the godlike sadly awry, poor fellow; only from a distance would you think The Beast not much different from any other man, although he wears a mask with a man's face painted most beautifully on it.

(p. 53)

The focus of the parody here is entirely different from the Márquez which I quoted at length earlier. This passage, with its labyrinthine syntax, its sophisticated vocabulary, and its fastidiously ironic tone, is mimicking classic realism. What causes the generic double-take in this case is that the subject matter is wrong-footingly at odds with the language in which it is being treated: the literary idiom is complex, but that idiom, nonetheless, is saying that its subject is worryingly simple. So classic realism, which works as a genre above all to celebrate human complexity, is being used against itself to describe caricatural flatness. The style resembles the mask which is referred to in the last quoted sentence – it is a surface which conceals an entirely different, and more frightening, reality.

What the generic instability of *The Bloody Chamber* most importantly suggests is that this classic realist idiom is too tainted – because of its cultural and historical associations – with an ideology that oppressively colonises and reifies those who are not its principal beneficiaries. The appetites of its beastly males are dedicated to commodifying and then devouring the innocent females. What saves them from this fate and bestows unexpected power upon them in the process of rescuing them from their innocence are the forms of generic empowerment which Carter insinuates into the stories. Alongside the fairy-tale discourse which destabilises the male's rationalist power, Carter introduces references to romance and Gothic which are much more congenial to the sensibility of the female protagonists than they are to the carnivorous males. Placed in these generic contexts, the heroines can draw upon structures of thought and feeling related to the power of desire. Wielding this power, the heroines soften and tame the beasts so that their interactions are enacted on an equal footing in which a mutual gender alienness is encountered with a vulnerability that unsettles both sexes:

He will gobble you up.

Nursery fears made flesh and sinew; earliest and most archaic of fears, fear of devourment. The beast and his carnivorous bed of bone and I, white, shaking, raw, approaching him as if offering, in myself, the key to a peaceable kingdom in which his appetite need not be my extinction.

He went still as stone. He was far more frightened of me than I was of him.

(p. 67)

Notes

1 Jacques Derrida, 'The Law of Genre', in W. J. T. Mitchell (ed.), *On Narrative* (Chicago: Chicago University Press, 1981), p. 52.
2 Jean-François Lyotard, *The Differend* (Minneapolis: University of Minnesota Press, 1988), p. xi.
3 Edwin Morgan, *Collected Poems* (Manchester: Carcanet, 1990), pp. 267–8.
4 Fredric Jameson, *Postmodernism or, The Cultural Logic of Late Capitalism* (London: Verso, 1991), p. 284.
5 Brian McHale, *Postmodernist Fiction* (London: Routledge, 1989), p. 59.
6 J. G. Ballard, *Crash* (London: Flamingo, 1993).
7 J. G. Ballard, 'Introduction to the French Edition of *Crash* (1974)', reprinted in *Crash* (London: Flamingo, 1993), p. 8.
8 Will Self, 'J. G. Ballard', in *Junk Mail* (London: Penguin, 1996), p. 345.
9 Paul Muldoon, *Selected Poems 1968–1983* (London: Faber and Faber, 1986), pp. 58–67.
10 John Haffenden, *Viewpoints: Poets in Conversation* (London: Faber and Faber, 1981), p. 139, henceforth *Viewpoints*.
11 Tom Stoppard, *Jumpers* (London: Faber, 1972).
12 Benedict Nightingale, *An Introduction to Fifty Modern British Plays* (London: Pan Books, 1982), p. 421.
13 Ian McEwan, *The Innocent* (London: Pan Books, 1990).
14 Ian McEwan, *Enduring Love* (London: Vintage, 1998).
15 Gabriel García Márquez, 'A Very Old Man with Enormous Wings', in Joseph F. Trimmer and C. Wade Jennings (eds), *Fictions* (Fort Worth: Harcourt Brace, 1998), pp. 555–9.
16 Salman Rushdie, *Imaginary Homelands: Essays and Criticism 1981–1991* (London: Granta Books, 1991), p. 301.
17 Walter Ong, *Orality and Literacy* (London: Routledge, 1988), p. 33.
18 Gabriel García Márquez, *One Hundred Years of Solitude* (London: Pan, 1978), p. 91.
19 Angela Carter, *The Bloody Chamber and Other Stories* (London: Penguin, 1979), p. 63.

4

Postmodern race

Profound historical changes including the end of empires and the rise of the black power movement in the USA have led to a highly significant increase in awareness about racial identity. 'Postcolonialism' is one of the most important theories to be applied to postmodern literature and to earlier texts which have been thereby deconstructed from a postmodern perspective. The second document in this book (pp. 158–61) is the 'Conclusion' to Frantz Fanon's classic text *The Wretched of the Earth*, written during the Algerian War (1954–62), in which Algerian guerrillas conducted an ultimately successful campaign against the forces of the French colonial power. Fanon was working in Algeria at the time as head of the psychiatric department of the Blida-Jonville Hospital, having trained previously in Paris and Lyons where his experiences of racist attitudes and stereotyping were formative for his later theorising.

Just as important, philosophically, were existentialism and Marxism which were important strands in French thought at the time. Fanon is extremely important for the way he brings these systems of thought (together with his own psychiatric knowledge) to bear upon the colonial experience. His psychiatric understanding of that experience is an important point of reference for Homi Bhabha, whom I discuss later; his Marxism and existentialism are important for the nuanced perspectives which they throw upon the early anti-colonial movement known as 'Negritude' which Fanon encountered first through having been taught (in Martinique where he grew up) by the poet Aimé Césaire who was one of its leaders. Negritude supported a separate black cultural identity. Fanon vacillated tellingly and importantly in his support for the movement, thereby foreshadowing a key debate in post-colonialism between those drawn to 'essentialist' notions of black identity, and those with postmodernist anxieties about such essentialism.

What would also become an important input into postmodernism in Fanon's work is identified by Jean-Paul Sartre when he draws attention to the alien light which is thrown by Fanon upon the West and its traditions.

Fanon refers to the self-proclaimed Western concern with the 'welfare of Man' but then indicts the West for hypocrisy: 'today we know with what sufferings humanity has paid for every one of their triumphs of the mind'. Sartre identifies in this the 'strip-tease' of Western humanism: 'There you can see it, quite naked, and it's not a pretty sight. It was nothing but an ideology of lies, a perfect justification for pillage; its honeyed words, its affectation of sensibility were only alibis for our aggressions.'[1]

So the postcolonial project has contributed to a postmodern undermining of Western humanism as it was defined in the Enlightenment. Similarly, Chinua Achebe's seminal essay on Conrad's *Heart of Darkness*, and Edward Said's pioneering work in his *Orientalism*, have led to a new awareness and scepticism about the monolithic cultural attitudes that prevailed before the Second World War. These new perspectives (combined with those described in the next chapter, on gender) form an important contribution to the thorough undermining of traditional hierarchies.

4.1 African-American literature

When Richard Wright published *Native Son* in 1940 he initiated a major change in American literature by introducing a newly political sense of the African-American experience. That political perspective had been lacking from the work, in the 1920s, of the 'Harlem Renaissance' (most prominently, Langston Hughes and Claude McKay). *Native Son* was designed to offend and even frighten white liberals with its crudely violent protagonist, Bigger Thomas, whose depiction is meant to illustrate the impact on African Americans of the social injustice which is inflicted upon them – he is formulaically the product of his environment.

African-American writers of the generation after Wright were indebted to his breaking of this new ground, but they reacted against his tendency to sacrifice literary subtlety in the process of imposing his polemical points. Race is still the key issue for James Baldwin and Ralph Ellison but in their work the perspectives upon it multiply as other identity issues are simultaneously raised. Where for Wright, as a communist, social and economic conditions are dominating factors, for Baldwin and Ellison they are only part of the point, and they are more American in their emphasis on individual expression. For them, as later for Toni Morrison, jazz is exemplary because of its roots in African-American experience but also because it transforms that experience through the patterns of variation it improvises minute by minute. James Baldwin's story 'Sonny's Blues' culminates in a moment of epiphanic transcendence as the jazz performance witnessed by the narrator is heard to recall a blues tradition and the history of social oppression that accompanied that tradition. But then a change is forced upon the ground of that music by the memory and imagination of the individual player:

> Sonny went all the way back, he really began with the spare, flat statement of the opening phrase of the song. Then he began to make it his. It was very beautiful because it wasn't hurried and it was no longer a lament. I seemed to hear with what burning he had made it his, with what burning we had yet to make it ours, how we could cease lamenting.[2]

Jazz is also important as a structural analogy in Ralph Ellison's great novel *Invisible Man* which was first published in 1952.[3] It works there to provide an aesthetic model for a fluid and open-ended novelistic form, but it also influences the novel's content by suggesting an improvisatory and perfor-mative model for identity. This links it to the novel's partial adoption of an existentialist outlook, but jazz turns out, in fact, to represent a more nuanced view of experience than the philosophy which was so fashionable in the 1950s and 1960s. As the quotation from Baldwin suggests, jazz is underpinned by a musical ground upon which its variations are played and that ground is the terrible oppression out of which the music arose. Existentialism tends to imply that identity can be freely invented by individuals and this ignores what for Ellison was still the important input from Richard Wright – that African-American identity inevitably continues to be linked to the legacy of slavery and to economic disadvantage imposed by systemic racism. Jazz is important because it implies an unresolved interaction between the historical ground and the contemporary improvisa-tion.

The most important political points in *Invisible Man* are made implicitly through its dialogue with the traditional assumptions of the *Bildungsroman*. The novel calls into question the tracing of 'psychological development' by depicting the impact on its protagonist of the racist assumptions of the institutions and individuals that he encounters. Above all, the novel insists that the protagonist's psychology is made irrelevant because white society marginalises him so thoroughly: it is this which makes him so invisible that he remains unnamed throughout. The liberal humanist assumptions of a *Bildungsroman* are accordingly deconstructed by the novel's depictions of how the protagonist is systematically drained of his humanity, so that he becomes 'a walking personification of the Negative' (p. 94); how he is turned into 'a thing and not a man; a child or even less – a black amorphous thing' (p. 95). This makes a nonsense of the idea that the protagonist could grow and mature into a fully rounded human being like Jane Austen's Emma or Dickens' David Copperfield.

This is above all because the protagonist is treated throughout as an object of use. The institution of slavery has disappeared but its culture and psychology continue in subtler, more insidious forms. So the protagonist's internal development is hardly considered: instead he is depicted as the almost helpless victim of external forces which constantly try to shape him according to the needs of the moment. He is treated throughout, not as an individual, but as a generalised representative of his race upon whom stereo-typical assumptions are relentlessly imposed. This turns him into a site of ideological struggle: a *tabula rasa* upon whom a variety of assumptions about African Americanness can be projected.

So the protagonist encounters a series of ideologies of race. These vary from the attitude of selfish advancement concealed under a posture of apparent submissiveness adopted by the college principal, Dr Bledsoe, to the extreme stance of black separatism adopted by Ras the Exhorter. Both attitudes, in their opposite ways, try to deny the hybridity of African-American identity: the first attempts to erase all trace of the African origin and to behave as though African Americans are simply subordinate Americans; the second seeks to deny the American experience of African Americans and to behave as though they are simply African. This novel acquires much of its complexity from the carefully inclusive way that it arbitrates between a variety of distortive simplifications such as these.

What these two simplifications share in common is that they are attributed to African-American individuals whose personal experience has forced them to pay full attention to racial ideology. Elsewhere in the novel Ellison depicts the attitudes of whites whose racial attitudes are casual assumptions. These include, most damagingly to the protagonist, the businessmen who reject him as an employee because of the letter he is carrying to them from Dr Bledsoe which, unknown to him, damns him in their eyes as a potential trouble-maker. Actually more conspicuous in the novel, however, are whites who treat the Invisible Man as a source of racist entertainment. So in an early scene (pp. 17–33) he is forced to engage in a 'battle royal' in the ballroom of a large hotel, to be blindfolded and fight against other blacks for the entertainment of his town's 'big shots'. Later in the novel a white woman called Sybil treats him as an object of her sexual fantasies concocted around the figures of Joe Louis and Paul Robeson (p. 516) in which he is 'Brother Taboo-with-whom-all-things-are-possible' (p. 517). In this she resembles another white woman who is excited by the fear he arouses in her with what she sees as his primitiveness: the 'tom-toms beating in [his] voice' (p. 413). Sybil calls him 'Anonymous brute 'n boo'ful buck' (p. 528). Her sexual fantasies are inextricable from assumptions about power – their transgressiveness involves the image of a rich white woman feeling an uncontrollable desire to be overpowered by a subservient black man, where the urge itself is experienced as so powerful that it can overturn conventional power relationships.

For the leftist organisation called the Brotherhood the Invisible Man can be used in ways that are in the end shockingly similar to this. They call upon his skills as an orator but it is his race above all which is useful to them as a weapon that can be deployed against the American establishment. They give him a new name and a new identity and so offer him a sense of self that will be as fulfilling as that of Frederick Douglass, who had taken this name in his role as an orator and thus 'became himself, defined himself' (p. 381). Ironically, though, his experience with the Brotherhood leads him instead in the direction of disintegration. What its members do is not in the end very dissimilar from what Bledsoe does because it involves them adopting a mask which simplifies them for political ends. As he looks back on his recent experiences he thinks that they 'seemed not to happen to me but to someone who actually bore my new name . . . and yet I am what they think I am' (p. 379).

The novel exposes the Brotherhood's ideology as a distortive simplification. Its grand narrative – its 'all-embracing idea' which gives the protagonist 'a vital role' and the world 'a new shape' in which 'everything could be controlled by our science' – is satirised as achieving this through a tunnel vision which conveniently tidies up 'loose ends' (p. 382). Ellison represents this with the glass eye of Jack, the protagonist's immediate superior. As Jack reprimands him and furiously tells him he must accept 'discipline', his glass eye erupts out of his face and he drops it into a glass of water (p. 474). This simultaneously represents the fissuring of self the Brotherhood inflicts on its members (the protagonist perceives it as a form of 'disembowelling') and the selective monolith which is its view of the world: 'So that is the meaning of discipline, I thought, sacrifice ... yes, and blindness' (p. 475). This image works all the more powerfully because it also forms part of an image cluster centred on blindness that recurs throughout the novel and which forms a symmetrical and interlocking pattern with an even more important (and eponymous) image cluster centred on invisibility.

By depicting such a wide range of attitudes to race *Invisible Man* creates an astonishingly sophisticated vision of the networks of power which operate to impose racist oppression. Ellison's critique of the Brotherhood is especially telling because it indicates his scepticism about the Marxist model espoused by Richard Wright. This scepticism is focused on the idea of a struggle between a clearly identifiable elite which holds all the power, and a powerless underclass which must be driven to rise up and overthrow that elite. Taken in the context of the whole novel, what Ellison's critique of the Brotherhood most resembles is Michel Foucault's critique of Marxism which it predates by almost twenty years.

In fact *Invisible Man* presents a Foucauldian model of social and political power in the sense that its synecdochic depiction of a wide range of institutions (education, business, healthcare, industry, the church) suggests how power is not held in one place but diffused across those institutions so that it operates in their interstices and across the gaps between them. The novel even satirically suggests that the Brotherhood itself operates as a part of this power network and it is made to resemble the rest of society in treating the protagonist as an object of use, or a 'natural resource' (p. 303). His encounter with institutions shows him as a Foucauldian 'subject'; he is the narrator of the novel and therefore the subject of most of its sentences: this, like his power as an orator, appears to make him linguistically powerful. But the novel depicts his repeated subjection to the racist perspectives of other characters, to the literal 'colouring' of their implied narratives, and to the unlocatable power of institutional structures.

One of the novel's great achievements is the insinuation into its narrative of a surrealism which is made to represent the multiple disorientations suffered by the Invisible Man as he is buffeted by one half-definable sphere of influence after another. An especially telling example of this political use of surrealism is in the scene where the protagonist ends up in hospital after an accident at Liberty Paints. Here he is threatened with a form of brain operation which will work like 'a prefrontal lobotomy', altering his identity so that it will conform to what society requires of it, since he is a machine that must be 'started again' (p. 232). Then he is subjected to an interrogation which degenerates, like a kind of sick joke, into a form of racial taunting: 'WHO WAS BUCKEYE THE RABBIT?' This is felt as a kind of medical torture. All of this constitutes a powerful representation of a form of subjection which closely resembles Foucault's account of how institutional power operates on individual subjects:

> the body is also directly involved in a political field; power relations have an immediate hold upon it; they invest it, mark it, train it, torture it, force it to carry out tasks, to perform ceremonies, to emit signs. This political investment of the body is bound up, in accordance with complex reciprocal relations, with its economic use; it is largely as a force of production that the body is invested with relations of power and domination; but, on the other hand, its constitution as labour power is possible only if it is caught up in a system of subjection . . .

the body becomes a useful force only if it is both a productive body and a subjected body.[4]

The only possible opposition to this is represented by the figure of Rinehart, who appears near the end of *Invisible Man* but still personifies the novel's coruscating, hallucinatory quality. Rinehart's multiple masks thoroughly subvert any sense of solidity and replace it with a 'vast seething, hot world of fluidity': 'Still, could he be all of them: Rine the runner and Rine the gambler and Rine the briber and Rine the lover and Rinehart the Reverend? Could he himself be both rind and hart?' (p. 498). Rinehart's multiple role-playing expresses an ironic awareness of the gap between racial appearance and reality: each role he adopts is a different black stereotype, but multiplying them calls into question the stereotypicality of each and so deconstructs racist caricature. He epitomises postmodernist man: he has no essence; he is all multiple surfaces.

4.2 Race and gender: Toni Morrison

The relationship between postmodernism and feminists is a fraught one, as I show in my chapter on 'Postmodern gender' but the relationship between postmodernism and women writers who focus upon race is even more fraught. The Chinese-American writer Maxine Hong Kingston complains about what she sees as the greyness of much contemporary writing: the fiction of what her interviewer Paula Rabinowitz calls 'the white, male, postmodernist establishment of writers, who have outlined the boundaries of what is considered contemporary writing'.[5] By contrast with those writers, Kingston feels an affinity with others, like herself, whose preoccupations are with gender and race; mentioning, in particular, Toni Morrison and Leslie Marmon Silko she says that, in their work, 'Nobody is alienated from life; everybody is warm. When I compare our work with some of the mainstream work, it seems as if many of them are only playing with words' (p. 184).

African-American feminists have expressed similar reservations at a theoretical level. As bell hooks has said: 'Should we not be suspicious of postmodern critiques of the "subject", when they surface at a historical moment when many subjugated people feel themselves coming to voice for the first time?'[6] Postmodernist theory engages hooks because it opposes essentialist attitudes; she is concerned to attack notions of essential blackness which are espoused both by white racists and by African Americans whose preoccupations with African roots and an authentic black identity are satirised in the figure of Ellison's Ras the Exhorter. However, she considers it an urgent necessity that feminists and African Americans be encouraged to shape an identity politics that will allow them to understand their histories, and she is deeply suspicious of a theorising which is conducted by a white male elite that is uninterested in the experience of marginalised groups. This theorising, as she sees it, questions the concept of identity so fundamentally and persistently that it disables that politics.

Toni Morrison is routinely discussed as a postmodernist writer, and it is true that she deploys a number of postmodernist narrative strategies and engages with characteristically postmodernist philosophical, and especially ontological, questions. Yet her preoccupation with African-American history challenges a number of key postmodernist tenets. Far from confirming the loss of the historical referent, Morrison's novels are determined acts of imaginative retrieval: *Beloved* works hard to evoke the actual conditions suffered by slaves; *Jazz* dwells on the sights and sounds of 1920s' Harlem; and *Paradise* refers, for example, to the Vietnam War, and to the impact on African-American emotional lives of the assassination of Martin Luther King. Morrison is one of the most important writers in the postmodern period precisely because she has invented a formidable body of work which is dedicated to drawing attention to the reality of African-American history – and done this in conscious opposition to the tendency of white America to marginalise or even to deny that reality.

What that body of work has cumulatively done is to find a depth where white sensibilities would prefer a shallowness; by insisting on an African-American presence in American history it has plumbed an ignored archaeology. As a critic, Morrison, in her book *Playing in the Dark*, has performed a similar feat by drawing attention to an African-American presence in American literature. That presence might unthinkingly have been dated only since the writings of African Americans themselves and thus to have seemed recent. But Morrison finds significant racial preoccupations and African-American characters in literature which predates those writers, and thus, again, finds a hidden depth:

> Just as the formation of the nation necessitated coded language and purposeful restriction to deal with the racial disingenuousness and moral frailty at its heart, so too did the literature, whose founding characteristics extend into the twentieth century, reproduce the necessity for codes and restriction. Through significant and underscored omissions, startling contradictions, heavily nuanced conflicts, through the way writers peopled their work with the signs and bodies of this presence – one can see that a real or fabricated Africanist presence was crucial to their sense of Americanness. And it shows.[7]

Fredric Jameson's insistence on 'a new depthlessness'[8] looks entirely misplaced in this context and this is all the more surprising given the cultural
importance of Morrison's archaeological project. It does suggest that the
postmodernism he is theorising applies only to a particular white and
affluent section of the Western population. Morrison's project amounts to a
challenge to the affectless postmodernist superficiality of that social group
whose sense of history is all 'pop images and simulacra' (p. 25). She does, in
fact, evolve her own form of postmodernism which is entirely different from
this and which is focused upon the painful difficulty of representing the
historical experiences which she represents: the paradoxical sense that they
are, as Jameson insists, 'forever out of reach' (p. 25) but that it is urgently
necessary to go on reaching for them.

Part of what Morrison does in response to this is to draw upon references
to allegory, so that the trilogy of novels *Beloved*, *Jazz* and *Paradise* are made
to refer to Dante's 'Inferno', 'Purgatorio' and 'Paradiso'. The point here is that
the allegorical idiom, by contrast with the symbolic one, displays the fact that
it is a form of representation – it is self-evidently a mechanistic construct. Paul
de Man's discussion of the theorising of symbol and allegory by Romantic
poets is useful for explaining this aspect of the idiom. He shows how the
'valorization of symbol at the expense of allegory' happens simultaneously
with the rise of 'an aesthetics that refuses to distinguish between experience
and the representation of this experience'.[9] The symbol is endowed with
'organic substantiality' (p. 193). Moreover, 'the material perception and the
symbolical imagination are continuous, as the part is continuous with the
whole' whereas 'the allegorical form appears purely mechanical' (p. 191).

An example of Morrison's deployment of allegory is its use in *Jazz*[10]
when she wants to stress that identity questions cannot be solved simply by
referring them to questions of origin. So she makes Joe Trace's name
allegorically significant. It is based on a childhood misunderstanding: he
was told that his parents 'disappeared without a trace' and so thought that
'the "trace" they disappeared without' was him (p. 124). Summing up his
identity totally in terms of his parental origin reduces him to the status of a
mere vestige. Wanting to retrace himself back to Wild, who lives without
clothes in a cave and is unable to speak, implies an entirely misguided
attempt to understand himself by reference to a natural origin rather than in
the much more complex terms of his social experience. But the most
damaging aspect of this is that it defines him entirely as a product of absence
and loss, and a key strand in the narrative is how Joe moves from having
Wild 'always on his mind' (p. 176) to his obsessive and finally destructive
love for Dorcas which can be seen, from this perspective, to arise from a
desperate attempt to fill an ontological void.

Morrison sums up the damaging distortiveness of this in a paragraph whose terms are explicitly allegorical. Here Joe is depicted, in his third attempt to find Wild, searching a hillside for a tree 'whose roots grew backward as though, having gone obediently into earth and found it barren, retreating to the trunk for what was needed' (p. 182). Joe is searching for his 'roots' but finds roots that represent the perverseness of his own obsessive retrospectiveness. Given the wider context of Morrison's concerns with race, there is an echo in this passage of the genealogical quest embodied in Alex Haley's *Roots*. Morrison's point is that identity can only be misunderstood when it is retraced in this way and this is confirmed allegorically by the rest of this paragraph which refers to the landscape below the tree where there is a river called 'Treason'. This can only be approached by terrain that threatens 'treachery' with its porous ground: 'A step could swallow your foot or your whole self.'

This landscape resembles the representative places in allegories like John Bunyon's *Pilgrim's Progress* and threatens to turn Joe Trace into a personification of the self misled and lost through obsessive preoccupation with 'roots'. Morrison's larger allegorical point, however, is that African Americans need to pass through this purgatorial transition to arrive at a more thorough self-determination. So the novel ends happily and proleptically by suggesting that Joe and Violet Trace have come to resemble 'real' characters who can be discussed in this idiom in an epilogue with Morrison herself intruding into the narrative: 'Busy, they were, busy being original, complicated, changeable – human, I guess you'd say' (p. 220).

What this suggests is the possibility – after postmodernism – of a renewed, but more circumspect, humanism. It is a tentative moment which Morrison has earned from her thorough deconstructing of liberal humanism in *Jazz* and, more angrily, in *Beloved* whose title indicates how the novel places itself in stark dialogue with the value which classic realism places upon love. Because Morrison's slaves are reduced to the status of things or animals and are not in possession of their own lives, they are tellingly deprived of that capacity to love which is such a central theme in the novelistic tradition:

> you protected yourself and loved small. Picked the tiniest stars out of the sky to own; lay down with head twisted in order to see the loved one over the rim of the trench before you slept . . . Anything bigger wouldn't do. A woman, a child, a brother – a big love like that would split you wide open in Alfred, Georgia. He knew exactly what she meant: to get to a place where you could love anything you chose – not to need permission for desire – well now, *that* was freedom.[11]

Where the characters of classic realism are accorded fully rounded humanity, these slaves are defined by absence and lack: they are 'trespassers among the human race', they are 'Watchdogs without teeth; steer bulls without horns; gelded workhorses whose neigh and whinny could not be translated into a language responsible humans spoke' (p. 125). The ending of *Jazz*, and the ending of *Beloved* also, tentatively suggest the possibility of a love which might reconstitute lost humanity – Paul D imagines that Sethe might heal his brokenness: 'The pieces I am, she gather them and give them back to me in all the right order' (pp. 272–3). This suggests that the mechanical constructedness of allegory, of postmodernist representation, might eventually be escaped – although this hope in the end is largely frustrated in *Paradise*.

4.3 Postcolonialism

Postcolonialism is often discussed as though it were a branch of post-modernism. But anti-colonialist writings predate postmodernism by some distance, and the politics of postcolonialism, like that of feminists and African Americans, is uneasy with the philosophical scepticism which is constitutive to postmodernist theory. That scepticism is linked to political pessimism: action becomes a deeply problematic prospect when human 'subjects' are plagued by radical epistemological and ontological doubts.

Salman Rushdie is therefore far too much of a postmodernist to satisfy the political expectations of the postcolonial critic Aijaz Ahmad, who considers that Rushdie's *Shame* invents a distorted political world in which Pakistanis are rendered incapable of resisting their tyrannical rulers. For Ahmad this is linked to the postmodernism of a Western elite to whom Rushdie is congenial because he depicts a world which resembles 'a super-market of packaged and commodified cultures ready to be consumed'.[12] This postmodernism has taken the 'the idea of a fragmented self, [and] the accompanying sense of unbelonging' which aroused terror in modernists, and turned it in 'a celebratory direction; the idea of belonging is itself seen now as a bad faith, a mere "myth of origins", a truth effect produced by the Enlightenment's "metaphysics of presence"' (p. 129).

However, postcolonialism has made a major contribution to post-modernist undermining of traditional hierarchies, and to its deconstruction of hegemonic assumptions and multiplying of alternative perspectives. An early example is Chinua Achebe's 'An Image of Africa: Racism in Conrad's *Heart of Darkness*', which dates originally from 1975. Here Achebe accuses Conrad of appropriating Africa for his own novelistic ends and completely ignoring what Africa means to Africans. He indicts Conrad of racism because, in his view, *Heart of Darkness* is an act of literary colonising in which Africa is transformed into an image to express an inner darkness which preoccupies Westerners: an image to express and therefore purge Western fears, and which in that process slurs Africa by imposing upon it alien and derogatory associations.

The most exciting aspect of more recent postcolonialism has been the inventiveness with which it has found practical uses for postmodernist theory. This is even reflected in the career of the most famous postcolonialist, Edward Said, who started out as a literary theorist but has since combined that activity with political activism on behalf of the Palestinian cause. His most celebrated book, *Orientalism*, is premised upon the concept of 'discourse' developed in the work of Michel Foucault where it forms part of a systematic analysis of the relationship of knowledge and power. That relationship is crucial to the postcolonial project, which is focused upon the political impact of modes of representation, and upon the ways that Western hegemonic thought constructs images of non-Western cultures in which their alienness is oppressively depicted as a sign of their inferiority or even their danger. For Said, Orientalism is a Foucauldian discourse:

> such texts can *create* not only knowledge but also the very reality they appear to describe. In time such knowledge and reality produce a tradition, or what Michel Foucault calls a discourse, whose material presence or weight, not the originality of a given author, is really responsible for the texts produced out of it.[13]

So Orientalism as a discourse evolved into an 'enormously systematic discipline by which European culture was able to manage – and even produce – the Orient politically, sociologically, militarily, ideologically, scientifically, and imaginatively during the post-Enlightenment period' (p. 3).

There is an important input from Foucault, also, in the work of the Indian postcolonialist Gayatri Spivak who, in her *A Critique of Postcolonial Reason*, draws upon his concept of the episteme:

> The episteme is not a form of knowledge (*connaissance*) or type of rationality which, crossing the boundaries of the most varied sciences, manifests the sovereign unity of a subject, a spirit or a period; it is the totality of relations that can be discovered, for a given period, between the sciences when one analyses them at the level of discursive regularities.[14]

Spivak deploys this concept, much as Said deploys the concept of 'discourse', to show how Western structures of thought have been violently imposed upon colonial peoples whose exotic otherness has thus been emphasised. She then shows how that perception of otherness has been used to enforce their subordination. She perceives the role of the postcolonial writer to involve opposition to these dominating structures, but she follows Foucault further than Said in continuing to insist that those structures are inescapable. (It is this pessimism about the effectiveness of political opposition that explains Ahmad's frustration with the postmodernist aspects of postcolonial writings.)

My sixth document (pp. 169–72) is an extract from Spivak and I discuss this in my chapter on 'Postmodern Nature'. However, Homi K. Bhabha is the postcolonial theorist whose work is most easily applicable to literary texts, especially in his theorising of 'hybridity' and 'liminality' which he deploys in order to oppose essentialist notions of identity, and to overcome dialectical forms of opposition and replace them with

> a space of translation: a place of hybridity, figuratively speaking, where the construction of a political object that is new, *neither the one nor the other* . . . The challenge lies in conceiving of the time of political action and understanding as opening up a space that can accept and regulate the differential structure of the moment of intervention without rushing to produce a unity of the social antagonism or contradiction.[15]

This suggests that the role that magic realism plays in postcolonial fiction may amount to an exemplary textual politics. This hybrid idiom hesitates self-consciously between the classic realism associated with the Western novelistic tradition and the primitivist mimicking of an oral form that incorporates fantastical writing. In the process it involves a form of liminality in drawing attention to the boundaries between the two discourses: the thresholds where they problematically collide. I discuss the hybridity of magic realism in my chapter on 'Postmodern genres', but there are clear signs that magic realism and the emphasis on its dialogic nature derived largely from Mikhail Bakhtin have influenced Bhabha's theorising of hybridity. He acknowledges the influence of Salman Rushdie on his own ideas about '"migrant" and minority space' (p. ix) and here he is evidently referring to Rushdie's description of migrants as defined by their otherness, as being 'people in whose deepest selves strange fusions occur, unprecedented unions between what they were and where they find themselves'.[16]

This is the most important premise of Rushdie's *The Satanic Verses* and leads him to his own explicit theorising about hybridity in that novel. So he has Saladin Chamcha associate himself, as a migrant, with a 'chimeran graft' he sees discussed on *Gardeners' World* – a tree growing in England which he thinks can take the place of a tree his father had chopped down in India:

> If such a tree were possible, then so was he; he, too, could cohere, send down roots, survive. Amid all the televisual images of hybrid tragedies – the uselessness of mermen, the failures of plastic surgery, the Esperanto-like vacuity of much modern art, the Coca-Colonization of the planet – he was given this one gift.[17]

This aspect of Rushdie is important for Bhabha as an example of a non-essentialist postcolonial identity, and he praises *The Satanic Verses* for its representation of 'the empowering condition of hybridity' (p. 227). For him a migrant disorientation is not only inevitable but can become the starting-point of a liberatory identity politics, and should therefore be celebrated, however much fundamentalists may angrily oppose it.

This view of postcolonial identity can also illuminate the contrast between Seamus Heaney, with his essentialist views of Irish identity, and Paul Muldoon, for whom the key metaphor is the hybrid. This opposes Heaney's metaphor of the poem as male heir (see, for example, 'Follower') with an emphasis on a bastard mingling of textual materials, on subversive miscegenation. So 'Mules'[18] provides a brief paradigm of Muldoon's canon which also wants 'the best of both worlds', evolves texts which are designedly 'neither one thing or the other' (a curious prefiguring of Bhabha), multiplies discourses and genres and hesitates between registers. The form of 'Mules' is also paradigmatic in this sense in its deployment of half-rhymes in a scheme that refuses to settle. The conjoining of 'foal' and, right at the end, 'fell' is especially telling and produces an unnerving, rather than a clinching effect.

However, the most significant rhyming pair are 'father' and 'other'. This is where Muldoon comes closest to a satirical intention and hints that, in general, his irony is often much less 'blank' than it appears to be. This too is where 'Mules' is linked to 'Immram' whose speaker's father is referred to as a 'mule' (p. 66). The primary meaning of 'mule' in this case is a carrier of drugs, but the word also refers to Muldoon's earlier poem and to how 'Immram' subverts notions of secure male lineage. Muldoon can be said to achieve this in a sense most importantly through the poem's form, which is itself a kind of 'mule' drawing upon references both to epic and to the prose style of Raymond Chandler. However, the hybridity of the form is also explicitly reflected in the content, and the speaker's search for fatherly origins is subverted from the start as he is informed that his father was an 'ass-hole' and that this makes an ass-hole out of him. His mockery of his father in 'Mules' is inevitably also self-mockery, especially because it is aimed at his father's sexuality, but here the point is made more clearly:

My grandfather hailed from New York State.
My grandmother was part Cree.
This must be some new strain in my pedigree.

(p. 58)

This parodically evoked notion of a hybrid origin is very close to the post-colonial image which Bhabha proposes. Similarly, 'Meeting the British'[19] is a contemptuous indictment of the damage caused to native cultures, but it focuses most on the bizarre troubling of identity that results from the intermingling of cultures: the Native American speaker of the poem finds himself 'calling out in French'.

Muldoon looks most towards the hybrid multiplying of cultural identities that are produced by colonialism. His poem 'Whim'[20] parodies Heaney's 'Act of Union' but makes the sex, as it were, significantly casual so that it does not glorify male potency, as Heaney does, as a side-effect of depicting colonial power. Instead the man is said to have 'got stuck into her' and then to have 'got stuck/ Full stop'. Then, much later, an ambulance is called and 'They were manhandled on to a stretcher/ Like the last of an endangered species'. That last image is *post*colonial to an extent Heaney never quite manages: this kind of colonial union is dying out everywhere. Because Muldoon is not at all secretly impressed by drives to territorial possession, he can be dismissive about both men and England, and moreover evoke how power can also inflict damage on those who possess it. The couple stuck together is a much more positive image than Heaney's act of union. This is partly because it is carnivalesque rather than heavy-breathing, but also because it takes for granted that the woman, Ireland, is the equal of the man, England. And, taken alongside Muldoon's other depictions of gender relations, it hints that both postcolonial and postmodern gender identities have come unstuck, and will be increasingly multiple and open to interrogation.

4.4 Postcolonial masculinity: Derek Walcott

The poetry of Heaney and Muldoon indicates how easily postcolonial issues can get entangled with gender issues. The Fanon document dates itself (1961) by its lack of self-consciousness about gender: he repeats the word 'man' and addresses himself to his brothers with no sense that he is excluding his colonial sisters. There is even a sense that these brotherly appeals represent a gender necessity, that he needs to feel masculine in the face of the colonial threat and that he wants to have that masculinity thoroughly confirmed by identifying in fraternal solidarity with other colonial males. This gender position has been analysed by Elleke Boehmer:

> The feminization of the male colonized under Empire had produced, as a kind of reflex, an aggressive masculinity in the men who opposed colonialism. Nationalist movements encouraged their members, who were mostly male, to assert themselves as agents of their own history, as self-fashioning and in control. Women were not so encouraged.[21]

The writings of the Caribbean poet Derek Walcott are continually marked by signs of the gender insecurity which is aroused in him by the colonial experience. This produces, in response, a defensive masculinity that exaggerates itself and which is analogous, in its poetic manifestation, to the political response that Boehmer identifies. The consistency of Walcott's gendered response to colonialism reveals with surprising clarity how thoroughly he wants to establish a masculine role in all his dealings with it. He is almost fanatical in immunising himself against anything that could be regarded as feminine in the colonial experience, and in refusing any role that is contaminated with feminine associations.

He achieves this largely through what he calls his 'Adamic' strategy: this guarantees his manliness in both technique (derived from a tradition which he himself regards, approvingly, as patriarchal) and subject matter (where he faces the rawness of the New World with fatherly authority). He regards many postcolonial writers as torturing themselves when they reject Western writing as 'the language of the master'[22] – by contrast, his strategy allows him to adopt that language as his own and thereby to acquire supreme paternal authority; to write as though he were in fact the first master and father, in a 'second Eden' where the apples 'have the tartness of experience'. This Adamic vision allows him, therefore, to have his apple and to eat it: he manages to be both the first writer *and* to draw upon the accumulated experience of his writerly forefathers.

The strategy which Walcott outlines in 'The Muse of History' leads him to imagine history being annihilated, and to acquire the 'elemental privilege of naming the new world' (p. 372). The implications of this are that Biodun Jeyifo places the emphasis wrongly in suggesting that Walcott wants to 'debunk' the 'epistemic, nomenclatural hegemony' of the West,[23] because this strategy in fact involves his *participation* in hegemonic naming. Jeyifo's analysis of the implications of this hegemony is accurate enough:

> 'white' domination is not only political and socio-economic, it is also, or aspires to total effectivity in the naming of things, in signifying and explanatory systems; in other words, it seeks to be an *epistemic* order of control and manipulation.

However, far from wishing to subvert this 'total effectivity', Walcott aspires to acquire it, and does so by placing himself in a 'filial' relationship to the West and, consequently, in a paternal relationship to the New World. He pictures himself, not as Caliban or Man Friday, but as Prospero, and in particular Crusoe, who appears repeatedly in his writings as an analogue of the poet, as he himself has explained in interviews:

> The Crusoe thing is inevitable because of his two conditions. One is the elation of being 'the monarch of all he surveys'. We are Crusoes: as poets, as novelists, as playwrights, we survey islands, and we feel they belong to us – not in a bad, godlike manner, but with that sense of exhilaration, of creative possession. The other side is the despair of Crusoe, the despair of always being alone. That is our true condition as writers.[24]

Walcott here identifies solely with fellow writers, not with others who have shared – as Friday prototypically did – in the colonial experience. Moreover, by taking Crusoe as his own prototype, he associates himself with what Jeyifo calls the West's 'epistemic, nomenclatural hegemony'. He is concerned precisely to acquire Crusoe's power to speak and write universal truths. Walcott therefore always equates Crusoe with Adam – thereby erasing his ideological and historical meaning in order to strengthen his epistemic meaning. The loss of Crusoe's ideological dimension is linked to Walcott's feeling that 'Race, despite what critics think, has meant nothing to me past early manhood. Race is ridiculous' (*Conversations*, p. 81). Most importantly, however, it works so that, in identifying with Crusoe, Walcott is identifying with a powerful male figure who, with literal originality, can linguistically engender all that he experiences, and who does so with unquestionable authority. To be a writer, for Walcott, is like being a colonist: to feel that the landscape you describe 'belongs' to you; that it is your 'creative possession' (*Conversations*, p. 63). As a writer, Walcott aspires to the condition of the patriarch.

So, in 'Crusoe's Journal', Walcott speaks of how

> the intellect appraises
> objects surely, even the bare necessities
> of style are turned to use,
> like those plain iron tools he salvages
> from shipwreck, hewing a prose
> as odorous as raw wood to the adze;
> out of such timbers
> came our first book, our profane Genesis

> whose Adam speaks that prose
> which, blessing some sea-rock startles itself
> with poetry's surprise,
> in a green world, one without metaphors[25]

This is a vision in which Crusoe/Adam can perceive, understand and evoke the phenomenal world masterfully and unmediatedly; the language he speaks is utterly transparent. The prose he deploys provides him with direct, unmetaphorical access to the world in its innocent greenness, so that it can smell like 'raw wood'. This is a language, certainly, and its artificiality is recognised because it is compared to carpentry which is repeatedly referred to by Walcott as a specifically masculine activity – for instance in *Omeros* when he says that 'Men are born makers, with that primal simplicity/ in every maker since Adam'[26] and then goes on to cite carvers, armourers and potters. But because of Crusoe's primacy, the hewing is erased; the prose is hewn but astonishingly retains its odorous rawness; the sea-rock is rendered poetically but is apprehended, through the poetry, as startlingly itself.

This is the sophisticated version of a gendered poetic in which readers encounter an author who identifies with Shabine, the poet hero of 'The Schooner Flight', a sailor who, like Walcott, has 'Dutch, nigger and English' (*CP*, p. 346) in him, and who leads a ruggedly adventurous life (Walcott's love of Conrad and Hemingway is in evidence here). When the cook on the ship snatches Shabine's poetry from his hand and starts throwing it about among the crew, and 'mincing me like I was some hen/ because of the poems' (p. 355) Shabine throws a knife at him which hits him in his calf:

> I suppose among men
> you need that sort of thing. It ain't right
> but that's how it is. There wasn't much pain,
> just plenty blood, and Vinnie and me best friend,
> but none of them go fuck with my poetry again.

> (p. 355)

This is all too obviously a defensive reaction to the charge that poetry is a sissy activity – to fuck with his poems is to make them feminine by placing them in a feminine sexual role. *More* obviously, though, it is a fantasy of the poet as Clint Eastwood or Arnold Schwartzenegger, the poet saying 'Make my day' or 'Hasta la vista, baby'.

Notes

1 Jean-Paul Sartre, 'Preface' to Frantz Fanon, *The Wretched of the Earth* (London: Penguin, 1967), p. 21.
2 James Baldwin, 'Sonny's Blues', in Joseph F. Trimmer and C. Wade Jennings (eds), *Fictions* (Fort Worth: Harcourt Brace, 1998), p. 237.
3 Ralph Ellison, *Invisible Man* (London: Penguin, 2001). Unless otherwise stated all references to Ellison are to this volume.
4 Michel Foucault, *Discipline and Punish*, trans. Alan Sheridan (London: Penguin, 1977), pp. 25–6.
5 Quoted in Deborah Madsen, 'The Racial Dominant: Postmodernism and American Ethnic Women's Fiction', in Steven Earnshaw (ed.), *Just Postmodernism* (Amsterdam: Rodopi, 1997), p. 150.
6 bell hooks, 'Postmodern Blackness', in Joseph Natoli and Linda Hutcheon, *A Postmodern Reader* (Albany: State University of New York Press, 1993), p. 515.
7 Toni Morrison, *Playing in the Dark: Whiteness and the Literary Imagination* (Cambridge, MA: Harvard University Press, 1992), p. 6.
8 Fredric Jameson, *Postmodernism or, The Cultural Logic of Late Capitalism* (London: Verso, 1991), p. 6.
9 Paul de Man, *Blindness and Insight* (London: Methuen, 1983), p. 188.
10 Toni Morrison, *Jazz* (London: Picador, 1993).
11 Toni Morrison, *Beloved* (London: Pan Books, 1988), p. 162.
12 Aijaz Ahmad, *In Theory: Classes, Nations, Literatures* (London: Verso, 1992), p. 128.
13 Edward Said, *Orientalism* (Harmondsworth: Penguin, 1985), p. 94.
14 Michel Foucault, *The Archaeology of Knowledge* (London: Tavistock Publications, 1974), p. 191.
15 Homi K. Bhabha, 'The Commitment to Theory', in *The Location of Culture* (London: Routledge, 1994), p. 25. All references to Bhabha are to this volume.
16 Salman Rushdie, 'The Location of Brazil', in *Imaginary Homelands: Essays and Criticism 1981–1991* (London: Penguin, 1992), pp. 124–5.
17 Salman Rushdie, *The Satanic Verses* (London; Vintage, 1998; first published, 1988), p. 406.
18 Paul Muldoon, *Selected Poems 1968–1983* (London: Faber, 1986), p. 34. Unless otherwise stated, all references to Muldoon are to this volume.
19 Paul Muldoon, *Meeting the British* (London: Faber, 1987), p. 16.
20 Paul Muldoon, *Why Brownlee Left* (London: Faber, 1980), pp. 7–8.
21 Elleke Boehmer, *Colonial and Postcolonial Literature* (Oxford: Oxford University Press, 1995), p. 224.
22 Derek Walcott, 'The Muse of History', in Bill Ashcroft, Gareth Griffiths and Helen Tiffin (eds), *The Post-Colonial Reader* (London: Routledge, 1995), p. 371.
23 Biodun Jeyifo, 'On Eurocentric Critical Theory: Some Paradigms from the Texts and Sub-Texts of Post-Colonial Writing', in Robert D. Hamner (ed.), *Critical Perspectives on Derek Walcott* (Washington, DC: Three Continents Press, 1993), p. 378.
24 Edward Hirsch, 'An Interview with Derek Walcott', in William Baer (ed.), *Conversations with Derek Walcott* (Jackson: University Press of Missouri, 1996), p. 63, henceforth *Conversations*.
25 Derek Walcott, *Collected Poems 1948–1984* (London: Faber, 1992), pp. 92–3, henceforth *CP*.
26 Derek Walcott, *Omeros* (New York: Farrar, Strauss, Giroux, 1990), p. 150.

|5|

Postmodern gender

The conditions of late capitalism have led to new perceptions of gender roles. As working conditions have changed, they have led to a shifting sense of gendered space; a move away from domestic space being considered 'feminine' by contrast with a work space, outside the home, which is occupied by men and masculine values. The rise of the women's movement is one of the key cultural shifts which mark the postmodern, and the accompanying feminist critique of 'essentialist' gender assumptions (linked to biology) has been of crucial importance in a newly unstable view of identity. Postmodern writers, both women and men, have responded markedly to these changes. Many postmodernist texts are explicitly feminist. Postmodernist texts by men are marked by a new awareness of gender issues, most explicitly in texts by gay men, but also – more than has been realised – in the work of straight males puzzled by what it now means to be 'masculine'.

What lies behind these changes is the movement from a rigid set of gender relations that became most dominant in high capitalism, and therefore modernism, to a much looser set associated with late capitalism and postmodernism. Some of the characteristics of the former were already present in early capitalism when it arose in the mid-fifteenth to the mid-seventeenth centuries in Western Europe: an increasing emphasis on what R. W. Connell calls 'the conjugal household',[1] on individualism, and on a view of both Western civilisation and masculinity as distinguished by their rationality which allowed the forging of 'a cultural link between the legitimation of patriarchy and the legitimation of empire' (Connell, p. 187). Culture became increasingly urban and entrepreneurial and its values – those associated with the 'Protestant ethic' – were overwhelmingly if implicitly gendered, so that masculinity became 'institutionalised' in the form of 'gendered work and power in the counting-house, the warehouse and the exchange' (Connell, p. 188).

These are the historical origins of an ideology which has embedded itself so deeply in the modern West and moulded the identities of men and women to such an extent that those identities have seemed inevitable and obvious. This ideology was so successful that it appeared to transcend history and established itself as common sense and natural. However, it strengthened its grip in the eighteenth century when social changes, most importantly industrialisation, resulted in 'an increasing separation of spheres, and a sharpening of the differences between male and female social roles',[2] as middle-class women were increasingly excluded from public life and dedicated themselves to household responsibilities. Many historians have argued that, as a result of this, the family became more sequestered and family life was characterised as 'private and sentimental, and defined as feminine, in opposition to the masculine world of public affairs' (Shoemaker, p. 7). Concurrently with this and largely as a consequence of these economic and social changes, concepts of the body and sexuality underwent a crucial shift:

> Thomas Laqueur has argued that . . . while in the early modern period female bodies were seen as essentially similar to men's but less fully developed, in the eighteenth century there developed a 'two-sex' model . . . The early modern view that lust was a fundamentally (though not exclusively) feminine vice was transferred to men, and women were increasingly seen as sexually passive . . . Changes in actual sexual practice are difficult to study, but a recent argument posits a parallel change: Henry Abelove and Tim Hitchcock have argued that over the eighteenth century heterosexual intercourse came to focus exclusively on vaginal penetration, excluding previous practices of fondling and mutual masturbation. Concurrently, sexual practices such as homosexuality and masturbation were increasingly condemned.
>
> (Shoemaker, p. 9)

This is worth quoting at length because it emphasises that gender characteristics and behaviour which tend now to be regarded, from a 'common-sense' point of view, as natural and inevitable are actually the products of history. In fact, it is the increasing knowledge and understanding of this that characterise our own period: it is a constitutive aspect of the postmodern that what had been established as gender norms and hierarchies have been increasingly called into question, most importantly by feminists.

To this extent postmodernism and feminism are in harmony with each other, and the varieties of highly theorised French feminism which have evolved in dialogue with poststructuralism, and especially in reaction to Jacques Lacan, are certainly postmodernist. The most important writers here are Luce Irigaray and Hélène Cixous, and the key concepts relate to a feminine body politics and its relationship to textuality – *jouissance* and its crucial role in *écriture féminine*. However, there are Anglo-American feminists who are chary of these theories, especially where they are connected to issues of identity, because they slip into essentialist assumptions in their explorations of the links between bodies and texts.

Feminism is also posed problems by the postmodernist habit of extreme philosophical scepticism. This tends to undermine the validity of any kind of moral or political pronouncement because it wants to disallow the possibility of a privileged position from which such pronouncements could be made. There are key arbitrations between postmodernism and feminism which are associated with Patricia Waugh and, more recently, Linda Hutcheon:

> Feminisms will continue to resist incorporation into postmodernism, largely because of their revolutionary force as political movements working for real social change. They go beyond making ideology explicit and deconstructing it to argue a need to change that ideology, to effect a real transformation of art that can only come with a transformation of patriarchal social practices.[3]

For Hutcheon the key problem is in representation and she quotes Jacques Derrida describing how it 'programs us and precedes us', how it 'constrains us, imposing itself on our thought through a whole dense, enigmatic and heavily stratified history' (Hutcheon, p. 151). The power of such representation programmes women into patriarchal distortions of femininity, requires them to submit to dominatingly masculine structures – to adopt purely postmodernist strategies would require women to acquiesce to such distortions. It is in response to this aesthetic problem that Hutcheon proposes the deployment of what she calls 'feminist postmodernist parody' (pp. 151–60), which can subvert consensual thinking. In this way, representation can be 'challenged and subverted'. Hutcheon finds the paradigm for this aesthetic in the visual art of Silvia Kolbowski and Barbara Kruger which, as Hutcheon says

> parodically inscribes the conventions of feminine representation, provokes our conditioned response and then subverts that response, making us aware of how it was induced in us. To work it must be complicitous with the values it challenges: we have to feel the seduction in order to question it and then to theorize the site of that contradiction. Such feminist uses of postmodern tactics politicize desire in the play with the revealed and the hidden, the offered and the deferred.

> (Hutcheon, p. 154)

5.1 Feminist fiction

What Linda Hutcheon calls 'the mastering gaze', which feminists have argued is 'inherently masculine' (p. 151) and which projects desire onto its feminine object, has been a key preoccupation of the feminist writing which has been so important in the postmodern period. It has become conspicuously important in the work of Joyce Carol Oates, whose career provides a helpful illustration of the growing power of feminist thought in contemporary culture. Oates started out preoccupied with spiritual issues and influenced by a Lawrentian and Nietzschean strain of modernist thinking, but she has become increasingly political and focused, in particular, on gender politics. So in *What I Lived For*[4] Oates creates a central character who is a self-destructively driven entrepreneur who routinely thinks of other people as objects of use. He feels this especially about women:

> hard to think of them as fellow citizens, like these feminists yammer-
> ing on about a woman's *personhood*, a woman isn't just tits and ass
> . . . Corky's bemused trying to consider a woman's *personhood* if it
> isn't her body what the fuck is it?
>
> (p. 223)

This idea is explored much further in Oates's recent novel *Blonde*,[5] a novelised biography of Marilyn Monroe which depicts her relentless reduction to a mere commodity, a 'foam-rubber sex doll' (p. 444). There are repeated references to dolls throughout and satirical anger directed at masculine reifications of women – no man in this book is exempted from this. Thus, one of Monroe's husbands, Arthur Miller, accurately identifies the origin of her commodification in 'capitalist-consumer culture' (p. 542), but he himself is depicted as not entirely innocent of it in his confusion of Monroe with his teenage lost love Magda.

Oates has been especially good at characterising teenage girls and young women and she has drawn upon the resources of the short story form to depict them undergoing difficult changes: awkward and baffled stages of development. The combination of this with her preoccupation with mascu-line predatoriness makes her famous story 'Where Are You Going, Where Have You Been?'[6] especially effective. Connie, at the start of the story, is a vain and frivolously self-involved fifteen-year-old but her encounter with the menacing Arnold Friend in a brilliantly executed scene at the end which occupies almost two-thirds of the story's length takes her, by implication, into a very unexpected development towards an ambiguous kind of self-sacrifice. Arnold Friend has masqueraded as a boy not much older than

Connie but turns out, during the encounter, to be much older and therefore much more dangerous. In finally agreeing to go with him and his equally louche companion, Connie is diverting the danger away from her parents and her sister.

It is an important part of Oates's range that she is able to depict the rawness and violence of a character like Arnold Friend – there is an important strain of social realism in her work including repeated descriptions of the urban squalor and menace of Detroit. However, the masculine predatoriness that most preoccupies her is usually of a more insinuating and subtle kind than that which drives the murderous villains of 'Where Are You Going, Where Have You Been?'. Most tellingly it involves a gender wrongheadedness in how her male characters think about women.

John Reddinger, in Oates's short story 'The Tryst',[7] resembles Corky, in the much later novel *What I Lived For*, in being a wealthy man in early middle age who regards adulterous sexual adventures as the automatic reward for his economic power. He reflects on his potency as an 'adult' in a passage near the start of the story when he is sunk in an autumnal reverie: this passage is fascinating because it shows Oates in transition, in 1976 when the story was first published, from her earlier writing into the angry politics of her later work. Reddinger's free indirect thought at this point resembles the consciousness of Jules in the 1969 novel *Them*[8] when this early character finds himself, for example, 'Sodden, satiated with the miracles of his own body . . . lacerated with having lived through so much' (p. 366).

This Lawrentian intensity is authorially sanctioned in Jules, but in Reddinger it is treated in a much more complex way. At this early point in the story it draws us into Reddinger's consciousness and encourages reader identification:

> His senses leaped, his eyes blinked rapidly as if he might burst into tears. In the autumn of the year he dwelt upon boyhood and death and pleasures of a harsh, sensual nature, the kind that are torn out of human beings, like cries; he dwelt upon the mystery of his own existence, that teasing riddle. The world itself was an intoxicant to him.
>
> (p. 63)

In Jules such ideas are treated sympathetically, but here they are stated in order to be eventually deconstructed by what the narrative reveals to be the consequences of Reddinger's outlook. The key point is that Oates's growing feminism treats this sensibility as specifically gendered. Her use of free indirect thought throughout the story presents Reddinger's point of view but simultaneously interrogates it from the point of view of the implied author. The effect is similar to that of dramatic monologue of the kind deployed in a feminist way by Carol Ann Duffy: in Bakhtinian terms, it introduces a dialogue of points of view which resembles the effects of parody as described by Linda Hutcheon.

Oates's free indirect speech is complicitous with Reddinger's point of view because it allows it expression and thus feels its (literal) seductiveness, however, it does this precisely 'in order to question it and then to theorize the site of that contradiction' (Hutcheon, p. 154). What this eventually reveals is that Reddinger has no idea about his girlfriend's 'personhood'. He is so exclusively focused upon her eccentric and girlish beauty that he fails to notice the terrible instability in her which leads, in the story's climactic scene, to her slashing herself with a razor in the bathroom of the marital home where he has complacently taken her.

5.2 Fiction and gender politics

Much of the feminist fiction writing in the postmodern period has been so explicitly political that it has mingled fictive modes with discursive ones and so has constituted one of the most important cultural forces in the period which have tellingly tested generic boundaries. I have dedicated a chapter to postmodern genres but it is worth dwelling here on how gender discussions have been influenced by this deliberate colliding of the fictive and the polemical. Fay Weldon, in *The Life and Loves of a She Devil*,[9] repeatedly pans out from the situation of her heroine Ruth to generalise about the situation of women. Ruth is abandoned by her husband but her response is immediately placed against a montage of such responses:

> 'What about me?' asked Ruth, and the words sped out into the universe, to join a myriad other 'what about me's' uttered by a myriad other women, abandoned that very day by their husbands. Women in Korea and Buenos Aires and Stockholm and Detroit and Dubai and Tashkent, but seldom in China, where it is a punishable offence.
>
> (pp. 45–6)

The commodification of women is repeatedly satirised. Ruth's husband, Bobbo, thinks that the tears of his mistress, Mary Fisher, must have 'an altogether stronger surface tension than his wife's and would surely be worth more on the open matrimonial market' (p. 23). Mary Fisher's servant Garcia, ogling Ruth and her huge size, is said to think of the term 'bulk buy' (p. 68).

When Ruth's revenge starts to work on Mary Fisher, the mistress is made to think for the first time about the burdens of domestic, as opposed to romantic, love: 'The material world surges in; tides of practical detail overwhelm the shifting sands of love' (p. 99). It is precisely these tides which afflict Martha in Weldon's short story 'Weekend',[10] and the practical details which dominate her life are listed minutely as she looks after her three children and her domineering husband Martin who performs no domestic duties at all, even though his job is no harder than Martha's. There is no question that this story is meant to be read synecdochically, that Martha's marriage is meant to evoke a whole society of others more or less like it, and that its mechanisms reveal how a whole gender system imposes a stifling role upon working wives and mothers and keeps them in line by making them feel anxious and guilty:

> Martin can't bear bad temper. Martin likes slim ladies. Diet. Martin rather likes his secretary. Diet. Martin admires slim legs and big bosoms. How to achieve them both? Impossible. But try, oh try, to be what you ought to be, not what you are. Inside and out.
>
> (p. 312)

The story ends with Martha's daughter Jenny having her first period and so entering the same system that oppresses her mother: 'Her daughter Jenny: wife, mother, friend' (p. 325).

Weldon's *The Life and Loves of a She Devil*, which I discuss in more detail in my chapter on 'Postmodern Nature', resembles a number of other polemical feminist texts in inventing a heroine whose physical powers both fascinate and intimidate men. So Jeanette Winterson's Dog-Woman[11] is a hideous monster whose gigantic size is deployed as a vengeful authorial weapon against males. Angela Carter's Fevvers[12] is a much subtler and more complex figure; her wings are celebratory and charged with the potential of feminine liberation in a 'New Age in which no women will be bound down to the ground' (p. 25). The crucial point about her is that she is a hybrid who transcends biology; she is 'neither one thing nor the other' (p. 76); she is 'Queen of ambiguities, goddess of in-between states, being on the border-line of species' (p. 80). *Nights at the Circus* is also a hybrid: it mingles generic expectations from the historical novel, from realist fiction, from 'magic realism', from fairy tale, from polemical feminism and so on, where the emphasis is on a bastard mingling of textual materials and subversive miscegenation. So Fevvers is herself a metafictional paradigm of the novel in which she is the focus and which is also 'neither one thing or the other', as it multiplies discourses and genres and hesitates between registers. The novel's feminism makes this hybridity also paradigmatic because it disrupts monolithic representations of gender and identity. Formally this point is enacted by the carnivalesque conjoining of comically diverse materials, the dialogic mingling of apparently irreconcilable idioms, so this stress on impurity is made exemplary and political.

5.3 Lesbian feminism: Adrienne Rich

Adrienne Rich is an important example of the political impact which writers have had in the postmodern period, when so many of them have been highly conscious that literature is inextricable from pressing issues of social and institutional power. Postmodern writers share, to an unprecedented extent, the sense that language is a political instrument.

To understand the extent of Rich's achievement it is necessary to read her essays alongside her poems – even aside from her stature as a poet, she is an important feminist theorist. Moreover, because in each genre she largely tackles a similar range of issues, reading her as both an essayist and a poet reveals how much she has struggled with the generic boundaries of poetry in order to make it say what she wants it to say. This has made her an experimental poet, unusually, *because* she is a political poet: because, that is, she has pushed and pulled at the edges of the poetic in order to charge it with political meaning, and to surprise political meaning with the vivid energy of the poetic. So at one extreme, as in 'Snapshots of a Daughter-in-Law',[13] she has bombarded the poem with all the resources available to her – imagery, allusion, irony, parody – while at the other she has chosen a minimalism in which the boundary between poetry and discursive prose is perilously in question, as, for example, in 'Heroines' (pp. 292–5), which discusses with deliberately prosaic starkness the social and economic position of nineteenth-century women.

Most of the difference between these two poems results from Rich's development away from self-conscious modernist textuality and irony to a plainer idiom of her own. 'Snapshots of a Daughter-in-Law' is indebted to modernist long poems like Ezra Pound's *Cantos* and William Carlos Williams' *Paterson* which incorporate quotations from diverse sources as part of their techniques of collage and montage, which interrogate how texts structure their linguistic materials. Rich adopts this mode but, crucially, redirects it so that language and textuality are held up for inspection now from an explicitly gendered perspective. Therefore, what had been merely an aesthetic strategy in male modernists becomes political when it is used by Rich. As she has said:

> Poetry is, among other things, a criticism of language. In setting words together in new configurations, in the mere, immense shift from male

to female pronouns, in the relationship between words created through echo, repetition, rhythm, rhyme, it lets us hear and see our words in a new dimension.[14]

In co-opting deconstructive montage for feminist ends, Rich explores the extent to which patriarchal values are, usually invisibly, written into the everyday relationships of words. By re-ordering those relationships ('through echo, repetition, rhythm, rhyme') she exposes those values and defamiliarises them.

As a result, more than any poet before her or even in her own time, Rich has questioned, in the process of constructing the poem, the extent to which poetry writing is a gender performance: how much the language and poetic form are shaped by the poet's gender. The impact of this questioning is felt with special acuteness because Rich has never doubted the ability of poetry to take on the most important, complex and abstract issues – the ones, that is, that are least poetry-friendly, and that are the most intractable to translation into poems. When she deals, in her essays, with the ramifying debates over gender essentialism, or the extensive psychological impact on women of what has been regarded as their appropriate work, the form copes easily. When she deals with the same subjects in her poems, the form balks. It is because of this that the form is called into question, and the nature of Rich's concerns ensures that the question asked is about gender. Does the form balk because it has been overwhelmingly a masculine form, and therefore does not want these questions asked?

In 'Shooting Script' (pp. 137–46) questions about poetry as a genre are joined by questions about film, so that the focus is particularly on the deployment of imagery. The pun on 'shooting' links the idea of masculine art with war and implies that it may be similarly obsessed with violent possession; its collocation with 'script' implies that masculine texts deploy language also as an instrument of territorial possessiveness, as well as wondering whether war is inevitably written into the masculine psyche. The twin concerns with the poetic and the filmic focus on the selection of isolated phenomena and their framing as images, and the poem suggests that this may be a deathly process. In the last section, Rich produces a series of brilliant images that deconstructs imagery:

> Whatever it was: the grains of the glacier caked in the boot-cleats; ashes spilled on white formica.
> The death-col viewed through power-glasses; the cube of ice melting on stainless steel.

These images might well appear as an arty montage in a film, or equally as examples, in twentieth-century poetry, of the kind of Imagist effect theorised by Ezra Pound, where each object is defined by being placed alongside another with contrasting colour, shape or texture, and where Pound's term for it, 'super-position',[15] unlike mere juxtaposition, gratuitously implies a kind of hierarchy (or objects performing missionary sex). However, the emphasis in the images on the draining of colour, and on dispersal and coldness, hint at numb sterility, at 'still life', in French called 'nature morte'. This isolating of phenomenal fragments is diagnosed as morbidly analytical, as driven by a need to murder to dissect.

What is crucial here is how these images are made to suggest a specifically masculine way of both perceiving and ordering perceptions, and how such apparently harmless processes are linked to much more sinister drives. 'Shooting Script' is concerned both with the Vietnam War and its media representation and concerned above all to draw attention to the alarming symmetry between them. Therefore, by defamiliarising the masculine symbolic that orders the poem's poetic and filmic imagery, 'Shooting Script' explores how the same sensibility is responsible for systemic violence. This exploration is already political but it is joined by another feature of the poem which is more so in being linked to Rich's larger programme for supplanting patriarchy; for 'Shooting Script' establishes a pattern of imagery which is designed to subvert its imagistic, eponymous hard news.

So the shooting script is associated with an analytical hardness that is linked to a form of voyeurism in its drive to use the gaze both to fix its object and control it. This inevitably distorts what it sees and reports: section 9 is a monologue spoken by a soldier who says that the newsreel footage appears to represent a different war from the one he experienced, which cannot be contained in this way: 'Someone has that war stored up in metal canisters, a memory he cannot use, somewhere my innocence is proven with my guilt, but this would not be the war I fought in' (p. 142). By contrast with the defining and containing imagery most thoroughly represented by these metal canisters, the poem introduces imagery of openness and fluidity. In fact, it does this in its first section in order to subvert the phallogocentric in advance. The first line complains, 'We were bound on the wheel of an endless conversation' (p. 137) and so introduces the poem's central concern with language as a prison-house. This idea is elaborated in the lines that follow but also opposed, as the poem's alternative pattern of imagery is also introduced, with references to the sea – 'A tide that ebbs and flows against a deserted continent' – and, more explicitly, to 'A cycle whose rhythm begins to change the meaning of words' (p. 138).

Taken together, these contrasting patterns of imagery suggest interplay and the possibility of change, and the image of the shell mediates between them. This is to some extent an image of containment but as such suggests an alternative to the image of the canisters which represent a complete enclosedness that is deathly. By contrast, the shell represents protectiveness which is also open-ended. Much of the message of the whole poem is epitomised in the contrasting gender associations of the two: the phallic hardness of the canisters versus the nurturing rotundity of the shell. Where the canisters represent armoured and static inwardness, the shell suggests the possibility of movement inwards and outwards, and the threshold of change. Most importantly, Rich uses it to imagine the potential for an altered language whose emphasis is on the provisional, on questioning rather than definition, referring to 'A shell waiting for you to listen' and 'The meaning that searches for its word like a hermit crab' (p. 138).

For similar reasons, at the end of section 10 Rich presents a series of images that insist on the refusal of the feminine to be seized and contained:

> You are spilt here like mercury on a marble counter, liquefying into many globes, each silvered like a planet caught in a lens.
> You are a mirror lost in a brook, an eye reflecting a torrent of reflections.
> You are a letter written, folded, burnt to ash, and mailed in an envelope to another continent.
>
> (p. 143)

These images again oppose the canister; they represent the opposite sensibility to those in section 14: the glacier grains in the boot-cleats, and so on. They are the response to men who attempt to possess women with crudely romantic strategies, and they oppose that attempt with a baffling elusiveness. Where the section 14 images are hard and fixed, the mercury is neither solid nor liquid, and its changeableness suggests that its possible meanings will not be contained or stilled. Similarly the burnt but posted letter suggests subversive eschewal of, and playful terrorism aimed against, conventional communication. Most importantly, the drowned mirror and the bombarded eye oppose the fixedness of the camera, and the Imagist poet, with a proliferation of shifting images; they bewilder voyeuristic control with movement and multiplicity. Therefore, what the shell does to language, these images do to the territorial ambitions of the framing gaze.

'Shooting Script' exemplifies what has been most important in Rich's achievement. Her poetic career has coincided with crucial advances made by feminism in terms of legislation for women's rights in Western countries, and in terms of much increased awareness of gender. She herself has played a large part in the latter and has been more influential than anyone else in promoting this awareness in the poetry world. 'Shooting Script' is only one example amongst many of how ambitiously and at the same time meticulously she explores cultural events (and their media or aesthetic representation) to expose how much they are specifically masculine forms of expression. From 1963 onwards, with the publication of *Snapshots of a Daughter-in-Law*, her poems always implicitly question poetry itself – down to its minutest generic details – for signs of what is gendered in its assumptions. Frequently, too, she makes these questions explicit, and they must always be read alongside her essays, especially those on women poets like Emily Dickinson and Elizabeth Bishop, where Rich's creative and polemical talents reinforce each other.

Rich is at her most convincing when she is asking such questions about gender, rather than attempting to make definitive statements about it. In this interrogative mode, for example, she can make a political point by deftly invoking a register which reveals how patriarchal assumptions are interwoven in the texture of language itself. So in 'Heroines' (pp. 292–5) she uses phrases such as 'without recourse' and 'bequeath property' like a form of free indirect speech to subvert this language and its users simultaneously. Such parodying of register is one of her most effective devices for interrogating masculine discourse, and introduces a dialogic effect for subtly political ends, thereby revealing how oppressively monologic that discourse has historically been.

5.4 Postmodern masculinity

In the postmodern period masculinity has been increasingly addressed as an issue. An increasing number of essays and books have been written during the last decade in which men have addressed the sort of gender questions previously associated with women theorists and critics. This entry of men into what was previously – as it were – a female intellectual sphere is itself important because it draws attention to the *genderedness* of the male author, and therefore to masculinity as a gender. This has a representative significance in opposing the assumption that had arisen in the culture that masculine values are not masculine but universal, and that masculinity is not a gender but a norm, not a perspective but the only coherent way to be and know.

This is a masculine self-consciousness which has arisen in response to feminism. It has led to an increasing amount and variety of work being done into what it means to be masculine, and into how masculinity has been historically and ideologically constructed. Many male writers in the period have depicted the ways that men respond to the demand to acquire a masculine identity as it has been traditionally understood. In other words, they have been concerned to explore their response to their need, as boys and men, to acquire the 'ideal masculine qualities', as David T. Evans puts it, of 'dominance, activity, autonomy, impersonality and rationality', and to acquire the appropriate sexuality with its focus on 'release, needs, experience, fantasy and achievement'.[16] To expand this further, this traditional male role involves

   a) 'no sissy stuff' – the avoidance of all feminine behaviours and traits;
   b) 'the big wheel' – the acquisition of success, status, and breadwin-
      ning competence;
   c) 'the sturdy oak' – strength, confidence and independence;
   d) 'give 'em hell' – aggression, violence and daring.[17]

Alice Jardine has listed what male authors should do 'after feminism'; she asks for a discourse that expresses

> men's relationship . . . to death, scopophilia, fetishism . . . the penis
> and balls, erection, ejaculation (not to mention the phallus), madness,
> paranoia, homosexuality, blood, tactile pleasure, pleasure in general,
> *desire* (but, please, not with an anonymously universal capital D)
> voyeurism, etc. Now this *would* be talking your body, not talking
> *about* it.[18]

Close attention to male writers in the postmodern period – and especially male poets – reveals that they have already been dealing with this relationship. One of the great challenges for these poets has been to respond to a male modernism with its roots in Ezra Pound's prescriptions for Imagism (imposed by contrast with late Romantic impressionism) and which imposes a demand for phallic hardness. This is the most helpful starting-point for discussing the gendered treatment of imagery in modern poetry. So Robert Lowell develops away from a creative outlook whose basis in a sinewy solidity has these modernist roots towards an increasing acceptance of oceanic fluidity. This shift in his characteristic imagery is symptomatic of a crucial shift in his gender attitudes – for the ocean, as Luce Irigaray indicates, is a crucially gendered image and she evokes this in her sardonic account of masculine attempts to tame, control and limit the sea:

> So this sea where he is, or at least seems to be, lost, that overwhelms
> him on every side and so puts his life in danger, what is she?
> Considered coldly, she consists of an *extended corporeal thing*.
> Probably immense. Which explains why the gaze at least is drowned,
> saturated in her. But from this place where he is now assured of
> existing, he can cut the sea into any number of pieces . . . The 'I' can
> subject the sea to a whole range of techniques that will transform her

into an *object of use*: into a means of transport for example . . .
Nonetheless, he must harden his heart to the glorious assault of her
colours, to the fascination of her sheer size, to the seduction of her
smells and sounds . . . Let him therefore call upon his will, *which also
has no bounds*, and disdain such ultimately secondary modes of being
in order to concentrate on the sea's essential attribute: extension . . .
The 'I' thinks, therefore this thing, this body that is also nature, that is
still the *mother*, becomes an extension at the 'I''s disposal for
analytical investigations, scientific projections, the regulated exercise
of the imaginary, the utilitarian practice of technique.[19]

The masculine discomfort and inhibition in the face of the sea which Irigaray
depicts are also in evidence in Lowell's response. As early as 'The Quaker
Graveyard in Nantucket',[20] he described man's agonised attempts to impose
his dominion over the sea which is an alien force whose 'high tide/ Mutters
to its hurt self, mutters and ebbs'. In 'Ocean', his description of the sea as
'one substance everywhere divisible' refers to the attempt to turn it into a
matter merely of 'extension' which can then be defined and quantified.

Surprisingly, Lowell does manage, in his later work, starting with 'Near
the Ocean',[21] to allow freer play to this oceanic imaginary and this produces
at least a partial cure for Lowell's gender sickness – and finally moderates
his obsessive working through a form of what Lynne Segal calls 'martial
masculinity' (referring not to Lowell, but to a condition which characterises
many men). This dominates his early work; Segal refers to it as an
'exaggerated, artificial, brittle and aggressive version of manhood'.[22] These
martial attitudes are linked to the desire for an autonomous masculinity,
which acquires special importance in the context of Lowell's repeated
writings about tyranny, which he himself diagnoses as a symptom of a
masculinity allowed to express itself with disastrous fullness.

One of Lowell's most remarkable achievements as a poet is that he diagnosed this tendency in himself, allowed it to express itself to a certain
cathartic extent in his work, but also learned how to distance himself from
it and counter its effects. His early work is characterised by what Gabriel
Pearson has called 'the omnipotence of manic verbal control'.[23] The poet
seems to want to tyrannise his material by obsessively man-handling it
through rhyme, heavy alliteration and compulsive punning into hard sinewy
shapes. The poetic technique does seem exaggeratedly virile and yet Lowell
learned to write entirely differently – and what is revealed in that process is
what motivated the early style in the first place. Confessional writing, like
the psychotherapy of which it is the creative kin, helps Lowell to know
himself and so to change. The hard shapes of the early poems seem to be

about fortifying and defending the poet, warding off any disturbing other-ness. Increasingly with *Life Studies*, and after that volume, the confessional Lowell allows in an otherness which also interrogates his gender identity.

As part of this process Lowell faces up to his fascination with omni-potence and tyranny and explores it repeatedly, especially in *History*. Ambivalence is a crucial feature here. The knowingness that lies behind this endeavour is linked to the interest in psychoanalysis and both are moti-vated, at least partly, by a desire to control whose sources are similar to those of Lowell's obsession with power. More disturbingly, the tyrants Lowell focuses on arouse in him – alongside his liberal feelings of repulsion and horror – obvious feelings of identification and excitement. This is all the more important because it is so closely tied up with his mental illness, his manic depression. Repeatedly, during his manic phases, Lowell (as well as becoming fixated on a younger woman) became obsessed with figures like Napoleon, Hitler or Mussolini:

> troublingly for those who cared for him, his enemies could all too easily construct from accounts of his delusions a portrait of Lowell as a sort of near fascist – How was it, they could disingenuously wonder, that this renowned spokesman for correct liberal causes persistently 'revealed', in mania, a fascination with tyrants and monsters of the right?
>
> (Hamilton, p. 343)

The omnipotence which the early Lowell exercises, through manic verbal control, over his poetic materials is exercised by these tyrants over the world itself – they can create the world around them in their own image. In Lowell's case the fascination with tyrants is linked to his fascination with violence and war, as in his poems on Napoleon,[24] and both fascinations are expressed in terms that stress that these are masculine preserves. In one of his poems about Vietnam, for example, the emphasis is specifically on the destructiveness of men: 'we was to burn and kill, then there'd be nothing/ standing, women, children, babies, cows, cats' (*History*, p. 199). The speaker of this poem is ordered to shoot a woman and finds she is holding a baby he 'thought was her gun. It kind of cracked me up.'

Much of the power of this writing comes from the complex feelings that are seen to lie behind it when it is taken in the context of Lowell's work as a whole. Taken in isolation, these poems seem to be simply about horror and protest but the obsessive repetition of this material reveals Lowell's feel-ings of guilty complicity in it – the disturbance he feels because his mind excitedly dwells on and returns to it. Lowell is involved in a psychological process that recognises elements of himself in these tyrants and also feverishly repudiates those elements. In doing so Lowell seems to be acutely aware of his own psychological motives: he is at the same time indulging his obsession and trying to shed a sickness.

It is in 'Near the Ocean' that the sources and effects of Lowell's 'martial masculinity' are worked through most fully, although the strain of this is evident in the poem's phantasmagoric difficulty. The figure of the powerful mother is represented first of all by Medusa, the sight of whose head is terrifying because, as 'Freud argues . . . it threatens by association with both castration and female genitalia'.[25] However, in a scene of dreamlike wish-fulfilment this powerful threat is shown being triumphantly overcome by a 'hero' who has killed the monster and 'lifts her head to please the mob'. This is a narcissistic fantasy of the son as Perseus – of the son, in other words, who responds to the threat of the mother's power by acquiring soldierly prowess and displaying it for the admiration of others. In the third stanza Lowell refers to the more general effects of martial masculinity when he suggests that the source of wars lies in this masculine repudiation of the feminine:

> Lost in the Near Eastern dreck,
> the tyrant and tyrannicide
> lie like the bridegroom and the bride;
> the battering ram, abandoned, prone,
> beside the apeman's phallic stone.

The reference to the bridegroom and the bride recalls a similar line in Lowell's two poems about the Spartan dead but its effect is the reverse of the celebratory one there – the shared maleness of the tyrant and tyrannicide produces a destructive impoverishment. It is paradoxical that they are like lovers because the dynamics of their purely male relationship produce a sterile cycle of violence represented by the encounter of two phalluses, the battering ram and the stone. In the terms of Gilbert and Gubar, Lowell is here relating sexual anxiety and societal breakdown,[26] but that is not because he wants the one to be read simply as the other, but because he wants to show, in his own way, that the personal is political. He is diagnosing a male sickness and indicating its social consequences.

Alongside the self-aggrandisingly mythic repudiation of the mother, Lowell places a more realist account of the son's desperate, half-guilty attachment to her, and his doomed attempts to replace her, ever afterwards, with his lovers. It is this element that then becomes the main subject of the poem, so that the references to tyranny and violence in 'Near the Ocean' are best seen as an element that Lowell tries to 'work through' so that he can move beyond them into a healthier accommodation of the feminine and an acceptance of the demands, however entangling, of mature sexual relationships. Nonetheless, the course of these relationships is necessarily envisaged as largely predetermined by the male's previous, deeply ambiguous, experiences with the mother, and dogged with consequent confusions between need and suspicion, desire and squeamish repulsion:

> then high delirious squalor, food
> burned down with vodka . . . menstrual blood
> caking the covers, when they woke
> to the dry, childless Sunday walk

There are misogynous images in 'Near the Ocean' but that is because it is a confessional poem *about* misogyny. That it is an attempt to work through these feelings is also evident from the fact that it is dedicated to Elizabeth Hardwick, Lowell's wife at the time.

What is perhaps most important about the poem is that it counters its own misogyny by explicitly associating feminine values with the ocean for the first time in Lowell's work. It is with the introduction, in its seventh stanza, of its oceanic references that 'Near the Ocean' grows lyrical (if still equivocally). And the growing presence of the ocean/woman association after this poem is the most important sign of the extent to which Lowell has worked through his martial masculinity. In 'Near the Ocean' it partly expresses masculine frustration at feminine unfixedness, but it also celebrates that same quality, and it is the celebratory note that is increasingly struck thereafter. It is precisely by contrast with phallic hardness that oceanic values are preferred. The battering ram and the phallic stone symbolise rigid responses to history: the ocean, on the other hand, collapses rigidities; 'grinding stones' it 'can only speak the present tense'.

So increasingly for Lowell the ocean is used to represent both the feminine and the overwhelming of pretentious masculine attempts at control. Through the linked figures of the mermaid and the dolphin, which dominate his later work, and an increased preoccupation with sexual love, Lowell learns not to harden his heart to the sea, to 'the seduction of her smells and sounds', and substitutes this healthy obsession for the previous sick one.

Notes

1 R. W. Connell, *Masculinities* (Cambridge: Polity, 1995), p. 186, henceforth Connell.
2 Robert B. Shoemaker, *Gender in English Society 1650–1850: The Emergence of Separate Spheres?* (Harlow: Longman, 1998), p. 6, henceforth Shoemaker.

3 Linda Hutcheon, *The Politics of Postmodernism* (London: Routledge, 1989), p. 168, henceforth Hutcheon.
4 Joyce Carol Oates, *What I Lived For* (London: Picador, 1995).
5 Joyce Carol Oates, *Blonde* (London: Fourth Estate, 2000).
6 In Joseph F. Trimmer and C. Wade Jennings (eds), *Fictions* (Fort Worth: Harcourt Brace), pp. 936–47.
7 Joyce Carol Oates, *A Sentimental Education: Stories* (New York: E. P. Dutton, 1982), pp. 62–74.
8 Joyce Carol Oates, *Them* (New York: Fawcett Crest, 1969).
9 Fay Weldon, *The Life and Loves of a She Devil* (Sevenoaks, Kent: Hodder and Stoughton, 1983).
10 Fay Weldon, 'Weekend', in Malcolm Bradbury (ed.), *The Penguin Book of Modern British Short Stories* (London: Penguin, 1988), pp. 309–25.
11 Jeanette Winterson, *Sexing the Cherry* (London: Vintage, 1990).
12 Angela Carter, *Nights at the Circus* (London: Picador, 1985).
13 Adrienne Rich, *The Fact of a Doorframe: Poems Selected and New 1950–1984* (New York: Norton, 1984) pp. 35–9. Unless otherwise stated all references to Rich's poems are to this book.
14 Adrienne Rich, *On Lies, Secrets, and Silence: Selected Prose 1966–1978* (London: Virago, 1980), p. 248.
15 Ezra Pound, 'Vorticism', *Fortnightly Review*, 1 September 1914, pp. 461–71.
16 David T. Evans, *Sexual Citizenship: The Material Construction of Sexualities* (New York: Routledge, 1993), p. 48.
17 R. Brannon, quoted in Nigel Edley and Margaret Wetherell, *Men in Perspective: Practice, Power and Identity* (Hemel Hempstead: Harvester Wheatsheaf, 1995), p. 77.
18 Alice Jardine, 'Men', in Alice Jardine and Paul Smith (eds), *Men in Feminism* (New York: Routledge, 1987), p. 61.
19 Luce Irigaray, *Speculum of the Other Woman* (Ithaca, NY: Cornell University Press, 1985), pp. 185–6.
20 Robert Lowell, *Poems 1938–1949* (London: Faber, 1950), pp. 18–24.
21 Robert Lowell, in *Near the Ocean* (London: Faber, 1967), p. 13.
22 Lynne Segal, *Slow Motion: Changing Masculinities, Changing Men* (London: Virago, 1990), p. 116.
23 Quoted in Ian Hamilton, *Robert Lowell: A Biography* (London: Faber, 1983), p. 105, henceforth Hamilton.
24 Robert Lowell, *History* (London: Faber, 1973), pp. 77–8, henceforth *History*.
25 Vereen M. Bell, *Robert Lowell: Nihilist as Hero* (Cambridge MA: Harvard University Press, 1983), p. 111.
26 Sandra M. Gilbert and Susan Gubar, 'Tradition and the Female Talent', in Nancy K. Miller (ed.), *The Poetics of Gender* (New York: Columbia University Press, 1986), p. 202.

|6|

Postmodern Nature

Postmodernism is urban and metropolitan. The New York poet Frank O'Hara said he was never comfortable unless there was a subway handy, and this camp anti-Nature stance is characteristically postmodern: much more thoroughly citified than the sensibility behind T. S. Eliot's *The Waste Land* with its montaged urban/natural contrasts. Eliot's satire arises out of his horror at the unnaturalness of modern culture, but in the postmodern this unnaturalness has intensified and established itself as a norm. For Fredric Jameson the superseding of Nature is a defining characteristic of postmodernism, which is the condition which is reached 'when the modernization process is complete and nature is gone for good'.[1]

Writers, like Jameson, with Marxist leanings tend to express ambiguous responses to this process. Walter Benjamin[2] analyses the reifications involved but also sees in the culture of mechanical reproduction the possibilities of a transformative politics which might lead to new, post-capitalist identities. Donna J. Haraway's half-ironic praise for 'cyborg' identities is similarly optimistic about the potential of the changed identities that technology might bring. She opposes the organicism of radical feminists such as Susan Griffin, Audré Lourd and Adrienne Rich, with their 'eco-feminism and feminist paganism', with a celebration of the ontological potential of late twentieth-century machines which call into question the boundaries between the organic and the mechanical, because they

> have made thoroughly ambiguous the difference between natural and artificial, mind and body, self-developing and externally designed, and many other distinctions that used to apply to organisms and machines. Our machines are disturbingly lively, and we ourselves frighteningly inert.[3]

(p. 152)

Teresa Brennan, by contrast, connects the superseding of Nature to the activities of a consumer capitalism which is so destructive that it produces a culture which is mentally ill:

> if nature is endlessly consumed in the pursuit of a totalizing course, then that course is dangerous for living; it constitutes a danger to one's own survival, as well as that of others. That, approximately, is the technical, legal definition of psychosis.[4]

Ecological attitudes espoused by writers as different as Ted Hughes, Adrienne Rich and Martin Amis lead to expressions of a similar horror. In their cases, however, the horror is combined with calls for a return to biological roots which arise from essentialist attitudes to the body and to gender. The very dominance of technology and urban artifice has led such writers to insist on the continuing importance of the natural world. In some there is a marked ecological concern, often significantly linked with a critique of 'masculine' values: Margaret Atwood in *Surfacing* and, strangely, the later Ted Hughes are both eco-feminists. Hughes is followed by Seamus Heaney in a celebration of Nature which takes an explicitly pagan and problematically gendered form. Also relevant here is the persistence in US culture and literature of a nostalgia for the wilderness and the frontier, evident even in sophisticates like John Updike and John Cheever, and crudely obvious in a book like Ken Kesey's *One Flew over the Cuckoo's Nest*.

6.1 Postcolonial Nature

In some of her recent work the postcolonial theorist Gayatri Spivak expresses similar anxieties to those theorised by Teresa Brennan. My sixth document is a remarkable example of this because the language in which it is expressed suggests a radical break from a postmodernist theorising with which the earlier Spivak was associated – given that, at the start of her career, she became famous as a translator and interpreter of the work of Jacques Derrida. It is true that, even from early on, Spivak's postcolonial and gender concerns politicised her attitude to deconstruction. Nonetheless, she is noted above all for her scepticism about the possibility of effective political action, given the thoroughly oppressive power with which Western hegemonic structures have been imposed on colonial peoples. For her, the extent to which such 'subaltern' peoples can speak is inevitably thoroughly limited.

All of these attitudes have been undergoing a subtle but important shift in Spivak's work. There is a starkly unpostmodernist earnestness in the language of this passage from Spivak's 'Afterword' (pp. 165–9) of her translation of the stories of the Bengali writer and political activist, Mahasweta Devi. The idiom here is the opposite of that wearily sophisticated irony employed by Fredric Jameson – as too is the content. Far from believing that Nature can be eschewed, Spivak is distraught at the damage inflicted upon it by the West's Enlightenment rationality and looks to oppose that destructiveness with an emphasis on ethical responsibility and – most remarkable of all – 'love'. Her point is that the threat to global ecology is so great that an almost hopeless undertaking is required, combining the efforts of previously irreconcilable forces – 'the silent gift of the subaltern' (the impossible but still necessary struggle of suppressed colonial people) and an Enlightenment reason reoriented so that its impact is *genuinely* rational.

6.2 Eco-feminism

Margaret Atwood's *Surfacing*[5] is a useful place to start a discussion of eco-feminism because its organicist ideology is so explicit and so articulately linked to other postmodern preoccupations, especially to gender and post-coloniality. Its title, however, is also a conspicuous signal of the extent to which this organicism is opposed to postmodernism, for 'surfacing' implies an image of lurking depths. This is important to these writers because it evokes the idea of values that persist beneath the veneer of 'civilised' existence, and which it is the business of writers to plunge into and uncover. So Adrienne Rich in 'Trying to Talk with a Man' declares that

> Sometimes I feel an underground river
> forcing its way between deformed cliffs
> an acute angle of understanding[6]

Here, the equating of 'understanding' with the 'underground river' draws attention to its etymology, suggesting a knowledge underlying the surface consensus associated with fertility rather than the desert, and which is literally 'subversive'. The exploratory quality of this is taken further in 'Diving into the Wreck' (pp. 162–4) which investigates the 'under' part, as it were, of 'understanding', with the assumed premise that there are modes of being and knowing that lie below the surface of ordinary experience. The power this image has for Rich is made especially clear by how it rears up again in an impassioned paragraph in her famous essay 'Compulsory Heterosexuality and Lesbian Existence', where she is arguing that there have been very elaborate and numerous measures imposed to ensure that women are sexually available to men, and that these measures in particular involve the 'rendering invisible of the lesbian possibility' which therefore becomes 'an engulfed continent which rises fragmentarily into view from time to time only to become submerged again'.[7] The drowned mirror, the underground river, the drowned ship, the engulfed continent: these are all crucial images for Rich of latent understanding which is related – especially because of the symbolic linking, traditionally, of women and water – to suppressed femininity.

These gender concerns are postmodern, but they are profoundly opposed to postmodernism which involves, as Jameson has pointed out, the eschewing of depth models (p. 12) and their replacement by multiple surfaces. Characteristically anti-postmodernist, too, is that the hankering for depth involves a symptomatic nostalgia which is represented in *Surfacing* by the premising of the narrative upon the protagonist's return to the scene of her childhood. This is accompanied by her quest there for her father whose disappearance symbolises the loss of a more 'natural' way of life which would not despoil the landscape but live in harmony with it. It also implies the loss of a nurturing masculinity which has been replaced by an aggressively technological patriarchy with predatory and colonising drives and obsessed with guns (p. 157). This is represented in the novel by the behaviour of the male characters, especially in the scene where they pressurise the wife of one of them, Anna, into performing in a pornographic film: here Joe, the protagonist's boyfriend, wields the camera 'like a bazooka or a strange instrument of torture' (p. 130).

Because the novel focuses upon the theme of return, it focuses also upon the landscape associated with that theme and evokes in vivid detail the remote island in the north of Canada where the protagonist grew up. The novel's setting is therefore very important in simply narrative terms but its importance is magnified by the ecological concerns which preoccupy it and which lead to repeated meditations on the relationship between the human and the natural. At the start of Chapter 17 this acquires a spiritual dimension, as the protagonist meditates on the heron that was senselessly killed by American tourists and visualises the flying heron as 'a bluegrey cross' and so associates it with Christ:

> anything that suffers and dies instead of us is Christ; if they didn't kill birds and fish they would have killed us. The animals die that we may live, they are substitute people, hunters in the fall killing the deer, that is Christ also. And we eat them, out of cans or otherwise; we are eaters of death, dead Christ-flesh resurrecting inside us, granting us life. Canned Spam, canned Jesus, even the plants must be Christ. But we

refuse to worship; the body worships with blood and muscle but the thing in the knob head will not, wills not to, the head is greedy, it consumes but does not give thanks.

(p. 134)

Those last sentences add another binary pair, body versus head, to the other which starts the passage, sacred versus profane. These are linked to the more conspicuous binary oppositions which dominate the novel: natural versus technological; feminine versus masculine; and even Canada versus the United States. All of these oppositions turn into the same opposition: feminine/natural/body/Canada versus masculine/techno-logical/head/USA. The former is violated by the latter. And each side of the binary opposition is further articulated by how the novel combines the different associations of its individual components, so that, for example, Canada's evocation as a colonised space feminises it and associates it with an original naturalness which is being invaded by a rationalist, masculinist culture which desecrates it.

This is the crucial idea in *Surfacing*. Its most important function is to bestow symbolic meaning on the feminine story of the protagonist in order that her experience can work as a synecdoche for the other oppressions which preoccupy the novel. This further demonstrates the key feminist idea that the personal is political. Her experience of abortion is therefore associated with the destructiveness represented by the assaults on Nature of rationalist masculinity: 'I was emptied, amputated; I stank of salt and antiseptic, they had planted death in me like a seed' (p. 138). This image of amputation is linked to an earlier one where she is compared to a woman in a magic trick who is sawn in half, but where the trick has gone wrong and she has actually come apart: 'I was the wrong half, detached, terminal. I was nothing but a head, or no, something minor like a severed thumb; numb' (p. 102). This Plathian image implies ontological insecurity as it does in Plath but it also forms part of an image cluster linked to the political themes I have been describing, so that personal amputation is made to symbolise the systemic amputation of Nature.

Despite all this, however, the novel moves towards a hesitantly optimistic ending. The protagonist chooses to get pregnant and this introduces an imagery of regeneration which suggests the possibility that the human destructiveness which had been the main focus might be transcended. This is most conspicuously signalled by the way the novel's eponymous image is reintroduced at the moment when the protagonist initiates the sex that will impregnate her. This time, significantly, it is applied to her abortion so that it implies that the death that had been planted in her will be replaced by life:

'I can feel my lost child surfacing within me, forgiving me, rising from the lake where it has been prisoned for so long' (pp. 155–6).

She welcomes the changes in her that pregnancy brings; unlike Plath she celebrates the sense it brings her of entering an overwhelmingly powerful natural process, so that the 'creature' in her 'sends out filaments' inside her (p. 162). More troublingly, this leads her first into a sense of pagan communion with chthonic gods (p. 175) and then to feel herself transforming into a furred animal, reminiscent of Ted Hughes' 'Wodwo'. This leads to the most memorable writing in *Surfacing* as Atwood tries to invent a language that evokes a fusion with natural things, a language beyond or before language: signifiers which are not signifiers but pure referent.

Something of this is present throughout the novel in an imagist tendency to leave out definite and indefinite articles: 'Slope of ground on either side, rock hung with creepers' (p. 161). In these passages near the end of *Surfacing*, however, there is something much more radical – an apparent attempt to use language to overcome the linguistic gap between the human and the natural. What makes these passages especially telling is that the attempt self-consciously breaks down, so that the language is deployed to make the point that it is impossible for humans to fuse unproblematically with Nature:

> From the lake a fish jumps
> An idea of a fish jumps
> A fish jumps, carved wooden fish with dots, carved wooden fish with dots painted on the sides, no, antlered fish thing drawn in red on cliffstone, protecting spirit.
>
> (p. 181)

This passage moves from an image that comes as close as language ever can to evoking, immediately, a natural thing (which, of course, can never be very close) to a greater and greater knowledge of human distance from natural things, leading to a reference to a human artefact which represents a fish but transforms it into a totemic hybrid. It is this sense of interference from language – that the novel form can very appropriately represent – which eventually leads the protagonist out of her creaturely state and back into a sane humanness. But it is also very important that she has learned self-transforming lessons from her fusion, however incomplete, with Nature.

6.3 Eco-feminism and the Goddess

The paganism to which *Surfacing* refers is a much more central idea in the work of Ted Hughes and Seamus Heaney. Hughes concludes his essay

'Poetry and Violence' with an optimistic statement of his own version of pagan eco-feminism. Cheered by 'New Age' interest in occult religions – which he relates to his own interests since the late 1950s – and the popularity of natural history broadcasts, he discerns a profound change which he sees, crucially, as feminising the culture:

> Along with this, maybe more visible in the US, countless changes have slowly but surely returned the Paleolithic world, the 'sacred' status, bringing with it, in the most curious fashion, the natural world's first and foremost representative – woman . . . It is the massive resurgence of something as archaic and yet as up to date – as timeless, and as global – as the 'sacred' biology of woman . . . And the universal movement in which all these different currents make one tide is the movement to save the earth by a reformed good sense and sensitivity.[8]

This recent harping on the feminine contrasts sharply with its absence in Hughes' early work. His early poems repeatedly enact and try to shed a masculine sickness which obsessively dwells on the twin themes of war and Nature red in tooth and claw and revealingly discuss each in terms of the other. The assumption behind this twinning of the themes is that which lies behind Hughes' work as a whole: the assumption that human behaviour is biologically driven; that it is shaped by instincts which are merely obscured by a veneer of civilisation. Tom Paulin gets it the wrong way around when he says that 'it is impossible not to view Hughes' fascination with elemental energy as expressing an impatience with the post-war consensus'[9]; in fact, that fascination with elemental energy always has much more priority in his work. Paulin is nonetheless right about the impatience and about its leading to the 'rage against peace and civility [that] erupts in "A Motorbike"' (p. 270). What is most disturbing about that poem,[10] however, is its assumption that war itself is a manifestation of elemental energy and in particular of masculine drives, so that peace can only be described negatively as not war, and as a state which emasculates and paradoxically takes the men prisoner. Thus, he says 'The shrunk-back war ached in their testicles' as though it were a suppressed desire, and that when the soldiers handed over their weapons they 'hung around limply' as though fighting were a kind of erection and not fighting were a kind of detumescence. The motorbike itself has spent six years 'outclassed' by the weapons of war, as though it were one of their kind but of a lower order, but it has also been 'Cramped in rust, under washing', so that it resembles one of Hughes' caged animals and represents the suppression of elemental energy, of 'thunder, flight, disruption'. A week after a young man bought it and kicked it into life he 'escaped/ Into a telegraph pole' while riding it. Taken together, all this imagery works to insist that war is a 'natural' activity for men who, deprived of it, will find compensatory outlets for their desire for it; a related implication is that the society of 'post-war consensus' is experienced by masculinity like bars around a jaguar or washing piled on a motorbike.

It is in this context that the priority Hughes gives to biology is revealed at its most damaging, and this is missed by Tom Paulin whose essay, otherwise, is the best writing there is on Hughes. Paulin's leftist outlook makes him focus on the social implications of Hughes' work: as he says, 'nature poetry is always a form of disguised social comment' (p. 252). This is generally revealing and valuable, especially given the tendency of commentators on Hughes, like Ekbert Faas and Keith Sagar,[11] to talk about him purely in his own anthropological and mythic terms. What Paulin ignores, however, is the extent to which Hughes' own terms are deployed specifically to privilege biology. To say 'The shrunk-back war ached in their testicles' is to make the larger point Hughes is always making through his insistence on that register – it is deliberately to soft-pedal the social (rhythmically the line is organised so that 'war' gets only a muted stress compared with the bodily words) and harp on the biological. Hughes' characteristic register is deployed against the privileging of 'social comment' (and, thereby, also, against the poetry of the Movement). Paulin wants the references to Nature in Hughes to be read analogically like those in Engels when he 'argues that active social forces work "exactly like natural forces"' (p. 272). In fact, however, Hughes does not distinguish between them: for him social forces *are* natural forces, or at least are the direct product of natural forces.

Hughes' poems in *Lupercal* present an extremely gendered view of Nature, and this becomes even clearer when they are compared with poems written by Sylvia Plath which date from a similar period in their marriage. Hughes is influenced by D. H. Lawrence in wanting a realignment of the human towards the natural and directs an angry satire against complacently 'civilised' ignorance of the natural processes which he sees as actually underlying human behaviour. As a result, Nature is treated by him with purposeful awe. Sylvia Plath also expresses awe but of a fearful rather than a wishful kind. Nature for her always involves the fear of being engulfed in processes of generation that lead to self-annihilation. In 'Morning Song'[12] the relationship between mother and baby is compared to that between a cloud and the pool of water it generates, which then mirrors the cloud's 'effacement' by the wind. Where Hughes' natural images express rigid and steely self-containment, Plath's express leakage and liquefaction: the 'spindling rivulets' in 'Parliament Hill Fields' (pp. 152–3) suggest that her miscarriage makes her feel as though part of herself is draining away. Where Hughes chooses a hawk as a dramatic monologuist, Plath chooses an elm (pp. 192–3): the man/predator is a masterful monolith, the woman/tree is anxiously multiple and at the same time fragmented. She is 'inhabited by a cry' which metaphorically evokes pregnancy as a horrifying invasion of the self, and the wind makes her 'break up in pieces that fly about like clubs'.

In *Wodwo* and *Crow* Hughes expresses increasing gender disturbance. 'The Warriors of the North' indicates that Hughes, very early on, invests his new self-consciousness about gender with more than a personal dimension. That poem's references to the Vikings' 'cash-down, beforehand revenge' and the 'iron arteries of Calvin' already prefigure the key idea of his work from this point on: that Protestantism represents a systemic rejection of the feminine which inflicts dire psychic consequences on Western culture and Nature. Hughes saw this as the constitutive theme of Shakespeare's work, and the central thesis of his *Shakespeare and the Goddess of Complete Being*[13] is that his whole oeuvre is shaped around a core myth which elaborately grieves over this loss:

> Since Shakespeare only ever chose one mythic subject – Venus and Adonis – and since he chose it for his first and (considering *Lucrece* as an automatic sequel) only long poem, one can believe that the image of the beautiful young Adonis, rejecting the voluptuous, besotted Goddess, then being bloodily, sumptuously slain by the Boar, before being restored as a flower between the breasts of the Goddess as she flies to heaven, was an obsessive nexus of images to which he was drawn by irresistible fascination.
>
> (pp. 39–40)

Hughes was convinced that Shakespeare spent his creative life writing variations on this theme, and he traces its presence with obsessive energy through most of his plays – though not, tellingly, in the history plays. What this whole endeavour does, repeatedly, is to transform political concerns into mythic ones and even Hughes seems unable to work this transformation where the politics are most conspicuous. (This again makes Paulin's emphasis on Hughes as a social commentator look misplaced.) This book certainly says far more about Hughes than it does about Shakespeare and what it suggests above all is the extent to which, during and after the writing of *Wodwo*, he realigned his gender views. When he says, for example, that 'the man who rejects the female, in moral, sexual revulsion, becomes in a moment the man who assaults and tries to destroy her' (p. 170), he is accounting for much of the violence that preoccupies his poems. When, too, he translates the Adonis myth into what he sees as its 'psycho-biological' meaning it takes him (via a reference to 'the light and dark of the womb's lunar cycle' and *The Wise Wound* by Penelope Shuttle and Peter Redgrove) to his preoccupation with the phallic mother.

The emphasis of both the Shakespeare book and Hughes' later poetry is to heal the violent divisiveness that arises from the 'peculiar division of the sexes' and their 'peculiar conflict'. This poetic ideology has had a marked impact on Hughes' successor Seamus Heaney, who systematically feminises the Irish landscape. So Michael Parker refers to how, in the third and fourth stanzas of 'At a Potato Digging', 'the poet draws a parallel between this contemporary scene of bowing, bending and stooping and the ancient obeisance paid to the Earth Mother, the source of all fertility'.[14] What has been insufficiently realised is the extent to which this gender ideology links Heaney to certain other male poets. Heaney's critics tend to be too focused on Ireland to recognise how much he has continued to share, in particular, with Ted Hughes. Terry Gifford and Neil Roberts are exceptions to this and indicate how Hughes, Heaney and Peter Redgrove share a number of preoccupations:

> The association of the female, mud or earth, and some form of rebirth, is common to all three . . . all of them embody, in varying degrees and proportions, a pervading critique of the masculine intellect, of the Platonic–Christian division between soul and body, and the rape of Nature by Western civilisation.[15]

What is most important, though, is how this ideology leads to a belief in what Hughes calls a Goddess of Complete Being. Heaney has a very similarly mythic model of history deployed in his case to account for a moment of change which initiates colonialism:

> the enmity can be viewed as a struggle between the cults and devotees of a god and a goddess. There is an indigenous territorial numen, a tutelar of the whole island, call her Mother Ireland, Kathleen ni Houlihan, the poor old woman, the Shan Van Vocht, whatever; and her sovereignty has been temporarily usurped or infringed by a new male cult whose founding fathers were Cromwell, William of Orange and Edward Carson, and whose godhead is incarnate in a rex or caesar resident in a palace in London.[16]

Critics have paid insufficient attention to the extent to which this political vision is coloured by gender assumptions linked to a pagan vision of Nature. This is crucial because the idea of the goddess is linked to the imposition of rigid gender categories. So when Heaney comes to write his 'bog people' poems he does so with assumptions very similar to those in the Hughes of *Crow* and after – assumptions derived from Carl Jung and Robert Graves'

White Goddess, based on a belief in a transcendent feminine principle which must be attended to if psychic divisions are to be healed. Heaney has described how these poems were inspired by P. V. Glob's *The Bog People* which argues that the bodies that were exhumed, having been preserved by peat,

> were ritual sacrifices to the Mother Goddess, the goddess of the ground who needed new bridegrooms each winter to bed with her in her sacred place, in the bog, to ensure the renewal and fertility of the territory in the spring. Taken in relation to the tradition of Irish political martyrdom for that cause whose icon is Kathleen ni Houlihan, this is more than an archaic barbarous rite: it is an archetypal pattern. And the unforgettable photographs of these victims blended in my mind with photographs of atrocities, past and present, in the long rites of Irish political and religious struggles.
>
> (*Preoccupations*, pp. 57–8)

The aesthetic assumptions behind the bog people poems arise from how they embody Heaney's masculine, yet eco-feminist response to the goddess – his own tribute to her. This has to be understood by reference to his own construction of the poet's role: a role which thoroughly expresses biological maleness and which is analogous to the male sex role as that is traditionally constructed. The bog people poems are constructed out of the relationship between the poet and the goddess who endorses the poet's masculinity but at the same time threatens it with her own power. It is this ambiguity which arouses the poet's creativity and links the goddess to the figure of the Muse as she is described by Robert Graves and whose meaning for Ted Hughes is described by Jacqueline Rose:

> we can recognise in this threatening, all-devouring female principle the imago of the phallic woman who, because she contains all things, threatens the man at the very core. According to this analysis, the idealisation of the woman is not contrary to the image of her as violent . . . the idealisation and the aggression are the fully interdependent and reverse sides of the same coin.[17]

Rose goes on powerfully to indict the damage that this fantasy of the feminine causes to women. However, it is also damaging to men because of the obsessive dynamic of domination and submission which it imposes and its sadomasochistic linking of sexuality with violence. Its deployment by Heaney to account for political atrocities is especially disturbing because it implies that those atrocities arise from a form of sexual compulsion. The assumptions here are again ones shared by Hughes – that history is psycho-biologically driven, and that it is essentially the product of instincts. What makes Heaney seem a much less dangerous poet than Hughes is that he characteristically dwells on sex rather than violence, but the bog people poems are memorable because they make a primordial peaty cocktail of the two.

The relationship between the poet and the goddess is sexual, but so too is the relationship between the poet and the bog people. As always when reading Heaney, there is a strong sense of the implied author: one of his most remarkable achievements has been to construct a version of himself as a poet which his readers recognise. This tends to draw attention away from the bizarreness of what is going on in these poems.

The sexual element in them is the most important key to their ambiguous effect on how the poet's maleness is perceived to respond. That is, the sexual element suggests that the male poet is masterful and in control but at the same time threatens that control. The poet is in control because he is constructed in the act of looking at the exhumed bodies:

> you were flaxen-haired,
> undernourished and your
> tar-black face was beautiful.
> My poor scapegoat,
>
> I almost love you
> but would have cast, I know,
> the stones of silence.
> I am the artful voyeur
>
> of your brain's exposed
> and darkened combs[18]

The gaze is poetico-sexual. The poet is a 'voyeur', which means that he can hold exciting material at arm's length and enjoy it while masterfully gauging and controlling his own response. The object of the gaze is hyperbolically the object of a male gaze – hyperbolically passive (being dead), hyperbolically reified (being turned into tar), hyperbolically submissive (being a 'scapegoat'), hyperbolically 'exposed' (because her brain is literally open). More than this, though, the poet is a voyeur who is 'artful'. His poem mimics an act of voyeurism, which is itself controlling, and controls it further by rendering it aesthetic. The little adulteress becomes an artefact to be contemplated; she is imagistically static, and her status as 'scapegoat' relates her to the controlling metaphor, derived from Jessie L. Weston, of T. S. Eliot's *The Waste Land*, where it also evokes pagan images in order to grieve over unnaturalness.

6.4 Nature and gender

The tendency of attitudes to Nature to get entangled with attitudes to
gender is further illustrated by two novels, one by Martin Amis, the other by
Fay Weldon: *London Fields*[19] and *The Life and Loves of a She Devil*.[20]
Amis's novel is premised upon an idea of pastoral innocence which has its
roots in Romanticism, but this pastoralism is under threat from a planetary
destructiveness which is directly attributed to masculine aggressiveness.
Feminists have been rightly troubled by Amis's depictions of women,[21] but
they have paid too little attention to how these depictions are linked, to
some extent with self-conscious symmetry, to caricatural simplifications of
masculinity.

That this is associated with one of the key themes of *London Fields* is
clear from the repetition of its references to 'Little Boy', the euphemistic
name bestowed with such astonishing insensitivity on the bomb dropped on
Hiroshima. This acquires more resonance in the context of the novel's
treatment of the theme of childhood and its contrasting of two babies:
Marmaduke, the son of Guy and Hope Clinch, and Kim, the daughter of
Keith and Kath Talent. The female baby is made to carry all of the associations of pastoral innocence and is treated with a lyricism that contrasts
significantly with the dominantly satirical writing; she has 'sweet breath and
faceted roundnesses, as tender as an eyeball' (p. 138); she is 'an *angel*'
(p. 102). The novel ends in this mode, poetically punning on the word
'impressions', referring to a baby's psychological impressionableness which
is also physically represented by the imprints made on its body by
fingerprints and clothes and a carpet's 'crenellations' (p. 470).

The 'Little Boy' references are further explicated in a passage where
Samson Young remembers playing as a five-year-old with his brother in
London Fields:

> Oh boys, you are heartbreaking and mysterious. The way you cock
> your weak bodies – to essay something, to dare something. Your love
> of war. Look! Watch! Oh, boys, why do you have to do this?
> But boys have to do this.
>
> (p. 323)

Children playing in fields ought to represent the most pastoral of images,
but the boys' compulsive aggressiveness transforms the scene so that it foreshadows all the massively cruel and sordid consequences of lost pastoral on
which this novel mostly focuses. And much of this is indicated in how the
cocking of their weak bodies suggests their striving to acquire fully phallic
power.

The caricaturing of Marmaduke works by a similar reversing of the innocent ideal so that he is already not only 'sexual' but even pornographic in his tastes (p. 158). He leers over a swimsuit advertisement, fellates his bottle, gropes his nannies and aspires to 'a career in child pornography: he knows it's out there, and he can tell there's a quick buck in it'. His aggression is not so much boyishly boisterous as a sinister foreshadowing of actual war: his nursery contains 'howitzers and grenade launchers and cartridge belts'. This paragraph escalates in characteristic Amis fashion so that a realist (if exaggerated) premise about boys' toys builds towards an outrageous climax in which Marmaduke is associated with nuclear war and said to favour the pre-emptive strike: 'Fight like hell for three days and then blow up the world' (p. 220).

This is confrontational satire of such an extreme kind that its status as comedy is in doubt, but it is a very important moment because it indicates the extent of the loss that is being depicted. Corruption of innocence on a scale that produces both pornography and nuclear war in the nursery is the result of the entropic 'planetary and twentieth century' circumstances (p. 141) which are referred to just after the domestic devastation inflicted by Marmaduke – 'broken glasses, chipped china, childblood, spilt milk, spilt milk' (p. 140). The entropy Amis identifies combines references to the trashing of two key Romantic values: innocence and Nature. The polluting of the natural environment is a repeated motif in *London Fields*, where it is associated with the obsessive theme of death, and is also made a routine part of the novel's setting – many of the novel's set scenes take place against the backdrop of metropolitan violence inflicted on the natural. So one of the most striking features of the style of this novel is displayed in those passages where Amis brings to bear his *fleur du mal* poetry to describe the symptoms of massive hurt suffered by the abused planet.

By contrast, Fay Weldon's outlook is closer to that of Donna J. Haraway in treating Nature as a force that needs to be quelled if its injustices are not to be perpetuated. On the last page of *The Life and Loves of a She Devil* she has her heroine declare that 'Nature gets away with far too much. It needs controlling' (p. 240). So the idea of transplanting your whole self, which Amis treats satirically, in *Money*, as a degenerate nightmare (though blackly comic), is proposed by Weldon as a liberating possibility. Amis's anti-hero John Self imagines going to California and being transformed: 'I am a robot, I am an android, I am a cyborg, I am a skinjob.'[22] For Amis, technology is a major part of the contemporary apocalyptic problem: for Weldon it is potentially the solution.

Weldon's heroine Ruth goes somewhere very like California and is transformed by plastic surgery on a scale resembling John Self's fantasy: her face and her torso are completely reconstructed; her height is drastically reduced. When one of her surgeons, Mr Ghengis, tightens Ruth's vagina and draws back her clitoris 'to heighten his patient's sexual response', it worries the other surgeon, Dr Black, because it seems 'an interference with the essential self'. But the postmodern implications of this extreme technological tampering with identity are made clear when Genghis replies that there is no essential self, and that it is 'all liable to change and flux, and usually the better for it' (p. 219).

However, Ruth's ontological project is too feminist in its political implications, and too existential in its philosophical implications, to be thoroughly postmodernist: it is not about subjecting her identity to flux but about fixing it in the form that she most desires. Philosophically, this is premised upon an existentialist belief that it is possible to make choices that will shape the self and its experiences; politically, it is premised upon an urgent insistence that women must recognise that such choices are available to them and so shake off the routine restrictions of their daily lives and make those choices. The anti-Nature polemic in *The Life and Loves of a She Devil* arises from anger at the extent to which those restrictions have been imposed as a result of women's traditional associations with Nature – how patriarchy has promoted a view of women as more firmly tied than men to the body and to natural cycles.

This is linked to a polemic against romance where Weldon joins with George Eliot in arguing against a form of writing that condemns women, as its major creators and consumers, to being generically pigeonholed as irrationally preoccupied with issues of desire and therefore ideologically blinded to their real political circumstances. Ruth's main enemy is Mary Fisher who stole her husband and who lives in a phallic tower (a reconstructed lighthouse), writing romances which have made her very wealthy and which send out a light which is treacherous: 'it spoke of clear water and faith and life when in fact there were rocks and dark and storms out there' (p. 180). Ruth tells her priest lover, Father Ferguson, that the real problem is not sex but love of the kind promoted in romantic fiction which is read by impoverished women whose emotional maturity is as a result endlessly delayed (p. 191).

So *The Life and Loves of a She Devil* carefully constructs an account of the forces at work which promote a gender ideology that is dependent upon consensual assumptions about the 'natural' role of women. The novel regards Christian belief as complicit with these views so that God is deployed as a conservative force; it is for this reason that Ruth declares that 'she was taking up arms against God Himself' (p. 82). Lady Bissop, one of Ruth's employers, insists that Ruth should learn to be happy with the body she has been given, and that 'a woman's function was to adjust herself to the times she lived in and the household she dwelt in, and that God worked His purposes out through the consent of the humble and faithful' (p. 144). It is against this background that Ruth sets out to construct herself as an anti-thetical fiction, a 'she-devil' designed to oppose the conservative forces of God and Nature.

The premise for this is that a woman is regarded as a she-devil if she refuses to accept the biological roles which patriarchy insists on imposing on her: 'Peel away the wife, the mother, find the woman, and there the she-devil is' (p. 44). In the fairy-tale register adopted in Chapter 15 this means that the wounded she-devil must temporarily retreat to her lair, in hiding from 'the ogre motherhood' (p. 76). The first stage of Ruth's revenge on Mary Fisher involves imposing on her the burdens of familial domestic-ity which had previously been her own encumbrance: she dumps her two unlovable children on Fisher and Ruth's absconded husband in their tower, and then evolves a strategy which results in Fisher's mother leaving her retirement home and also going to live with her daughter's newly extended ménage. The animosity between the two Fisher women confirms the novel's satirical hostility towards maternity, which is raised to a higher intensity when Ruth encourages a single mother to sell her children, and to an even higher one when Ruth in the end feels no maternal feelings at all for her son and daughter.

'The Death of Love' was one of the titles that Martin Amis contemplated for the novel that became *London Fields* (see his prefatory 'Note'), and it is a major theme of that novel, connected to its horrified depiction of an apocalyptically unnatural culture. Fay Weldon, by contrast, is only half-ironic when she welcomes the idea and has Ruth 'sing a hymn to the death of love and the end of pain' (p. 160). The contrast again arises from a stark gender opposition between the two writers: for Amis, love represents an indisputably positive value; for Weldon it is charged with the associations of a biological slavery which her she-devil is vowed to escape, however fantastically. This makes Weldon the least gender essentialist of novelists and this is why she satirises the 'separatist feminists' whose commune Ruth joins in Chapter 29: they are 'sodden by the muddy flood of purgatory wastes' (p. 199); their ecological version of feminism is too bound up with the traditional associations between women and the earth, and therefore with a traditional bondage.

When Ruth looks at her body and thinks she will be 'glad to be rid of it', she does so because it has 'so little to do with her nature' (p. 209) – but there the word is used confrontationally to stress a contrast between human 'nature' and the natural world, between a human sense of self and a biological destiny imposed upon it. This is a contrast which Ted Hughes and Seamus Heaney would not acknowledge because their emphasis is always upon the psycho-biological view which explains human behaviour by reference to instincts, however suppressed by civilisation. It is against such constructions of human nature, and the gender ideology that accompanies them, that Weldon wields the weapon of her she-devil, for 'She-devils are beyond nature: they create themselves out of nothing' (p. 131).

Notes

1 Fredric Jameson, *Postmodernism or, The Cultural Logic of Late Capitalism* (London: Verso, 1991), p. ix.
2 Walter Benjamin, 'The Work of Art in the Age of Mechanical Reproduction', in *Illuminations* (London: Pimlico, 1999).
3 Donna J. Haraway, 'Simians, Cyborgs, and Women: A Cyborg Manifesto', in *Simians, Cyborgs and Women; The Reinvention of Nature* (London: Free Association Books, 1991), p. 174.
4 Teresa Brennan, *History After Lacan* (London and New York: Routledge, 1993).
5 Margaret Atwood, *Surfacing* (London: Virago, 1979).
6 Adrienne Rich, *The Fact of a Doorframe: Poems Selected and New 1950–1984* (New York: Norton, 1984), p. 149.
7 Adrienne Rich, *Blood, Bread and Poetry: Selected Prose 1979–1985* (London: Virago, 1987), p. 50.
8 Ted Hughes, 'Poetry and Violence', in William Scammell (ed.), *Winter Pollen: Occasional Prose* (London: Faber, 1994), p. 267.
9 Tom Paulin, 'Laureate of the Free Market? Ted Hughes', in *Minotaur: Poetry and the Nation State* (London: Faber, 1992), p. 270.
10 Ted Hughes, *Moortown* (London: Faber, 1979), p. 104.
11 Ekbert Faas, *Ted Hughes: The Unaccommodated Universe* (Santa Barbara: Black Sparrow Press, 1980). Keith Sagar (ed.), *The Achievement of Ted Hughes* (Manchester: Manchester University Press, 1983).
12 Sylvia Plath, *Collected Poems* (London: Faber, 1981), p. 156.
13 Ted Hughes, *Shakespeare and the Goddess of Complete Being* (London: Faber, 1992).
14 Michael Parker, *Seamus Heaney: The Making of the Poet* (Basingstoke: Macmillan, 1993), p. 70.
15 Terry Gifford and Neil Roberts, 'Hughes and Two Contemporaries: Peter Redgrove and Seamus Heaney', in Sagar, *The Achievement of Ted Hughes*, p. 93.
16 Seamus Heaney, *Preoccupations: Selected Prose 1968–1978* (London: Faber, 1980), p. 57, henceforth *Preoccupations*.
17 Jacqueline Rose, *The Haunting of Sylvia Plath* (London: Virago, 1991), p. 151.
18 Seamus Heaney, *New Selected Poems 1966–1987* (London: Faber, 1990), p. 72.
19 Martin Amis, *London Fields* (London: Penguin, 1990).
20 Fay Weldon, *The Life and Loves of a She Devil* (Sevenoaks, Kent: Hodder and Stoughton, 1983).
21 See, for example, Laura L. Doan, '"Sexy Greedy is the Late Eighties": Power Systems in Amis's *Money* and Churchill's *Serious Money*', *The Minnesota Review: A Journal of Committed Writing*, 34–5 (Spring 1990), pp. 69–79.
22 Martin Amis, *Money* (London: Penguin, 1985), p. 329.

|7|

Postmodern realism

This chapter's title could easily be taken as an oxymoron because extreme postmodernists like Jean Baudrillard deny the reality of social and political experience. In doing so they are expressing a view which may already be regarded as implicit in much postmodernist theory in its tendency towards extreme scepticism about knowledge and being. These implications in postmodernism have led Marxists like Alex Callinicos, Christopher Norris and Terry Eagleton to attack postmodernist theory as a reactionary force. Callinicos insists that most of the social conditions of the modern period are still very much in evidence, and attacks theories about 'postindustrialism' originated by Daniel Bell, doubting his premise of a move from manufacturing to service industries. He sees these changes as either 'greatly exaggerated' or 'the consequences of much longer-term trends or specific to the particular, and highly unstable economic conjuncture of the 1980's'. More relevant to these changes, as far as he is concerned, are 'the combination of the disillusioned aftermath of 1968 throughout the Western world and the opportunities for an "overconsumptionist" lifestyle offered upper white-collar strata by capitalism in the Reagan–Thatcher era'.[1] Callinicos's point about the continuing importance of social conditions that arise from a modernist capitalist economy is supported by the number of texts in the postmodern period which vividly reflect the truth of social and working conditions in an identifiably realist idiom.

7.1 Defamiliarised realism: Toni Morrison and Philip Roth

Postmodernism has become so prominent, has attracted so much attention, that it has tended to obscure the extent to which realism has still been widely deployed in the postmodern period. Toni Morrison, for example, is routinely discussed in predictably postmodernist terms, but this is distortive because it ignores how much this important writer draws – in novels like *Song of Solomon* and *Tar Baby* – upon realist techniques to aid her in evoking what African Americans have had to struggle against in order to be regarded as fully human. Morrison appropriates realism but deploys it in contexts which subvert its liberal humanist premises. Because she is dealing with the experience of African Americans, her subject matter is radically at odds with that of the white tradition and therefore does not arouse the consensual response upon which realism conventionally depends. Because her subject matter subversively denies the assumption (as Elizabeth Deeds Ermarth puts it) of 'the uniformity at the base of human experience and the solidarity of human nature',[2] it interrogates realism itself: the experiences being described are precisely *not* uniform with what white readers, or even their ancestors, have experienced. What Morrison's realist depiction of these historical experiences evokes is not solidarity but disorienting disparity. It is not surprising, then, that critics have tended not to pay enough attention to how much Morrison operates in a realist idiom because this defamiliarised realism can easily blend into the postmodernist and magic realist idioms for which she is more famous. But Morrison cannot be properly understood unless the place of realist strategies in her work is properly recognised.

Another interesting case in this context is Philip Roth whose work has been driven by a combination of realism and satire. What these modes share is their concern with getting at the truth of postwar American social and political experience, a concern which receives especially brilliant expression in his three novels of the 1990s – *Sabbath's Theatre, American Pastoral* and *I Married a Communist*. The comparative muting of this concern in his metafictional novels of the mid-1970s to the mid-1980s – novels such as *My Life as a Man, The Professor of Desire,* and *The Counterlife* – seems to me to account for their comparative lack of persuasiveness. Roth's talents, though extensive, are not best suited to the multiplying of these self-reflexive labyrinths.

It is a preoccupation with the fictiveness of fiction that leads Roth to these metafictional novels of the late 1970s and 1980s. Eventually, however, it leads, because of Roth's dissatisfaction with mere fictiveness, to the social realism of *American Pastoral* and *I Married a Communist*. In inventing the character of Swede, Roth seems to have been driven by a wish to invent someone fundamentally different from the writer personae who multiply in his fictions (Zuckerman, Kepesh, Tarpanol, etc.) – someone beyond the doubts that trouble writers; someone like the doctors, pornographers and chauffeurs who, according to Zuckerman, are 'all confidence'.[3] What the novel focuses on is the process whereby Swede's confidence is shattered, so that he acquires – shockingly against his will – a subjectivity at odds with himself. Where before his 'discontents were barely known', he awakes 'in middle-age to the horror of self-reflection'.[4]

In stark contrast to the postmodernism of the Rothian 1980s, *American Pastoral* adopts a documentary style at times, especially when it deals with the glove industry in which Swede has spent his working life: this involves an enjoyment of economic facts for their own sake and of the detail of factory work. Something like this mode is in evidence throughout Roth's career – he has always had a remarkable facility for realist notation deployed, for example, to evoke the details of rooms, personal possessions, physical appearance. The difference here is in the thematic prominence given to this material: the emphasis it acquires has political motives.

To acquire this significance fully, however, it has to be connected to the character of Swede. It is significant that it is the externals of Swede's life, like his prowess as a sports star and his marriage to a beauty queen, which characterise him. It is the point of Swede that it is these externals which define his identity rather than subjectivity which Zuckerman at first thinks has been erased in him in the process of achieving his 'perfection': 'There had to be a substratum, but its composition was unimaginable' (p. 20). The documentary style therefore helps to evoke Swede as a man of action rather than thought and to imply in him a specifically American kind of innocence. *American Pastoral* establishes Swede's 'perfection' as its premise and associates that perfection with this mode of documentary realism. In doing so it draws upon the assumptions of that mode, which are that human beings can be rationally understood by reference to their social conditions: their actions, and the motives of those actions, are thoroughly comprehensible when placed in that context. However, having established this premise, Roth spends the rest of the novel exploding it by introducing a grotesque incomprehensibility which makes a nonsense of decent reasonableness because

> [Swede's] daughter was an insane murderer hiding on the floor of a room in Newark, his wife had a lover who dry-humped her over the sink in their family kitchen, his ex-mistress had knowingly brought disaster upon his house, and he was trying to propitiate his father with on-the-one-hand-this and on-the-other-hand-that.
>
> (p. 358)

Much of the motive for Roth's grotesque satire lies in the sense that only a wildly non-realist mode can deal with a reality as grotesquely aberrant as this. In *American Pastoral*, however, his strategy is radically different because he wants to establish a sense of stable normality in order to register the extent of the grotesque deviation from that normality. To that end he starts out by establishing Swede as a kind of *tabula rasa*. Though Jewish, Swede has such an 'unconscious oneness with America' that the Jew in him seems erased alongside any irrationality or temptations or mischief (p. 20). It is on this blank page that the grotesqueness writes itself and he becomes 'history's plaything' (p. 87). So Roth establishes realism as a mode in order to make his deviation from it more significant: the rationality on which realism is based is invaded by its opposite, a kind of madness which he sees as specifically American: 'the indigenous American berserk' (p. 86). Swede searches his past endlessly to explain why his only child Merry has turned into an insane terrorist, but nothing he comes up with can rationally explain it.

The sense that everything is 'disconnected' is the source of another aesthetic problem for novelists who, in constructing their texts, must find connections everywhere and in everybody. Roth's crucial point in making Swede and his wife such paragons who nonetheless produce a bizarre horror is extreme disconnectedness – a level of randomness so wide-ranging it becomes a structural principle. The key point is that the social and economic factors are so widely disconnected from what arises out of them: the painstaking evocation of those facts serves to reveal how little they explain and how divergent the effect is from any discernible cause.

7.2 'Dirty realism': Raymond Carver

Realism is important to both Morrison and Roth because they interrogate it and juxtapose it with other fictive modes. However, there have been a number of writers in the postmodern period who are much more thoroughly committed to realism and who, for this reason, sometimes make explicitly anti-postmodernist statements. Some of these writers have been grouped together as 'minimalists' or 'dirty realists': Richard Ford, Bobbie Ann Mason, Tobias Wolff and, above all, Raymond Carver.

Introducing a collection of short stories with his co-editor Tom Jenks, Carver is dismissive about fiction which is 'self-reflexive, fabulist, magic realist' and advocates fiction with 'a strong narrative drive, with characters we could respond to as human beings': he champions 'the lifelike – that is to say . . . realistically fashioned stories that may even in some cases approximate the outlines of our own lives'.[5] Some of the context for this outlook is suggested in Carver's review of a book by Donald Barthelme when he talks about how, when he was in college, Barthelme was highly fashionable and everybody tried to imitate him. Carver is at pains to express his admiration for Barthelme, but it is clear that the main thrust of his argument is against a modish postmodernism which led Barthelme's imitators to write what Carver regards as an impoverished, flippantly anti-humanist fiction:

> The characters are dropped into silly situations where they are treated by their creators with the most extreme irony, or even downright contempt. They are never to be found in situations that might reveal them as characters with more or less normal human reactions. To allow the characters to express any emotion, unless it can be ridiculed, is unthinkable. It is impossible for the characters even to see, much less accept, responsibility for their actions. There is a feeling that anything goes in the stories, that is, nothing in the story has to make sense, or has any more pertinence, value or weight than anything else. This world is on the skids, man, so everything is relative, you know.
>
> (*No Heroics Please*, pp. 167–8)

Carver was uninterested in theory, but this is a cogent diagnosis of the negative impact on some fiction writing of postmodernist assumptions. The flattening of hierarchies of meaning and postmodernist 'depthless-ness' – unless it is manipulated with precise and pointed purpose – can erase so many of fiction's traditional strengths that it is left fatuously directionless.

However, it is above all in his story-writing practice that Carver makes these points most forcefully. His references to his early encounters with Barthelme's work, and his reaction against the influence of the ludic and fabulatory strategies of writers like Barthelme, make it clear that he was, from an early age, thoroughly aware of postmodernist fiction and chose to make his own work radically different from it. In doing so he evolved a form of realism that, far from being atavistic, shows all the signs of coming self-consciously *after* postmodernism. Randolph Paul Runyon is making a point similar to this when he refers to Carver's self-reflexivity, so that the stories in a Carver collection 'refer to each other in ways that seem to refer to their doing so'[6] and when he points out how much happens in the interstices and silences in Carver's texts.

But Carver's absorption of postmodernism is much more easily discerned than this because it is conspicuous in stories like 'Collectors' and 'Why, Honey?',[7] which both have self-reflexive fun with the habit fiction has of withholding and then selectively disclosing information. 'Why, Honey?' turns on the sort of short story trick which Carver explicitly scorned.[8] It takes the form of a letter written by an aging woman replying to a letter by someone, probably a journalist, who has discovered she is the mother of a man whose activities are repeatedly reported by the media. Her feelings of shame about her son, and her descriptions of his cruel and anti-social behaviour as an adolescent, trick the reader into thinking the son is now a notorious criminal, perhaps a serial killer. The twist at the end of the story – when it turns out that the son is a famous politician – resembles those at the end of stories by de Maupassant. What takes it closer to postmodernism is that the twist is deployed satirically so that it is made to ask questions about the ambiguities of celebrity, and the extent to which celebrity is constructed by media fabulation.

'Collectors' is narrated by an unemployed man who is expecting 'to hear from up north' (p. 90), presumably about a job, though even this is left open to question. What remains more crucially undisclosed is whether the narrator is called Mr Slater because a letter does in the end arrive addressed with that name but is pocketed by the other character in the story, Aubrey Bell, a man who calls on the narrator because Mrs Slater has won a free vacuuming and carpet shampoo. The sharp sense of frustration all this arouses in the reader is compounded by the irrelevancies introduced by Bell with his references to Auden and Rilke: these resemble the unsettling evasions of a Pinter character. There are further Pinteresque echoes in the idea of an enigmatic stranger entering the territory of an equally enigmatic protagonist, and in an oblique dialogue which shifts attention away from the realist setting onto a plane where larger philosophical issues seem to be at stake, and where an atmosphere of futility imposes that half-comic experience of existential emptiness which was labelled 'absurd' in the 1960s.

This story is significant because the aimlessness of its central character is repeatedly echoed throughout the rest of Carver's work. What is telling is that, in this early story, that theme is enacted by a narratorial aimlessness which resembles the silliness that Carver condemns in Barthelme's imitators and whose impact is to treat the narrator with an obvious irony of which the later Carver would have disapproved. It does not treat him with 'downright contempt', but it allows him insufficient respect to suggest much of an emotional or moral life. This is telling because it indicates the trajectory of Carver's career – the same trajectory suggested by the distance he travelled to reach 'A Small Good Thing' from its prototype 'The Bath' (which appeared in *What We Talk About When We Talk About Love*). The early version is ambiguous, ironic, open-ended; the later is measured, fully explanatory, probing in substantial detail the emotional lives of its characters.

Nonetheless, the presence of these postmodernist elements in Carver's first book of short stories (*Will You Please Be Quiet Please?*) provides a clue to their deliberately more muted, but still significant, input into Carver's more mature and most characteristic work. That work is not founded upon realist innocence but upon a postmodernist knowledge deployed in the cause of a renewed attention to the substantial impact on lived experience of social and economic conditions. This is a form of realism which is very distant from the liberal humanism of classic realism: it is spiked with postmodernist *ennui* and terminal exhaustion, and it depicts its corner of the postmodern condition with at least as much vividness as more obviously postmodernist writing.

The most important key to its specific impact is in its repeated depiction of alcoholism where the realism of the depiction is guaranteed for us as readers by our extra-textual knowledge of Carver's own problems with alcohol. This is another example of the impact of the craving for the real which I described in the Introduction as one of the paradoxical conditions of the postmodern. It is impossible, when reading Carver's characterisations of alcoholics, not to refer them mentally to a biographical knowledge of Carver's own struggles with alcoholism. This introduces into the reading of these stories a form of generic double-take – fictive versus biographical. However, while this appears to substantiate realism, the frequency of the references to alcoholism raises it to the status of a representative condition. Given the nature of addiction, Carver's alcoholics are inevitably condemned to watch themselves as they attempt to struggle out of the limitations of self which that addiction imposes. So the narrator of 'Where I'm Calling From' says:

> I sit down on the front steps and light a cigarette. I watch what my hand does, then I blow out the match. I've got the shakes. I started out with them this morning. This morning I wanted something to drink. It's depressing, but I didn't say anything about it to J.P. I try to put my mind on something else.

(p. 240)

The self-consciousness of these selves intensifies because they are selves which have lost control of their selves; as readers we watch these characters watching themselves so that self-reflexivity multiplies. So while Carver's idiom is realist, this most characteristic of his themes requires a form of ontological spectatorship that acquires important postmodern implications.

However, it is important in the context of a larger discussion of postmodernism that the greatest achievement of Raymond Carver – who is certainly one of the most important writers in the postmodern period – was the invention of a fictive idiom which is entirely at odds with postmodernist fictive idioms. Most tellingly, his idiom is not deconstructive. It does not

arouse disbelief in its readers by drawing attention to its own constructedness, on the contrary, its plainness encourages the reader to believe that its
characters are real people in real situations.

The size of Carver's achievement can best be measured by pointing out
that his invention of this idiom suggests a highly viable alternative to the
response made by postmodernist writers to major literary precursors – in
other words it suggests a different way of coming after modernism. His
work owes obvious debts to Hemingway and Joyce but it draws upon them
for its own ends which are determined by the subject matter of the late
twentieth century. The stark objectivity of Hemingway's prose is recalled
by the plainness of Carver's style, as in these opening sentences of 'A Small
Good Thing': 'Saturday afternoon she drove to the bakery in the shopping
center. After looking through a loose-leaf binder with photographs of cakes
taped onto the pages, she ordered chocolate, the child's favourite' (p. 308).
This input from Hemingway links Carver to an austerely mimetic
modernist aesthetic practised by short story writers preoccupied with
impersonal terseness, and by Imagist poets like Ezra Pound and Marianne
Moore preoccupied with quasi-scientific rigour. Statements of emotion are
fastidiously avoided and sentimentality is regarded with horror. This is
drawn upon as a resource in 'A Small Good Thing' in its focus on the
parents of a small child as he dies slowly after being run over by a hit-and-
run driver: the narrative voice is so matter-of-fact at the start of the story
that it seems almost cruel, especially in its references to the child as 'the
birthday boy' (p. 309).

Carver also resembles Hemingway in constantly hinting at an underlying
sense of existential emptiness – this is explicit in Hemingway's story 'A
Clean Well-Lighted Place'. In both writers it is linked to a sharp sense of the
limits of what can be said which to some extent justifies the label of
minimalism: the strategic use of terse, simple sentences depicting an action
or reporting mostly simple speech implies a stark reductiveness. The deployment of the short story form is also significant in this context. Hemingway
wrote novels as well as short fiction but Carver limited himself to poems and
short stories and the implication is that only fragmentary insights are
possible – any bigger picture is out of reach. Carver's characters similarly
refer repeatedly to their own inability to say what needs to be said; either
they fall into silence or they start to speak and then frustratedly refer to the
insufficiency of what can be said. The reason for the father's decline in 'The
Third Thing that Killed My Father Off' is, despite the story's title, left open
to question; it is attributed to three different things by the narrative, most
prominent of which is the death of Dummy. However, Dummy's role
acquires a significance which is more representative because the question-

ableness of the eponymous decline is evoked by Dummy's inability to speak, so that this becomes a story about being unable to tell the story.

Frequently, Carver's lapses into silence evoke a baffled sense of futility and hollowness: 'What's there to tell?' the narrator of 'Boxes' says at the end of the story (p. 346) as he contemplates another restless, and apparently pointless, move of house and location made by his mother, this time to California, so far away that he will probably never see her again. 'Feathers', similarly, ends with references to a new distance, this time metaphorical, between the narrator and his wife, and between the narrator and his friend Bud. The story depicts them at a dinner party all talking to each other, but time has passed and things have, partly inexplicably, changed, and now the narrator is 'careful' what he says to Bud, and he and his wife 'talk less and less' (pp. 290–1).

Where the novel relies, in order to generate its length, on the depiction of complex and substantial interrelationships, the short story can effectively enact the aborting or collapse of relationships by its own formal habit of trailing off into silence. This is certainly a frequent effect in Carver's work which also relies on brevity to depict severe lack of emotional depth and responsiveness in characters who lack the richness to occupy an expansive novelistic space. This is where Carver crucially differs from Hemingway. The modernist precursor focuses on heroic, or at least skilfully purposeful action, as a way of imposing meaning on what would otherwise be existentially empty: his 'clean well-lighted place' is a refuge from the darkness of nothingness, of 'nada'. Similarly, in 'Big Two-Hearted River', the fishing skills which Nick deploys in a burnt landscape which acquires mythic associations are dwelt upon with a loving detail which suggests the stoic imposition of a satisfying shape to an existence which would otherwise too closely resemble the symbolic 'swamp' which Nick avoids and where 'the fishing would be tragic'.[9]

Carver's characters are a sad contrast to the Hemingway ideal. The figure of the alcoholic is again representative, here, of Carver's focus upon characters who are purposeless and self-divided, who either cannot see how to act for the best or who know what they should do but are hobbled by adverse circumstances (especially poverty) or by weak character. Hemingway's focus on action contrasts with Carver's focus on passivity and stasis. Carver's poem 'No Heroics, Please' suggests Carver's own knowledge of this contrast because it juxtaposes two images in a two-stanza poem. The first stanza refers to the heroic figure of Dr Zhivago from Pasternak's modernist epic; the second evokes its contemporary opposite by describing the impact of the sound of jazz from a topless bar – how 'the rising and falling saxophone/ . . . drains away the strength/ To resist' (*No Heroics, Please*, p. 99).

Almost all Carver's characters are drained of their strength. Much of this has happened to them because of the postmodern social conditions which Carver evokes with careful realism; the contrast with Hemingway suggests that those conditions have exerted an especially debilitating effect on the gender identity of Carver's males. Nick's activities are clearly designed to represent a role model for a masculine identity that expresses itself through effective action. But the meretricious and dilapidated urban conditions Carver's men occupy offer them little scope for heroics compared with Hemingway's burnt and mythic terrain. They are anyway thoroughly drained of the ability to make life choices of the sort required for the existential hero; they are inert victims who allow things to happen to them. The fishermen of 'So Much Water So Close to Home' are given a chance to act well when they find the naked body of a female murder victim floating in the water; instead, one of them

> waded into the water and took the girl by the fingers and pulled her, still face down, closer to shore, into shallow water, and then took a piece of nylon cord and tied it around her wrist and then secured the cord to tree roots, all the while the flashlights of the other men played over the girl's body.
>
> (p. 175)

And then they continue to fish.

Given the overwhelmingly defeated atmosphere of Carver's stories, his deployment of Joycean 'epiphany' acquires particular importance because it tempers what would otherwise be unrelieved pessimism. The fastidious eschewal of this modernist device by mainstream postmodernist writers is part of their flattening of hierarchical structures of meaning: the focus on an isolated moment or image is too heavily (even solemnly) laden with significance to be tolerated by their sceptical fiction, and the vestigial religious associations of epiphany are also suspect. Carver's take on this flattening is characteristically negative when he complains that in Barthelmian fiction nothing has 'any more pertinence, value, or weight than anything else' (*No Heroics, Please*, p. 168). For Carver, by contrast, it is very important that there are turning-points in people's lives, and these are the repeated focus of his work. The influence he acknowledges in this context, rather than Joyce, is Chekhov. On his wall, he says

> I have a three-by-five . . . with this fragment of a sentence from a story by Chekhov: '. . . and suddenly everything became clear to him.' I find these words filled with wonder and possibility. I love their simple clarity, and the hint of revelation that's implied. There is mystery, too.

What has been unclear before? Why is it just now becoming clear? What's happened? Most of all – what now? There are consequences as a result of such sudden awakenings. I feel a sharp sense of relief – and anticipation.

(*Call If You Need Me*, p. 88)

This is the dominant structural principle of Carver's work. He often makes it explicit: the last sentences of 'Fat' are 'My life is going to change. I feel it' (p. 54). The narrator of 'Feathers' says that the change that happened to him and his wife 'was like something that happened to other people, not something that could have happened to us' (p. 290). However, whether explicitly or not, Carver uses the short story form repeatedly to examine the process of life changes and to highlight an incident that either precipitated the change, or which represented the forces that caused that change. The short story form can preserve ambiguity by holding things in reserve; its brevity gives its writer the permission to freeze the narrative at a point which retains an element of the fragmentary. Carver draws upon this formal capacity to retain 'mystery', especially about what role the incident actually played. The narrator's wife, Fran, is sure that the dinner party upon which 'Feathers' focuses was 'the beginning of the change' (p. 290) that happened to them. The narrator himself disagrees, so that the relationship between the incident and the change is left open to an interpretation which must explore how and why the narrator and his wife were influenced by the example of domestic life which was presented to them by their hosts. In the process of this interpretation, the reader is required to think about much larger questions about how changes happen: about the interactions between objective events and subjective readiness – subjective potential for change – which produce those changes.

Carver is right to acknowledge Chekhov as an influence in the context of this structural principle as that influence was by far the most important for the international practice of the short story in the twentieth century. However, there are key moments in Carver's work where the influence of the Russian writer is combined with a more specific input from James Joyce. Discussion of epiphany becomes particularly appropriate where Carver's depiction of turning-points acquires a quasi-religious element of transcendence, as it does at the end of 'Cathedral' and 'A Small Good Thing'. These are important because these culminating epiphanies oppose the tendency of the short story to short-circuit a narrative with downbeat irony so that any potential expansiveness is abruptly narrowed. This effect in the short story can produce a monotonous structure that leads repetitively to a pessimistic conclusion. By contrast, the endings of these two stories are an ironic surprise because they offer unexpected hope. The baker at the end of 'A Small Good Thing' excuses himself to the parents he has tormented by confessing his guilt and asking forgiveness, and by offering them bread in a gesture that acquires sacramental associations. The narrator of 'Cathedral', who resents the presence in his house of a blind man who comes to visit, is amazed when that visit leads to him drawing a cathedral and then leading the blind man's hands over the drawing, so that the two of them together are made to feel a cathedral's spaciousness and meaning:

> I put in windows with arches. I drew flying buttresses. I hung great doors. I couldn't stop. The TV station went off the air. I put down the pen and closed and opened my fingers. The blind man felt around the paper. He moved the tips of his fingers over the paper, all over what I had drawn, and he nodded.

(pp. 306–7)

7.3 David Mamet

Like Raymond Carver's short stories, David Mamet's plays are best understood as a form of realism which has absorbed the lessons of postmodernism. Mamet's most influential precursor is Harold Pinter whose impact on Mamet's work is most conspicuous in the deployment of what appears to be an unadornedly naturalistic dialogue which mimics the repetitions, pauses, syntactical confusions, evasions and inconsequentialities of 'real' speech. A crucial difference, however, is that in Pinter the treatment of this dialogue is edged continually with parody: an 'absurd' effect is produced by introducing what seems a starkly untheatrical language into the theatre. Its impact is like a linguistic 'ready-made'; like the theatrical equivalent of Duchamp's exhibiting of a urinal. Part of its point, in other words, is metatheatrical in drawing attention to what constitutes 'dialogue' in a play and to how that dialogue is artificial in its deployment as a means of unravelling character and driving plot. Pinter is postmodernist in his eschewal of such unravelling, which is replaced by mystifications and evasions which make their own points about stories and characters.

Literature develops in response to historical changes, but it also develops in response to its own internal demands. There comes a point when it is clear that a literary style has made its point and something different is required; certainly by 1980 the elements of parody in this Pinteresque style had exhausted their expressive potential. Mamet's success as a playwright has arisen most conspicuously from his development of a Pinteresque dialogue in a realist direction and away from parodic self-consciousness. He has achieved this by drawing upon other influences from his own American background. His mimicry of real speech has a greater specificity than Pinter's because it is closely tied to his own upbringing in Chicago. His experience as a screen-writer has helped him to invent a style of dialogue which is terse, direct and spiked with street knowledge. And he has drawn upon a powerful strand of politically committed American drama with influences from Clifford Odets and Arthur Miller, as well as upon the realist (as opposed to expressionist) aspects of the work of Eugene O'Neill and Tennessee Williams.

Arthur Miller's *Death of a Salesman* is often referred to by critics of Mamet's *Glengarry Glen Ross*. Both plays centre on the figure of the salesman as representative of the obsessively commercial values of American culture and the dehumanising impact of those values on the psychology of individuals. However, Miller's play aspires to the condition of tragedy, whereas Mamet's is thoroughly aware that tragic heroism is impossible in postmodern culture, and that the prevailing social conditions make such a status unattainable for any individual, let alone a salesman. In its tone and structure Mamet's play would be more accurately described as a desperate comedy.

Mamet's characters, moreover, are driven by a psychology which suggests that the characters of O'Neill and Williams are their direct antecedents in the sense that his salesmen are in the grip of powerful illusions whose unreality is made progressively apparent. It is this theme (reality versus 'pipe-dreams') which is theatrically rendered in plays like *Long Day's Journey Into Night* and *A Streetcar Named Desire* by the generic clash between expressionism and realism. This theme is recurrent in American drama; it is also pivotal in Edward Albee's *Who's Afraid of Virginia Woolf?* where the protagonists must save themselves and their marriage by exorcising from their lives the false and destructive consolation of their imaginary child and make the existential choice of living without illusions.

The thematic, as well as stylistic, importance of realism in *Glengarry Glen Ross* is only understood when it is seen against the background of this American theatrical tradition which is related to the impact of the 'American Dream' and its endlessly tantalising offer of a life entirely different from the one that is currently being lived. Odets and Miller are important to Mamet, not stylistically, but because their political commitment made their plays aware that capitalism feeds upon these illusions and drives individuals into ferocious and self-defeating competition with each other. Mamet's salesmen sell 'real estate' but its value is illusory; it is fabricated by their sales talk. This represents how an exchange value can be constructed (if only briefly) with no basis in real or use value. In the course of this transaction, in which the commodity is worthless, the customers are commodified – they become 'leads' to be competed for by the salesmen. This competition resembles a game show in which the winner gets a Cadillac, the one in second place gets a set of steak knives, and the losers lose their jobs.

What makes the play compelling theatre is its focus on sales talk as performance. There is a Pinteresque input in this because it is premised upon a knowledge of how language gets deployed, not as a means of communication, but as a weapon wielded in a complex power game. With sales talk designed to sell worthless real estate this point is even more pointed because it produces a metatheatrical punning on theatrical illusion: the salesmen are really actors, but such salesmen are always actors anyway. Their theatrical talk is designed to produce suspension of disbelief, but real sales talk creates belief designed to shift a product. In this process, the salesman sells himself. So Roma, in Act 1, Scene 3, makes his sale by wooing Lingk with a vivid, earthy and passionate version of himself that makes financial enrichment seem like merely an aspect of a larger, existential enrichment:

> I don't know. For *me*, I'm saying, what it is, it's probably not the orgasm. Some broads, forearms on your neck, something her *eyes* did. There was a *sound* she made . . . or, me, lying in the, I'll tell you: me lying in bed: the next day she brought me *café au lait*. She gives me a cigarette, my balls feel like concrete. Eh? What I'm saying, What is our life: (*Pause*) it's looking forward or it's looking back. And that's our life. That's *it*. Where is the *moment*?[10]

Roma makes the sale, but he turns out, ironically, to have been more successful in selling himself. Lingk later wants to reverse the sale but is desperate not to lose, in the process, what he has been tricked into thinking is Roma's friendship.

Roma intensifies the element of performance later when he enlists the help of Levene in an elaborate pretence in which Levene plays the part of a highly important businessman and associate of Roma's who is investing in Roma's properties. Lingk has entered the office to withdraw from the sale and becomes the audience to this performance which is concocted in order to undermine Lingk's resolve. In a postmodernist work such confusions of theatrical illusion with actual fact would multiply to the point where the two would become indistinguishable. What is conspicuous in *Glengarry Glen Ross* is that such confusions are carefully limited and are, in the end, studiously resolved. In terms of generic structure the play resembles a whodunnit and – unlike postmodernist re-readings of this genre – it fully explains all its mysteries. This satisfaction of generic expectations affirms a sense of a solidly believable reality which is used (as in plays by O'Neill and Williams) to oppose the dangerous illusions which obsess its characters. This realism also allows the play to construct a privileged position from which it is possible to make moral and political judgements.

7.4 C. K. Williams: The questioning gaze

Questioning is the most characteristic mode of the mature work of the poet C. K. Williams and replaces the tendency towards statement (and overstatement) in his mostly unsuccessful first two volumes. It is his switch to this mode and his simultaneous finding of the perfect form to express it, in his long free verse lines, that facilitate the astonishing leap forward in quality that he makes with his third volume *With Ignorance*.[11] The assertiveness and expressionism of his earliest work are too frenetic and unfocused. These poems are undermined by their formal flux and unpunctuated slither so that they seem to be slipping through their own fingers; their form evokes an elusiveness that their content is constantly and unsuccessfully trying to master.

Elusiveness is the most recurrent quality of the subjects of Williams' mature poems but one that is now admitted and often assumed and focused upon interrogatively. The form that he invents for himself and which is his most distinctive poetic achievement allows him to introduce a prosaic inclusiveness alongside a discursive idiom which he deploys to question the nuanced ramifications of his subject. This makes Williams' use of the long line the opposite of Whitman's. Where Whitman deploys it to reach out and encompass all experience in the embrace of transcendentalist acceptance, Williams uses it to locate experience with painstakingly realist precision but also to hold it at arm's length and analyse it with troubled scepticism.

The posture he adopts is one of looking and then questioning what he sees, but this very posture is also reflected upon as the poem simultaneously looks at and questions the poet and his poetic posture. This self-consciousness and self-reflexiveness indicate the influence of postmodernist thinking in Williams, but these elements are deployed, in the end, to thoroughly realist effect because they are handled unironically, even earnestly, and are used to make the poem work harder to grasp the referent. Getting beyond the self into the real is especially crucial because the poems worry about their own voyeurism which troubles Williams, in particular, because he wants to invent a notion of the gaze which is creatively sympathetic.

This is so important to him because it is so thoroughly bound up with his own notion of what poetry should do, and with his own most repeated poetic strategy which starts from looking, often at what a stranger is doing, and then following the ramifications of his response to what he sees. The volume *Flesh and Blood* is composed entirely of eight-line poems that mostly show this process at its starkest, almost like notebook starting-points for his longer poems. 'The Dirty Talker: D Line, Boston'[12] starts by describing a man ('shabby, tweedy, academic') old enough to be the father of the woman he is talking to, but standing too close to her for that. So he thinks they are lovers and that he is ending their affair but that the girl is refusing to let him go. This then seems to explain the spasms in her shoulders which he thought at first were laughter. But then:

> We were in a station now, he pulled back half a head from her the
>   better to behold her,
> then was out the hissing doors, she sobbing wholly now so that finally
>   I had to understand –
> her tears, his grinning broadly in – at *me* now though, as though I
>   were a portion of the story.

This is characteristic, then, of Williams' work in finding its material in something closely observed in a city environment and then painstakingly interpreting it. As elsewhere there is some discomfort in the sense of the poet observing a moment in someone else's life, and this is increased because we as readers are made to participate in the act of observing. There is tension in the implied covertness of this, like watching the sympathetic hero of a film searching someone's flat as its owner is approaching. Here again there is the edge of voyeurism I have referred to and it is here especially acute because the 'dirty talker' is engaged in what may worryingly be regarded as an analogously creepy activity involving an unwanted intrusion. When this man looks back at the poet in the last line, this sense of dismaying complicity is confirmed when this makes Williams feel as though he were 'a portion of the story'.

This self-reflexiveness is characteristic of Williams in his insistence that he can have no privileged position from which to judge what his poems report – the judgements that he makes are necessarily compromised by his own emotional investment in what he is seeing. This is made clearer by his account of his early poetic career in 'My Mother's Lips' (pp. 178–9) where he describes being the subject of his mother's ventriloquy, as she 'seemed to be saying under her breath the very words I was saying as I was saying them', so that he is anxious that she actually '*caused*' what he said. The next step in development Williams describes is being alone in a hotel declaiming his earliest poems from a window. This attempt to acquire his own 'voice' is paralleled with his earlier wish to speak for himself, so that he is shown at the end of the poem learning to be his own man as a poet. What is most characteristic of Williams, though, is that in this very moment of becoming himself he stresses how this is involved with being drawn out of himself 'and beyond' – the acquisition of his poetic identity involves transcending the boundaries of identity. His mature poems can be read as consistently enacting this and showing that autonomy is both impossible and irrelevant. Their consistent concern with looking and questioning places them on the far threshold of self, or on the meeting-point of selves.

This means that some of the most memorable moments in Williams' poems are when the objects of his gaze suddenly return that gaze. These are moments of mutual recognition which still retain crucial elements of the unknown – they enact how selves interact with significantly limited mutual understanding and how that understanding can suddenly grow and also increase self-understanding. In 'The Dirty Talker' this takes the form of a shock of potential self-recognition. In 'Bread' Williams describes how he and a grocer were apparently the only people still living in a neighbourhood subject to urban renewal, and how one day Williams shouted at some boys misbehaving on the grocer's roof. Then their eyes met and the grocer smiled and Williams smiled back, 'as though we were lovers, as though, like lovers, we'd made speech again/ and were listening as it gutted and fixed the space between us' (p. 152). In 'From My Window' Williams watches a man pushing the wheelchair of a Vietnam veteran until they both tumble over and the man has to haul his friend back into the wheelchair – and then 'leans against the cyclone fence, suddenly staring up at me, as though he'd known/ all along, that I was watching'. The men in both these poems are observed in moments that are curiously touched with intimacy to such an extent that they take on a sexual edge. The grocer is rubbing himself with the cream 'he used to use on his breasts'; the veteran's friend accidentally jerks off the paraplegic's jeans so that his shrivelled penis is revealed.

This deliberately raises the question of the poet's voyeurism – part of the impact of these poems arises from the discomfort they arouse. Much of their importance, however, comes from how they draw on this discomfort to question interrelationships; the poems transcend voyeurism in the end because of the fastidious realism with which they enact the investment of each individual self in other selves and so suggest an entirely different model of interaction. Where voyeurism requires the object of the gaze to be fixed at a stable distance, Williams' poems destabilise the gaze so that its objects are brought suddenly and humanly close. This means that what starts as 'lust of the eye' is transformed into 'regard'.

In this way, the neediness that lies behind the gaze in Williams' poems is referred to as motivating their 'lust of the eye' – the poet's fragility leads him to look at others with a vulnerability that may seem creepy. However, it is largely by admitting this that they transcend mere voyeurism and enact genuine moments of human contact and understanding that involve the interaction of vulnerabilities, which motivate both the desire to look and the need to be looked *at*. This is why the meeting of gazes is so representatively important; when, in 'Bob', Williams meets the gaze of the eponymous retired hit man, he says:

> It's impossible to tell how much that glance weighed: it was like
>   having to lift something,
> something so ponderous and unwieldy that you wanted to call for
>   someone to help you.

Notes

1 Alex Callinicos, *Against Postmodernism: A Marxist Critique* (London: Polity Press, 1989), p. 7.
2 Elizabeth Deeds Ermarth, *Realism and Consensus in the English Novel: Time, Space and Narrative* (Edinburgh: Edinburgh University Press, 1998), p. 65.
3 Philip Roth, *Zuckerman Unbound* and *The Anatomy Lesson* collected in *Zuckerman Bound* (London: Vintage, 1998), p. 488.
4 Philip Roth, *American Pastoral* (London: Vintage, 1998), p. 85.
5 Raymond Carver (with Tom Jenks), 'Fiction of Occurrence and Consequence', in Raymond Carver, *No Heroics Please* (London: Harvill, 1991), pp. 147, 148.
6 Randolph Paul Runyon, *Reading Raymond Carver* (Syracuse, New York: Syracuse University Press, 1992), p. 9.
7 Raymond Carver, *Where I'm Calling From: The Selected Stories* (London: Harvill, 1993), pp. 90–6, 97–102. Unless otherwise stated, all subsequent references to Carver are to this volume.
8 Raymond Carver, 'On Writing', in *Call If You Need Me: The Uncollected Fiction and Prose* (London: Harvill, 2000), p. 88.
9 Ernest Hemingway, 'Big Two-Hearted River', in Joseph F. Trimmer and C. Wade Jennings (eds), *Fictions* (Fort Worth: Harcourt Brace, 1998), p. 663.
10 David Mamet, *Glengarry Glen Ross* (London: Methuen, 1984), p. 24.
11 First published in 1972 and reprinted in C. K. Williams, *Poems 1963–1983* (Newcastle upon Tyne: Bloodaxe, 1988). Unless otherwise stated all page numbers refer to this volume.
12 C. K. Williams, *Flesh and Blood* (New York: Farrar Strauss Giroux, 1987), p. 6.

Documents

1 From Ferdinand de Saussure, 'Nature of the linguistic sign', *Course in General Linguistics* (1974; first published 1915)

1. *Sign, Signified, Signifier*

Some people regard language, when reduced to its elements, as a naming-process only – a list of words, each corresponding to the thing that it names. For example:

This conception is open to criticism at several points. It assumes that ready-made ideas exist before words; it does not tell us whether a name is vocal or psychological in nature (*arbor*, for instance, can be considered from either viewpoint); finally, it lets us assume that the linking of a name and a thing is a very simple operation – an assumption that is anything but true. But this rather naïve approach can bring us near the truth by showing us that the linguistic unit is a double entity, one formed by the associating of two terms.

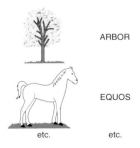

We have seen in considering the speaking-circuit that both terms involved in the linguistic sign are psychological and are united in the brain by an associative bond. This point must be emphasized.

The linguistic sign unites, not a thing and a name, but a concept and a sound-image.[1] The latter is not the material sound, a purely physical thing, but the psychological imprint of the sound, the impression that it makes on our senses. The sound-image is sensory, and if I happen to call it 'material,' it is only in that sense, and by way of opposing it to the other term of the association, the concept, which is generally more abstract.

The psychological character of our sound-images becomes apparent when we observe our own speech. Without moving our lips or tongue, we can talk to ourselves or recite mentally a selection of verse. Because we regard the words of our language as sound-images, we must avoid speaking of the 'phonemes' that make up the words. This term, which suggests vocal activity, is applicable to the spoken word only, to the realization of the inner image in discourse. We can avoid that misunderstanding by speaking of the *sounds* and *syllables* of a word provided we remember that the names refer to the sound-image.

The linguistic sign is then a two-sided psychological entity that can be represented by the drawing:

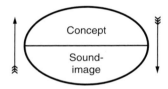

The two elements are intimately united, and each recalls the other. Whether we try to find the meaning of the Latin word *arbor* or the word that Latin uses to designate the concept 'tree,' it is clear that only the associations sanctioned by that language appear to us to conform to reality, and we disregard whatever others might be imagined.

Our definition of the linguistic sign poses an important question of terminology. I call the combination of a concept and a sound-image a *sign*, but in current usage the term generally designates only a sound-image, a word, for example (*arbor*, etc.). One tends to forget that *arbor* is called a sign only because it carries the concept 'tree,' with the result that the idea of the sensory part implies the idea of the whole.

1 The term sound-image may seem to be too restricted inasmuch as beside the representation of the sounds of a word there is also that of its articulation, the muscular image of the phonational act. But for F. de Saussure language is essentially a depository, a thing received from without. The sound-image is par excellence the natural representation of the word as a fact of potential language, outside any actual use of it in speaking. The motor side is thus implied or, in any event, occupies only a subordinate role with respect to the sound-image. [Ed.]

Ambiguity would disappear if the three notions involved here were designated by three names, each suggesting and opposing the others. I propose to retain the word *sign* [*signe*] to designate the whole and to replace *concept* and *sound-image* respectively by *signified* [*signifié*] and *signifier* [*signifiant*]; the last two terms have the advantage of indicating the opposition that separates them from each other and from the whole of which they are parts. As regards *sign*, if I am satisfied with it, this is simply because I do not know of any word to replace it, the ordinary language suggesting no other.

The linguistic sign, as defined, has two primordial characteristics. In enunciating them I am also positing the basic principles of any study of this type.

2. Principle I: The Arbitrary Nature of the Sign

The bond between the signifier and the signified is arbitrary. Since I mean by sign the whole that results from the associating of the signifier with the signified, I can simply say: *the linguistic sign is arbitrary*.

The idea of 'sister' is not linked by any inner relationship to the succession of sounds *s-ö-r* which serves as its signifier in French; that it could be represented equally by just any other sequence is proved by differences among languages and by the very existence of different languages: the signified 'ox' has as its signifier *b-ö-f* on one side of the border and *o-k-s* (*Ochs*) on the other.

No one disputes the principle of the arbitrary nature of the sign, but it is often easier to discover a truth than to assign to it its proper place. Principle I dominates all the linguistics of language; its consequences are numberless. It is true that not all of them are equally obvious at first glance; only after many detours does one discover them, and with them the primordial importance of the principle.

One remark in passing: when semiology becomes organized as a science, the question will arise whether or not it properly includes modes of expression based on completely natural signs, such as pantomime. Supposing that the new science welcomes them, its main concern will still be the whole group of systems grounded on the arbitrariness of the sign. In fact, every means of expression used in society is based, in principle, on collective behavior or – what amounts to the same thing – on convention. Polite formulas, for instance, though often imbued with a certain natural expressiveness (as in the case of a Chinese who greets his emperor by bowing down to the ground nine times), are nonetheless fixed by rule; it is this rule and not the intrinsic value of the gestures that obliges one to use them. Signs that are wholly arbitrary realize better than the others the ideal of the semiological process; that is why language, the most complex and universal of all systems of expression, is also the most characteristic; in this sense linguistics can become the master-pattern for all branches of semiology although language is only one particular semiological system.

The word *symbol* has been used to designate the linguistic sign, or more specifically, what is here called the signifier. Principle I in particular weighs against the use of this term. One characteristic of the symbol is that it is never wholly arbitrary; it is not empty, for there is the rudiment of a natural bond between the signifier and the signified. The symbol of justice, a pair of scales, could not be replaced by just any other symbol, such as a chariot.

The word *arbitrary* also calls for comment. The term should not imply that the choice of the signifier is left entirely to the speaker (we shall see below that the individual does not have the power to change a sign in any way once it has become established in the linguistic community); I mean that it is unmotivated, i.e. arbitrary in that it actually has no natural connection with the signified.

In concluding let us consider two objections that might be raised to the establishment of Principle I:

1) *Onomatopoeia* might be used to prove that the choice of the signifier is not always arbitrary. But onomatopoeic formations are never organic elements of a linguistic system. Besides, their number is much smaller than is generally supposed. Words like French *fouet* 'whip' or *glas* 'knell' may strike certain ears with suggestive sonority, but to see that they have not always had this property we need only examine their Latin forms (*fouet* is derived from *fāgus* 'beech-tree,' *glas* from *classicum* 'sound of a trumpet'). The quality of their present sounds, or rather the quality that is attributed to them, is a fortuitous result of phonetic evolution.

As for authentic onomatopoeic words (e.g. *glug-glug*, *tick-tock*, etc.), not only are they limited in number, but also they are chosen somewhat arbitrarily, for they are only approximate and more or less conventional imitations of certain sounds (cf. English *bow-wow* and French *ouaoua*). In addition, once these words have been introduced into the language, they are to a certain extent subjected to the same evolution – phonetic, morphological, etc. – that other words undergo (cf. *pigeon*, ultimately from Vulgar

Latin *pīpiō*, derived in turn from an onomatopoeic formation): obvious proof that they lose something of their original character in order to assume that of the linguistic sign in general, which is unmotivated.

2) *Interjections*, closely related to onomatopoeia, can be attacked on the same grounds and come no closer to refuting our thesis. One is tempted to see in them spontaneous expressions of reality dictated, so to speak, by natural forces. But for most interjections we can show that there is no fixed bond between their signified and their signifier. We need only compare two languages on this point to see how much such expressions differ from one language to the next (e.g. the English equivalent of French *aïe!* is *ouch!*). We know, moreover, that many interjections were once words with specific meanings (cf. French *diable!* 'darn!' *mordieu!* 'golly' from *mort Dieu* 'God's death', etc.).[2]

Onomatopoeic formations and interjections are of secondary importance, and their symbolic origin is in part open to dispute.

3. *Principle II: The Linear Nature of the Signifier*

The signifier, being auditory, is unfolded solely in time from which it gets the following characteristics: (a) it represents a span, and (b) the span is measurable in a single dimension; it is a line.

While Principle II is obvious, apparently linguists have always neglected to state it, doubtless because they found it too simple; nevertheless, it is fundamental, and its consequences are incalculable. Its importance equals that of Principle I; the whole mechanism of language depends upon it. In contrast to visual signifiers (nautical signals, etc.) which can offer simultaneous groupings in several dimensions, auditory signifiers have at their command only the dimension of time. Their elements are presented in succession; they form a chain. This feature becomes readily apparent when they are represented in writing and the spatial line of graphic marks is substituted for succession in time.

Sometimes the linear nature of the signifier is not obvious. When I accent a syllable, for instance, it seems that I am concentrating more than one significant element on the same point. But this is an illusion; the syllable and its accent constitute only one phonational act. There is no duality within the act but only different oppositions to what precedes and what follows.

---

2 Cf. English *goodness!* and *zounds!* (from *God's wounds*). [Tr.]

2 From Frantz Fanon, 'Conclusion', *Wretched of the Earth* (1963)

Come, then, comrades; it would be as well to decide at once to change our ways. We must shake off the heavy darkness in which we were plunged, and leave it behind. The new day which is already at hand must find us firm, prudent and resolute.

We must leave our dreams and abandon our old beliefs and friendships of the time before life began. Let us waste no time in sterile litanies and nauseating mimicry. Leave this Europe where they are never done talking of Man, yet murder men everywhere they find them, at the corner of every one of their own streets, in all the corners of the globe. For centuries they have stifled almost the whole of humanity in the name of a so-called spiritual experience. Look at them today swaying between atomic and spiritual dis-integration.

And yet it may be said that Europe has been successful in as much as everything that she has attempted has succeeded.

Europe undertook the leadership of the world with ardour, cynicism and violence. Look at how the shadow of her palaces stretches out ever farther! Every one of her movements has burst the bounds of space and thought. Europe has declined all humility and all modesty; but she has also set her face against all solicitude and all tenderness.

She has only shown herself parsimonious and niggardly where men are concerned; it is only men that she has killed and devoured.

So, my brothers, how is it that we do not understand that we have better things to do than to follow that same Europe?

That same Europe where they were never done talking of Man, and where they never stopped proclaiming that they were only anxious for the welfare of Man: today we know with what sufferings humanity has paid for every one of their triumphs of the mind.

Come, then, comrades, the European game has finally ended; we must find something different. We today can do everything, so long as we do not imitate Europe, so long as we are not obsessed by the desire to catch up with Europe.

Europe now lives at such a mad, reckless pace that she has shaken off all guidance and all reason, and she is running headlong into the abyss; we would do well to avoid it with all possible speed.

Yet it is very true that we need a model, and that we want blueprints and examples. For many among us the European model is the most inspiring. We have therefore seen in the preceding pages to what mortifying set-backs such an imitation has led us. European achievements, European techniques and the European style ought no longer to tempt us and to throw us off our balance.

When I search for Man in the technique and the style of Europe, I see only a succession of negations of man, and an avalanche of murders.

The human condition, plans for mankind and collaboration between men in those tasks which increase the sum total of humanity are new problems, which demand true inventions.

Let us decide not to imitate Europe; let us combine our muscles and our brains in a new direction. Let us try to create the whole man, whom Europe has been incapable of bringing to triumphant birth.

Two centuries ago, a former European colony decided to catch up with Europe. It succeeded so well that the United States of America became a monster, in which the taints, the sickness and the inhumanity of Europe have grown to appalling dimensions.

Comrades, have we not other work to do than to create a third Europe? The West saw itself as a spiritual adventure. It is in the name of the spirit, in the name of the spirit of Europe, that Europe has made her encroachments, that she has justified her crimes and legitimized the slavery in which she holds four-fifths of humanity.

Yes, the European spirit has strange roots. All European thought has unfolded in places which were increasingly more deserted and more encircled by precipices; and thus it was that the custom grew up in those places of very seldom meeting man.

A permanent dialogue with oneself and an increasingly obscene narcissism never ceased to prepare the way for a half delirious state, where intellectual work became suffering and the reality was not at all that of a living man, working and creating himself, but rather words, different combinations of words, and the tensions springing from the meanings contained in words. Yet some Europeans were found to urge the European workers to shatter this narcissism and to break with this unreality.

But in general the workers of Europe have not replied to these calls; for the workers believe, too, that they are part of the prodigious adventure of the European spirit.

All the elements of a solution to the great problems of humanity have, at different times, existed in European thought. But Europeans have not carried out in practice the mission which fell to them, which consisted of bringing their whole weight to bear violently upon these elements, of modifying their arrangement and their nature, of changing them and, finally, of bringing the problem of mankind to an infinitely higher plane.

Today, we are present at the stasis of Europe. Comrades, let us flee from this motionless movement where gradually dialectic is changing into the logic of equilibrium. Let us reconsider the question of mankind. Let us reconsider the question of cerebral reality and of the cerebral mass of all humanity, whose connexions must be increased, whose channels must be diversified and whose messages must be re-humanized.

Come, brothers, we have far too much work to do for us to play the game of rear-guard. Europe has done what she set out to do and on the whole she has done it well; let us stop blaming her, but let us say to her firmly that she should not make such a song and dance about it. We have no more to fear; so let us stop envying her.

The Third World today faces Europe like a colossal mass whose aim should be to try to resolve the problems to which Europe has not been able to find the answers.

But let us be clear: what matters is to stop talking about output, and intensification, and the rhythm of work.

No, there is no question of a return to Nature. It is simply a very concrete question of not dragging men towards mutilation, of not imposing upon the brain rhythms which very quickly obliterate it and wreck it. The pretext of catching up must not be used to push man around, to tear him away from himself or from his privacy, to break and kill him.

No, we do not want to catch up with anyone. What we want to do is to go forward all the time, night and day, in the company of Man, in the company of all men. The caravan should not be stretched out, for in that case each line will hardly see those who precede it; and men who no longer recognize each other meet less and less together, and talk to each other less and less.

It is a question of the Third World starting a new history of Man, a history which will have regard to the sometimes prodigious theses which Europe has put forward, but which will also not forget Europe's crimes, of which the most horrible was committed in the heart of man, and consisted of the pathological tearing apart of his functions and the crumbling away of his unity. And in the framework of the collectivity there were the differentiations, the stratification and the bloodthirsty tensions fed by classes; and finally, on the immense scale of humanity, there were racial hatreds, slavery, exploitation and above all the bloodless genocide which consisted in the setting aside of fifteen thousand millions of men.

So, comrades, let us not pay tribute to Europe by creating states, institutions and societies which draw their inspiration from her.

Humanity is waiting for something other from us than such an imitation, which would be almost an obscene caricature.

If we want to turn Africa into a new Europe, and America into a new Europe, then let us leave the destiny of our countries to Europeans. They will know how to do it better than the most gifted among us.

But if we want humanity to advance a step farther, if we want to bring it up to a different level than that which Europe has shown it, then we must invent and we must make discoveries.

If we wish to live up to our peoples' expectations, we must seek the response elsewhere than in Europe.

Moreover, if we wish to reply to the expectations of the people of Europe, it is no good sending them back a reflection, even an ideal reflection, of their society and their thought with which from time to time they feel immeasurably sickened.

For Europe, for ourselves and for humanity, comrades, we must turn over a new leaf, we must work out new concepts, and try to set afoot a new man.

3 From Jean-François Lyotard, 'The referent, the name', *The Differend: Phrases in Dispute*, trans. Georges Van Den Abbeele, vol. 46 of *Theory and History of Literature* (1988)

93. 'It's not for nothing that Auschwitz is called the "extermination camp".' Millions of human beings were exterminated there. Many of the means to prove the crime or its quantity were also exterminated. And even the authority of the tribunal that was supposed to establish the crime and its quantity was exterminated, because the constitution of the Nuremburg tribunal required an Allied victory in the Second World War, and since this war was a kind of civil war resulting from a lack of consensus over legitimacy in international relations, the criminal was able to see in his judge merely a criminal more fortunate than he in the conflict of arms. The differend attached to Nazi names, to *Hitler*, to *Auschwitz*, to *Eichmann*, could not be transformed into a litigation and regulated by a verdict. The shades of those to whom had been refused not only life but also the expression of the wrong done them by the Final Solution continue to wander in their indeterminacy. By forming the State of Israel, the survivors transformed the wrong into damages and the differend into a litigation. By beginning to speak in the common idiom of public international law and of authorized politics, they put an end to the silence to which they had been condemned. But the reality of the wrong suffered at Auschwitz before the foundation of this state remained and remains to be established, and it cannot be established because it is in the nature of a wrong not to be established by consensus. What could be established by historical inquiry would be the quantity of the crime. But the documents necessary for the

validation were themselves destroyed in quantity. That at least can be established. The result is that one cannot adduce the numerical proof of the massacre and that a historian pleading for the trial's revision will be able to object at great length that the crime has not been established in its quantity. – But the silence imposed on knowledge does not impose the silence of forgetting, it imposes a feeling. Suppose that an earthquake destroys not only lives, buildings, and objects but also the instruments used to measure earthquakes directly and indirectly. The impossibility of quantitatively measuring it does not prohibit, but rather inspires in the minds of the survivors the idea of a very great seismic force. The scholar claims to know nothing about it, but the common person has a complex feeling, the one aroused by the negative presentation of the indeterminate. *Mutatis mutandis*, the silence that the crime of Auschwitz imposes upon the historian is a sign for the common person. Signs are not referents to which are attached significations validatable under the cognitive regimen, they indicate that something which should be able to be put into phrases cannot be phrased in the accepted idioms. That, in a phrase universe, the referent be situated as a sign has as a corollary that in this same universe the addressee is situated like someone who is affected, and that the sense is situated like an unresolved problem, an enigma perhaps, a mystery, or a paradox. – This feeling does not arise from an experience felt by a subject. It can, moreover, not be felt. In any case, how can it be established that it is or is not felt? One comes up against the difficulties raised by idiolects. The silence that surrounds the phrase, *Auschwitz was the extermination camp* is not a state of the mind [*état d'âme*], it is the sign that something remains to be phrased which is not, something which is not determined. This sign affects a linking of phrases. The indetermination of meanings left in abeyance [*en souffrance*], the extermination of what would allow them to be determined, the shadow of negation hollowing out reality to the point of making it dissipate, in a word, the wrong done to the victims that condemns them to silence – it is this, and not a state of mind, which calls upon unknown phrases to link onto the name of Auschwitz. – The 'revisionist' historians understand as applicable to this name only the cognitive rules for the establishment of historical reality and for the validation of its sense. If justice consisted solely in respecting these rules, and if history gave rise only to historical inquiry, they could not be accused of a denial of justice. In fact, they administer a justice in conformity with the rules and exert a positively instituted right. Having placed themselves, moreover, in the position of plaintiffs, who need not establish anything, they plead for the negative, they reject proofs, and that is certainly their right as the defense. But that they are not worried by the scope of the very silence they use as an argument in their plea, by this does one recognize a wrong done to the sign that is this silence and to the phrases it invokes. They will say that history is not made of feelings, and that it is necessary to establish the facts. But, with Auschwitz, something new has happened in history (which can only be a sign and not a fact), which is that the facts, the testimonies which bore the traces of *here*'s and *now*'s, the documents which indicated the sense or senses of the facts, and the names, finally the possibility of various kinds of phrases whose conjunction makes reality, all this has been destroyed as much as possible. Is it up to the historian to take into account not only the damages, but also the wrong? Not only the reality, but also the meta-reality that is the destruction of reality? Not only the testimony, but also what is left of the testimony when it is destroyed (by dilemma), namely, the feeling? Not only the litigation, but also the differend? Yes, of course, if it is true that there would be no history without a differend, that a differend is born from a wrong and is signaled by a silence, that the silence indicates that phrases are in abeyance of their becoming event [*en souffrance de leur événement*], that the feeling is the suffering of this abeyance [*cette souffrance*]. But then, the historian must break with the monopoly over history granted to the cognitive regimen of phrases, and he or she must venture forth by lending his or her ear to what is not presentable under the rules of knowledge. Every reality entails this exigency insofar as it entails possible unknown senses. Auschwitz is the most real of realities in this respect. Its name marks the confines wherein historical knowledge sees its competence impugned. It does not follow from that that one falls into non-sense. The alternative is not: either the signification that learning [*science*] establishes, or absurdity, be it of the mystical kind.

4 From Edwin Morgan, *Collected Poems* (1990)

Message Clear

```
      am                  i
                                      if
    i am                         he
          he r          o
          h       ur    t
          the re             and
          he       re       and
          he re
      a                  n    d
          the r                   e
    i am      r                       ife
                       i n
                 s       ion and
    i                       d      i e
       am    e res    ect
       am    e res    ection
                         o            f
            the                      life
                         o            f
        m    e              n
               sur e
            the               d      i e
    i           s
                 s    e t    and
    i am the    sur         d
       a    t    res    t
                         o            life
    i am  he r                        e
    i a               ct
    i           r   u      n
    i    m    e  e      t
    i                   t              i e
    i           s      t    and
    i am th              o       th
    i am      r              a
    i am the    su       n
    i am the    s        on
    i am the    e    rect on      e  if
    i am       re         n    t
    i am          s        a         fe
    i am          s    e   n     t
    i      he  e                d
    i    t  e  s       t
    i           re          a  d
       a    th  re          a  d
       a          s    t on      e
       a    t    re          a  d
       a    th  r         on      e
    i           resurrect
                               a      life
    i am                  i  n        life
    i am       resurrection
    i am the resurrection and
    i am
    i am the resurrection and the life
```

5 From Julia Kristeva, 'Approaching abjection', *Powers of Horror: An Essay on Abjection* (1982)

No Beast is there without glimmer of infinity.
No eye so vile nor abject that brushes not
Against lightning from on high, now tender, now fierce.
                    Victor Hugo, *La Légende des siècles*

NEITHER SUBJECT NOR OBJECT

There looms, within abjection, one of those violent, dark revolts of being, directed against a threat that seems to emanate from an exorbitant outside or inside, ejected beyond the scope of the possible, the tolerable, the thinkable. It lies there, quite close, but it cannot be assimilated. It beseeches, worries, and fascinates desire, which, nevertheless, does not let itself be seduced. Apprehensive, desire turns aside; sickened, it rejects. A certainty protects it from the shameful – a certainty of which it is proud holds on to it. But simultaneously, just the same, that impetus, that spasm, that leap is drawn toward an elsewhere as tempting as it is condemned. Unflaggingly, like an inescapable boomerang, a vortex of summons and repulsion places the one haunted by it literally beside himself.

When I am beset by abjection, the twisted braid of affects and thoughts I call by such a name does not have, properly speaking, a definable *object*. The abject is not an ob-ject facing me, which I name or imagine. Nor is it an ob-ject, an otherness ceaselessly fleeing in a systematic quest of desire. What is abject is not my correlative, which, providing me with someone or some-thing else as support, would allow me to be more or less detached and autonomous. The abject has only one quality of the object – that of being opposed to *I*. If the object, however, through its opposition, settles me within the fragile texture of a desire for meaning, which, as a matter of fact, makes me ceaselessly and infinitely homologous to it, what is *abject*, on the contrary, the jettisoned object, is radically excluded and draws me toward the place where meaning collapses. A certain 'ego' that merged with its master, a superego, has flatly driven it away. It lies outside, beyond the set, and does not seem to agree to the latter's rules of the game. And yet, from its place of banishment, the abject does not cease challenging its master. Without a sign (for him), it beseeches a discharge, a convulsion, a crying out. To each ego its object, to each superego its abject. It is not the white expanse or slack boredom of repression, not the translations and transfor-mations of desire that wrench bodies, nights, and discourse; rather it is a brutish suffering that 'I' puts up with, sublime and devastated, for 'I' deposits it to the father's account [*verse au père – père-version*]: I endure it, for I imagine that such is the desire of the other. A massive and sudden emergence of uncanniness, which, familiar as it might have been in an opaque and forgotten life, now harries me as radically separate, loathsome. Not me. Not that. But not nothing, either. A 'something' that I do not recognize as a thing. A weight of meaninglessness, about which there is nothing insignificant, and which crushes me. On the edge of non-existence and hallucination, of a reality that, if I acknowledge it, annihilates me. There, abject and abjection are my safeguards. The primers of my culture.

THE IMPROPER/UNCLEAN

Loathing an item of food, a piece of filth, waste, or dung. The spasms and vomiting that protect me. The repugnance, the retching that thrusts me to the side and turns me away from defilement, sewage, and muck. The shame of compromise, of being in the middle of treachery. The fascinated start that leads me toward and separates me from them.

Food loathing is perhaps the most elementary and most archaic form of abjection. When the eyes see or the lips touch that skin on the surface of milk – harmless, thin as a sheet of cigarette paper, pitiful as a nail paring – I experience a gagging sensation and, still farther down, spasms in the stomach, the belly; and all the organs shrivel up the body, provoke tears and bile, increase heartbeat, cause forehead and hands to perspire. Along with sight-clouding dizziness, *nausea* makes me balk at that milk cream, separates me from the mother and father who proffer it. 'I' want none of that element, sign of their desire; 'I' do not want to listen, 'I' do not assimilate it, 'I' expel it. But since the food is not an 'other' for 'me,' who am only in their desire, I expel *myself*, I spit *myself* out, I abject *myself* within the same motion through which 'I' claim to establish *myself*. That detail, perhaps an insignificant one, but one that they ferret out, emphasize, evaluate, that trifle turns me inside out, guts sprawling; it is thus that *they* see that 'I' am in the process of becoming an other at the expense of my own death. During that course in which 'I' become, I give birth to myself amid the violence of sobs, of vomit. Mute protest of the symptom, shattering violence of a convulsion that, to be sure, is inscribed in a symbolic system, but in which, without either wanting or being able to become integrated in order to answer to it, it reacts, it abreacts. It abjects.

The corpse (or cadaver: *cadere*, to fall), that which has irremediably come a cropper, is cesspool, and death; it upsets even more violently the one who confronts it as fragile and fallacious chance. A wound with blood and pus, or the sickly, acrid smell of sweat, of decay, does not *signify* death. In the presence of signified death – a flat encephalograph, for instance – I would understand, react, or accept. No, as in true theater, without makeup or masks, refuse and corpses *show me* what I permanently thrust aside in order to live. These body fluids, this defilement, this shit are what life withstands, hardly and with difficulty, on the part of death. There, I am at the border of my condition as a living being. My body extricates itself, as being alive, from that border. Such wastes drop so that I might live, until, from loss to loss, nothing remains in me and my entire body falls beyond the limit – *cadere*, cadaver. If dung signifies the other side of the border, the place where I am not and which permits me to be, the corpse, the most sickening of wastes, is a border that has encroached upon everything. It is no longer I who expel, 'I' is expelled. The border has become an object. How can I be without border? That elsewhere that I imagine beyond the present, or that I hallucinate so that I might, in a present time, speak to you, conceive of you – it is now here, jetted, abjected, into 'my' world. Deprived of world, therefore, I *fall in a faint*. In that compelling, raw, insolent thing in the morgue's full sunlight, in that thing that no longer matches and therefore no longer signifies anything, I behold the breaking down of a world that has erased its borders: fainting away. The corpse, seen without God and outside of science, is the utmost of abjection. It is death infecting life. Abject. It is something rejected from which one does not part, from which one does not protect oneself as from an object. Imaginary uncanniness and real threat, it beckons to us and ends up engulfing us.

It is thus not lack of cleanliness or health that causes abjection but what disturbs identity, system, order. What does not respect borders, positions, rules. The in-between, the ambiguous, the composite. The traitor, the liar, the criminal with a good conscience, the shameless rapist, the killer who claims he is a savior. . . . Any crime, because it draws attention to the fragility of the law, is abject, but premeditated crime, cunning murder, hypocritical revenge are even more so because they heighten the display of such fragility. He who denies morality is not abject; there can be grandeur in amorality and even in crime that flaunts its disrespect for the law – rebellious, liberating, and suicidal crime. Abjection, on the other hand, is immoral, sinister, scheming, and shady: a terror that dissembles, a hatred that smiles, a passion that uses the body for barter instead of inflaming it, a debtor who sells you up, a friend who stabs you. . . .

In the dark halls of the museum that is now what remains of Auschwitz, I see a heap of children's shoes, or something like that, something I have already seen elsewhere, under a Christmas tree, for instance, dolls I believe. The abjection of Nazi crime reaches its apex when death, which, in any case, kills me, interferes with what, in my living universe, is supposed to save me from death: childhood, science, among other things.

THE ABJECTION OF SELF

If it be true that the abject simultaneously beseeches and pulverizes the subject, one can understand that it is experienced at the peak of its strength when that subject, weary of fruitless attempts to identify with something on the outside, finds the impossible within; when it finds that the impossible constitutes its very *being*, that it *is* none other than abject. The abjection of self would be the culminating form of that experience of the subject to which it is revealed that all its objects are based merely on the inaugural *loss* that laid the foundations of its own being. There is nothing like the abjection of self to show that all abjection is in fact recognition of the *want* on which any being, meaning, language, or desire is founded. One always passes too quickly over this word, 'want', and today psychoanalysts are finally taking into account only its more or less fetishized product, the 'object of want'. But if one imagines (and imagine one must, for it is the working of imagination whose foundations are being laid here) the experience of *want* itself as logically preliminary to being and object – to the being of the object – then one understands that abjection, and even more so abjection of self, is its only signified. Its signifier, then, is none but literature. Mystical Christendom turned this abjection of self into the ultimate proof of humility before God, witness Elizabeth of Hungary who 'though a great princess, delighted in nothing so much as in abasing herself'.

The question remains as to the ordeal, a secular one this time, that abjection can constitute for someone who, in what is termed knowledge of castration, turning away from perverse dodges, presents himself with his own body and ego as the most precious non-objects; they are no longer seen in their own right but forfeited, abject. The termination of analysis can lead us there, as we shall see. Such are the pangs and delights of masochism.

Essentially different from 'uncanniness', more violent, too, abjection is elaborated through a failure to recognize its kin; nothing is familiar, not even the shadow of a memory. I imagine a child who has swallowed up his parents too soon, who frightens himself on that account, 'all by himself', and, to save himself, rejects and throws up everything that is given to him – all gifts, all objects. He has, he could have, a sense of the abject. Even before things for him *are* – hence before they are signifiable – he drives them out, dominated by drive as he is, and constitutes his own territory, edged by the abject. A sacred configuration. Fear cements his compound, conjoined to another world, thrown up, driven out, forfeited. What he has swallowed up instead of maternal love is an emptiness, or rather a maternal hatred without a word for the words of the father; that is what he tries to cleanse himself of, tirelessly. What solace does he come upon within such loathing? Perhaps a father, existing but unsettled, loving but unsteady, merely an apparition but an apparition that remains. Without him the holy brat would probably have no sense of the sacred; a blank subject, he would remain, discomfited, at the dump for non-objects that are always forfeited, from which, on the contrary, fortified by abjection, he tries to extricate himself. For he is not mad, he through whom the abject exists. Out of the daze that has petrified him before the untouchable, impossible, absent body of the mother, a daze that has cut off his impulses from their objects, that is, from their representations, out of such daze he causes, along with loathing, one word to crop up – fear. The phobic has no other object than the abject. But that word, 'fear' – a fluid haze, an elusive clamminess – no sooner has it cropped up than it shades off like a mirage and permeates all words of the language with nonexistence, with a hallucinatory, ghostly glimmer. Thus, fear having been bracketed, discourse will seem tenable only if it ceaselessly confront that otherness, a burden both repellent and repelled, a deep well of memory that is unapproachable and intimate: the abject.

6 From Donna Landry and Gerald Maclean (eds), Gayatri Spivak's Translator's preface and afterword to Mahasweta Devi, 'Imaginary Maps', *The Spivak Reader* (1996)

In the contemporary context, when the world is broadly divided simply into North and South, the World Bank has no barrier to its division of that world into a map that is as fantastic as it is real. This constantly changing map draws economic rather than national boundaries, as fluid as the spectacular dynamics of international capital. One of the not inconsiderable elements in the drawing up of these maps is the appropriation of the Fourth World's ecology. Here a kinship can be felt through the land-grabbing and deforestation practiced against the First Nations of the Americas, the destruction of the reindeer forests of the Suomis of Scandinavia and Russia, and the tree-felling and eucalyptus plantations on the land of the original nations, indeed of all the early civilizations that have been pushed back and away to make way for what we call the geographic lineaments of the map of the world today.

Upon the body of this North-South world, and to sustain the imaginary map-making of the World Bank, yet another kind of unification is being practiced as the barriers between international capital and the fragile national economies of the South are being removed. The possibility of social redistribution in these states, uncertain at best, is disappearing even further.

In this context, it is important to notice that the stories in this volume are not only linked by the common thread of profound ecological loss, the loss of the forest as foundation of life, but also of the complicity, however apparently remote, of the power lines of local developers with the forces of global capital. This is no secret to the initiative for a global movement for non-Eurocentric ecological justice. But this is certainly a secret to the benevolent study of other cultures in the North. And here a strong connection, indeed a complicity, between the bourgeoisie of the Third World and migrants in the First cannot be ignored. We have to keep this particularly in mind because this is also the traffic line in Cultural Studies. Mahasweta's texts are thus not only of substantial interest to us, but may also be a critique of our academic practice. Is it more or less 'Indian' to insist on this open secret?

What follows is not a romanticization of the tribal. Indeed, 'Pterodactyl' is a critique of any such effort. The following paragraphs outline a dream based on the conviction that large-scale mind change is hardly ever possible on grounds of reason alone. In order to mobilize for non-violence, for example, one relies, however remotely, on building up a conviction of the 'sacredness' of human life. 'Sacred' here need not have a religious sanction, but simply a sanction that cannot be contained within the principle of reason alone. Nature is no longer sacred in this sense for civilizations based on the control of Nature. The result is global devastation due to a failure of ecology. It is noticeable that the less advantaged groups among the Indian tribals still retain this sense as a matter of their cultural conformity, if only because they have been excluded from the mainstream. It is also true that more self-conscious First Nation groups such as the Canadian Native American Movement use this possibility of cultural conformity precisely to mobilize for ecological sanity as well as against historical injustice. What we are dreaming of here is not how to keep the tribal in a state of excluded cultural conformity but how to construct a sense of sacred Nature which can help mobilize a general ecological mindset beyond the reasonable and self-interested grounds of longterm global survival.

Indeed, if this seems an impractical dream, we should perhaps learn a lesson from the other side. In the World Bank's Environmental Report for the fiscal year 1992, we read:

The World's remaining indigenous peoples – estimated to number more than 250 million in seventy countries – possess knowledge fundamental to the sustainable management of resources in these regions. . . . In cooperation with the Center for Indigenous Knowledge, the Environmental Department prepared a Bank discussion paper entitled *Using Indigenous Knowledge in Agricultural Development* (Warren 1991). Region-specific technical papers are being prepared to support the implementation of the directive.

World Bank assistance comes at the request of governments. These stories prepare us to take a critical stance toward such 'assistance'. Within that framework, we should remind ourselves that the preparation of 'technical papers' that will extract methods from so-called 'indigenous knowledge' will not be accompanied by any change of mindset in the researchers. By contrast, we draw out from literary and social texts some impossible yet necessary project of changing the minds that innocently support a vicious system. That is what 'learning from below' means here. Mahasweta writes in 'Pterodactyl' that the tribals remain largely spectators as India moves toward the twenty-first century. Assia Djebar has written that women remained largely spectators as Algeria moved toward Independence. 'If only one could cathect [*investir*] that single spectator body that remains, encircle it more and more tightly in order to forget the defeat!' she writes. This wish is another version of ethical singularity. It should not be conflated with romanticizing the tribal as figure for the Unconscious.

Having seen, then, the powerful yet risky role played by Christian liberation theology, some of us have dreamt of animist liberation theologies to girdle the perhaps impossible vision of an ecologically just world. Indeed the name 'theology' is alien to this thinking. Nature 'is' also super-nature in this way of thinking and knowing. (Please be sure that I am not positing some generalized 'tribal mind'.) Even 'super' as in 'supernatural' is out-of-the-way. For Nature, the sacred other of the human community is, in this thinking, also bound by the structure of ethical responsibility of which I have spoken in connection with women's justice. The pterodactyl is not only the ungraspable other, but also the ghost of the ancestors that haunts our present and our future. We must learn 'love' (a simple name for ethical responsibility-in-singularity), as Puran does in 'Pterodactyl', in viewing the impossibility of communication. No individual-transcendence theology, being just in this world in view of the next – however the next is underplayed – can bring us to this.

Indeed, it is my conviction that the inter-nationality of ecological justice in that impossible, undivided world cannot be reached by invoking any of the so-called 'great' religions of the world, because the history of their 'greatness' is too deeply imbricated in the narrative of the ebb-and-flow of power. In the case of Hindu India – a terrifying phrase – no amount of reinventing the nature poetry of the *Rg-Veda* will, in this view, suffice to undo that history. I have no doubt that we must *learn* to learn from the original practical ecological philosophers of the world, through the slow, attentive, mind-changing (on both sides) ethical singularity that deserves the name of 'love' – to supplement necessary collective efforts to change laws, modes of production, systems of education and health care. This for me is the lesson of Mahasweta, activist/journalist *and* writer. This relationship, a witnessing love and a supplementing collective struggle, is the relationship between her 'literary' writing and her activism. Indeed, in the general global predicament today, such a supplementation must become the relationship between the silent gift of the subaltern and the thunderous imperative of the Enlightenment to 'the public use of Reason', however hopeless that undertaking might seem. One filling the other's gap.

1945–1998

Timeline of key events and publications

1945   6 and 9 August, American planes drop atomic bombs on Hiroshima and Nagasaki, Japan
The Second World War ends
Syria and Lebanon become independent from France

1946   Invention of the first civilian computers

1947   India and Pakistan become independent of Britain
Tennessee Williams, *A Streetcar Named Desire*

1948   The Russians cut road and rail links to Berlin, precipitating the 'Berlin Crisis'. The Berlin airlift begins as a result of this, and the East and West are locked in a confrontation. This signals the start of the Cold War
F. R. Leavis, *The Great Tradition*
Norman Mailer, *The Naked and the Dead*

1949   First successful test of atomic bomb by Soviet Union
Simone de Beauvoir, *Le deuxième sexe*
Arthur Miller, *Death of a Salesman*
George Orwell, *1984*

1950   The USA intervenes in Korea to prevent communism spreading from the north into the south

1951   TV broadcasting begins across the USA
J. D. Salinger, *The Catcher in the Rye*

1952   Ralph Ellison, *Invisible Man*

1953   Death of Joseph Stalin, followed by a power struggle in the USSR
Francis Crick and James Watson discover the 'double helix' (DNA)
Jorge Luis Borges, *Labyrinths*

1954   The French are expelled from Vietnam
        Nasser seizes power in Egypt
        The hunt for Communist infiltrators in the US government is
        extended by Senator Joseph McCarthy
        Outbreak of the Algerian war for independence
        William Golding, *Lord of the Flies*

1955   Vladimir Nabokov, *Lolita*

1956   The Suez crisis. Britain and France, together with Israel, make an
        abortive attempt to overthrow the Egyptian government and its
        revolutionary leader, Colonel Nasser. This signals the end of the
        ability of the colonial countries to exercise their former powers
        Hungarian revolution suppressed by invading Soviet forces
        Fidel Castro starts Cuban revolution
        Samuel Beckett, *Waiting for Godot*
        Allen Ginsberg, *Howl*

1957   The Common Market begins, comprising France, the German
        Federal Republic, Italy, the Netherlands, Belgium and Luxembourg
        Eugene O'Neill, *Long Day's Journey into Night*

1958   Chinua Achebe, *Things Fall Apart*

1959   Robert Lowell, *Life Studies*
        William Burroughs, *Naked Lunch*

1960   Congo crisis: independence from Belgium is followed by civil war
        Sharpeville massacre: South African police fire on anti-apartheid
        demonstrators killing over sixty and wounding more than a
        hundred
        Nigeria becomes independent from Britain
        John Updike, *Rabbit Run*
        Harold Pinter, *The Caretaker*

1961   Anti-Castro Free Cuban forces, supported by the USA, launch Bay
        of Pigs invasion, which fails
        The East German government builds the Berlin Wall
        Joseph Heller, *Catch-22*

1962   The Cuban missile crisis. In response to the presence of US missiles
        in Turkey, Khrushchev, the Soviet leader, places missiles in Cuba. A
        nuclear war appears imminent but both sides finally back down and
        withdraw their missiles
        Edward Albee, *Who's Afraid of Virginia Woolf?*
        Rachel Carson, *Silent Spring*

1963   Martin Luther King heads March on Washington for Jobs and
        Freedom
        President Kennedy is assassinated

Nelson Mandela is tried in South Africa under the Suppression of Communism Act

Hannah Arendt, *Eichmann in Jerusalem: A Report on the Banality of Evil*

Frantz Fanon, *The Wretched of the Earth*

Thomas Pynchon, *V*

Adrienne Rich, *Snapshots of a Daughter-in-Law*

1964   The Palestine Liberation Organization (PLO) is formed

Saul Bellow, *Herzog*

Philip Larkin, *The Whitsun Weddings*

1965   Black Power leader Malcolm X is assassinated

The beginning of the Vietnam War, which lasts until 1975

Sylvia Plath, *Ariel*

1966   Thomas Pynchon, *The Crying of Lot 49*

1967   Six Day War between Israel and Arab states

Civil war breaks out in Nigeria

First heart transplant operation performed by Dr Christiaan Barnard

Jacques Derrida, *Of Grammatology* published in French (1977 in English)

John Barth, *The Sot-Weed Factor*

Gabriel García Márquez, *One Hundred Years of Solitude*

1968   The 'Prague Spring': Soviet forces invade Czechoslovakia and overthrow the regime of Alexander Dubcek which had passed liberal reforms

The 'events of May': students demonstrate in Paris and this is followed by a national strike of workers which threatens the government of General de Gaulle. Other student demonstrations follow across the world, from Berkeley and Mexico City in the West to Warsaw, Prague and Belgrade in the East

1969   'Troubles' begin in Northern Ireland

John Berryman, *The Dream Songs*

Philip Roth, *Portnoy's Complaint*

Kurt Vonnegut, *Slaughterhouse 5*

Robert Coover, *Pricksongs and Descants*

1970   End of Nigerian Civil War

Four students at Kent State University shot dead by the National Guard

1971   General Idi Amin becomes dictator in Uganda

President Richard Nixon and Henry Kissinger initiate 'détente' with the Soviet Union

1972   Republican demonstrators are fired upon by British troops in Londonderry ('Bloody Sunday')

1973   The oil crisis. The OPEC countries steeply raise the price of oil, with enormous economic consequences
        Yom Kippur War between Israel, backed by the USA, on one side, and Egypt and Syria, supplied by the Soviets, on the other
        The Watergate scandal, which eventually brings down President Richard Nixon
        Chilean president, Salvador Allende, is overthrown and killed by the army led by General Augusto Pinochet and supported by the CIA
        Thomas Pynchon, *Gravity's Rainbow*
        Edwin Morgan, *From Glasgow to Saturn*
1974   Constitutional crisis in the USA caused by the Watergate hearings
1975   The Khmer Rouge seize power in Cambodia
        Video recorders and floppy disks are introduced for home use
        Donald Barthelme, *The Dead Father*
        E. L. Doctorow, *Ragtime*
1976   Mao Zedong dies
1977   In New York the first cases of AIDS are diagnosed
1978   The first 'test-tube baby' is born
        Edward Said, *Orientalism*
1979   Margaret Thatcher is elected prime minister in Britain
        Jean-François Lyotard, *The Postmodern Condition*
        Angela Carter, *The Bloody Chamber*
        Derek Walcott, *The Star-Apple Kingdom*
        V. S. Naipaul, *A Bend in the River*
1980   The Green Party is formed in West Germany
        Iraq invades Iran
        'Solidarity' movement formed in Poland
        Zimbabwe, under the independent majority rule of Robert Mugabe, replaces Rhodesia
        William Golding, *Rites of Passage*
1981   Ronald Reagan becomes American president
        Islamic fundamentalist assassinates President Sadat of Egypt
        Salman Rushdie, *Midnight's Children*
1982   Falklands War between Britain and Argentina
        Walter Abish, *How German Is It*
        Julia Kristeva, *Powers of Horror: An Essay on Abjection*
        Bobby Ann Mason, *Shiloh and Other Stories*
1983   President Reagan denounces the Soviet Union as an 'evil empire'
        Raymond Carver, *Cathedral*
1984   Famine in Ethiopia
        In Britain the protracted miners' strike leads to the defeat, by the

government of Margaret Thatcher, of one of the most powerful unions

Don Delillo, *White Noise*

1985   Mikhail Gorbachev becomes president in the Soviet Union and initiates *perestroika* (economic and political restructuring) and *glasnost* (openness)

Paul Auster, *City of Glass*

Douglas Dunn, *Elegies*

1986   Chernobyl nuclear reactor explodes

1986–7 Superpower summits in Reykjavik and Washington, involving Mikhail Gorbachev and Ronald Reagan. These effectively end the Cold War

1987   Palestinian 'Intifada' begins against Israeli rule in the occupied territories

Stock market crashes

1988   Soviet troops begin to withdraw from Afghanistan

Henry Gates, *The Signifying Monkey*

Toni Morrison, *Beloved*

Tony Harrison, *Selected Poems*

Carol Ann Duffy, *Selling Manhattan*

1989   Tiananmen Square massacre in Beijing

Communist rule ends in Eastern European countries such as Poland, Hungary, Czechoslovakia and East Germany

Fatwa issued against Salman Rushdie

1990   Iraq invades Kuwait

Nelson Mandela is released from prison

1991   American military action against Iraq is supported by twenty-eight countries, including Saudi Arabia, Egypt and Syria

The end of the Soviet Union

The disintegration of Yugoslavia precipitates war between its ethnic factions

Fredric Jameson, *Postmodernism or, The Cultural Logic of Late Capitalism*

World wide web launched

1992   Bosnia recognised by the European Community; violence between the ethnic factions continues

The first Earth Summit meets in Rio de Janeiro to discuss environmental issues

Famine in Somalia

1993   War in Somalia

Joint Declaration on Northern Ireland, established by the British prime minister John Major and the Irish prime minister Albert Reynolds, calls for an end to sectarian violence

1994   The Cairo Agreement establishes Palestinian self-rule
        War begins in Chechnya. Russian warplanes bomb the Chechen
        capital, Grozny
        Apartheid ends in South Africa. Nelson Mandela becomes the first
        black president
        Homi K. Bhabha, *The Location of Culture*
1995   Fighting intensifies in Bosnia until an agreement is finally reached
        War in Rwanda
1996   The IRA ends its ceasefire and carries out a bombing campaign on
        the British mainland, injuring 220 people in the centre of
        Manchester
        Boris Yeltsin becomes the first democratically elected president of
        Russia
        The Taliban Islamic militia seizes control in Afghanistan
        The Dayton Peace Treaty ends the fighting in the former Yugoslavia
1997   The 'El Niño' effect produces extreme weather conditions which
        intensify environmental anxieties
        Princess Diana dies
        Peace treaty signed between Russia and Chechnya
        Power transferred in Hong Kong from Britain to China
1998   Toni Morrison *Paradise*

Bibliography of literary texts

Walter Abish, 'The English Garden', in *In the Future Perfect* (London: Faber, 1984).

Walter Abish, *How German Is It* (London: Faber, 1982).

Martin Amis, *Money* (London: Penguin, 1985).

Martin Amis, *London Fields* (London: Penguin, 1990).

John Ashbery, *Selected Poems* (London: Paladin, 1987).

Margaret Atwood, *Surfacing* (London: Virago, 1979).

Paul Auster, *The New York Trilogy* (London: Faber, 1987).

J. G. Ballard, *Crash* (London: Flamingo, 1993).

Samuel Beckett, *Waiting for Godot* (London: Faber, 1965; first published 1956).

John Berryman, *Selected Poems 1938–1968* (London: Faber, 1972).

A. S. Byatt, *Possession* (London: Vintage, 1991).

Angela Carter, *The Bloody Chamber and Other Stories* (London: Penguin, 1979).

Angela Carter, *Nights at the Circus* (London: Picador, 1985).

Angela Carter, 'Flesh and the Mirror', in Malcolm Bradbury (ed.), *The Penguin Book of Modern British Short Stories* (London: Penguin, 1988).

Raymond Carver, *Where I'm Calling From: The Selected Stories* (London: Harvill, 1993).

Don Delillo, *White Noise* (London: Picador, 1985).

Ralph Ellison, *Invisible Man* (London: Penguin, 2001).

Gabriel García Márquez, *Leaf Storm and Other Stories* (London: Harper Collins, 1971).

Gabriel García Márquez, *One Hundred Years of Solitude* (London: Picador, 1978).

Seamus Heaney, *New Selected Poems 1966–1987* (London: Faber, 1990).

Paul Hoover (ed.), *Postmodern American Poetry* (New York: Norton, 1994).

Ted Hughes, *New Selected Poems 1957–1994* (London: Faber, 1995).

Robert Lowell, *Poems 1938–1949* (London: Faber, 1950).

Robert Lowell, *Near the Ocean* (London: Faber, 1967).

Robert Lowell, *History* (London: Faber, 1973).

David Mamet, *Glengarry Glen Ross* (London: Methuen, 1984).

Bobbie Ann Mason, *Shiloh and Other Stories* (London: HarperCollins, 1982).

Ian McEwan, *The Innocent* (London: Pan Books, 1990).

Ian McEwan, *Enduring Love* (London: Vintage, 1998).

Edwin Morgan, *Collected Poems* (Manchester: Carcanet, 1990)

Toni Morrison, *Beloved* (London: Pan Books, 1988).

Toni Morrison, *Jazz* (London: Picador, 1993).

Paul Muldoon, *Selected Poems 1968–1983* (London: Faber and Faber, 1986).

Joyce Carol Oates, *Them* (New York: Fawcett Crest, 1969).

Joyce Carol Oates, *A Sentimental Education: Stories* (New York: E. P. Dutton, 1982).

Joyce Carol Oates, *What I Lived For* (London: Picador, 1995).

Joyce Carol Oates, *Blonde* (London: Fourth Estate, 2000).

Frank O'Hara, *Collected Poems* (New York: Knopf, 1979).

Sylvia Plath, *Collected Poems* (London: Faber, 1981).

Adrienne Rich, *The Fact of a Doorframe: Poems Selected and New 1950–1984* (New York: Norton, 1984).

Philip Roth, *Portnoy's Complaint* (London: Vintage, 1995; first published 1968).

Philip Roth, *Sabbath's Theatre* (London: Vintage, 1996).

Philip Roth, *Zuckerman Unbound* and *The Anatomy Lesson* collected in *Zuckerman Bound* (London: Vintage, 1998).

Philip Roth, *American Pastoral* (London: Vintage, 1998).

Salman Rushdie, *Midnight's Children* (London: Vintage, 1995).

Salman Rushdie, *The Satanic Verses* (London; Vintage, 1998; first published, 1988)

Tom Stoppard, *Jumpers* (London: Faber, 1972).

Derek Walcott, *Omeros* (New York: Farrar, Strauss, Giroux, 1990)

Derek Walcott, *Collected Poems 1948–1984* (London: Faber, 1992).

Fay Weldon, *The Life and Loves of a She Devil* (Sevenoaks, Kent: Hodder and Stoughton, 1983).

Fay Weldon, 'Weekend', in Malcolm Bradbury (ed.), *The Penguin Book of Modern British Short Stories* (London: Penguin, 1988), pp. 309–25.

C. K. Williams, *Flesh and Blood* (New York: Farrar Strauss Giroux, 1987).

C. K. Williams, *Poems 1963–1983* (Newcastle upon Tyne: Bloodaxe, 1988).

Jeanette Winterson, *Sexing the Cherry* (London: Vintage, 1990).

Suggestions for further reading

1 Readers

Thomas Docherty (ed.), *Postmodernism: A Reader* (Brighton, 1993).
Patricia Waugh (ed.), *Postmodernism: A Reader* (London, 1992).

2 Accounts of postmodernism

Perry Anderson, *The Origins of Postmodernity* (London, 1998).
Hans Bertens, *The Idea of the Postmodern* (London, 1995).
Christopher Butler, *Postmodernism: A Very Short Introduction* (Oxford, 2002).
Nigel Wheale (ed.), *The Postmodern Arts* (London and New York, 1995).

3 Postmodernist theory

Andrew Benjamin (ed.), *The Lyotard Reader* (Oxford, 1989).
Jean Baudrillard, *Simulations* (New York, 1983).
Jean Baudrillard, *America* (London, 1988).
Alex Callinicos, *Against Postmodernism* (London, 1990).
Jürgen Habermas, *The Philosophical Discourse of Modernity: Twelve Lectures*, trans. Frederick Lawrence (Cambridge, 1992).
Fredric Jameson, *Postmodernism or, The Cultural Logic of Late Capitalism* (London, 1991).
Jean-François Lyotard, *The Postmodern Condition: A Report on Knowledge*, trans. Geoff Bennington and Brian Massumi (Manchester, 1984).
Jean-François Lyotard, *The Differend* (Minneapolis, 1988).

4 Postmodern race

Henry Louis Gates, *The Signifying Monkey* (New York, 1989).
bell hooks, *Talking Back: Thinking Feminist, Thinking Black* (Boston, 1989).
Toni Morrison, *Playing in the Dark: Whiteness and the Literary Imagination* (London, 1992).

5 Postcolonialism

Chinua Achebe, *Hopes and Impediments* (London, 1975).
Aijaz Ahmad, *In Theory* (London, 1992).
Bill Ashcroft, Gareth Griffiths and Helen Tiffin (eds), *The Post-Colonial Reader* (London, 1995).
Homi K. Bhabha, *The Location of Culture* (London, 1994).
Elleke Boehmer, *Colonial and Postcolonial Literature* (Oxford, 1995).
Frantz Fanon, *The Wretched of the Earth* (New York, 1963).
Donna Landry and Gerald Maclean (eds), *The Spivak Reader* (London, 1996).
Edward Said, *Orientalism* (Harmondsworth, 1985).

6 The postmodern self

Michèle Barrett, *The Politics of Truth* (Cambridge, 1991).
Jacques Derrida, *Positions* (Chicago, 1981).
Paul du Gay, Jessica Evans and Peter Redman (eds), *Identity: A Reader* (London, 2000).
Michel Foucault, *The History of Sexuality* (Harmondsworth, 1981).
Julia Kristeva, *Powers of Horror: An Essay on Abjection* (New York, 1982).
Jacques Lacan, *Ecrits: A Selection* (London, 1977).

7 Postmodern gender

Judith Butler, *Gender Trouble* (New York, 1990).
Hélène Cixous and Catherine Clement, *The Newly Born Woman*, trans. Betsy Wing (Manchester, 1987).
R. W. Connell, *Masculinities* (Cambridge, 1995).
Luce Irigaray, *Speculum of the Other Woman* (New York, 1985).

Jacqueline Rose, *Sexuality in the Field of Vision* (London, 1986).
Lorna Sage, *Women in the House of Fiction: Post-War Women Novelists* (London, 1992).

8 On postmodernist literature

Theo D'haen and Hans Bertens (eds), *British Postmodern Fiction* (Amsterdam, 1993).
Paul Hoover (ed.), *Postmodern American Poetry: A Norton Anthology* (New York, 1994).
Linda Hutcheon, *A Poetics of Postmodernism: History, Theory, Fiction* (London, 1988).
Linda Hutcheon, *The Politics of Postmodernism* (London, 1989).
Roger Luckhurst and Peter Marks (eds), *Literature and the Contemporary* (Harlow, Essex, 1999).
Brian McHale, *Postmodernist Fiction* (London, 1987).
Brian McHale, *Constructing Postmodernism* (London, 1992).
Susan Sontag, *Against Interpretation* (New York, 1967).

Index